BURT
LANCASTER

*Other titles by Michael Munn and published
by Robson Books*

Trevor Howard
Charlton Heston: A Biography
The Hollywood Murder Casebook
Hollywood Rogues
Clint Eastwood: Hollywood's Loner
The Hollywood Connection
Stars at War

BURT LANCASTER

· The Terrible-Tempered Charmer ·

Michael Munn

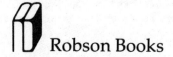
Robson Books

First published in Great Britain in 1995 by Robson Books Ltd, Bolsover House, 5–6 Clipstone Street, London W1P 7EB

British Library Cataloguing in Publication Data
A catalogue record for this title is available from the British Library

ISBN 0 86051 970 8

Photoset in North Wales by Derek Doyle & Associates, Mold, Clwyd. Printed in Great Britain by St Edmundsbury Press, Bury St Edmunds, Suffolk

For Peter and Judy
– from baby brother

Contents

A Brief Foreword   ix

 1   An Irish Temper   1
 2   Sometimes a Sergeant   15
 3   Hollywood Brains   24
 4   Work Hard, Play Hard   35
 5   Some Enchanted Evening   44
 6   Shelley's Regret   55
 7   Caricature of a He-Man   63
 8   Kissing in the Sea   72
 9   Being God   81
10   Back on the Trapeze   93
11   Smell of Success   104
12   An Actor Like Mr Olivier   114
13   A Popular Victory   128
14   Locked In   138
15   Perfectly Mysterious Man   147
16   Great Buddies   156
17   Western Sunset   163
18   From Swimming Pools to the Ocean   174
19   Smoking Ears   186
20   The Light of Experience   196
21   When in Rome   203

22   Autumn Years   213
23   A Hero in Scotland   225
24   A Tough Guy   235

Afterword   246
Bibliography   248
Filmography   250
Index   270

A Brief Foreword

In 1972 I met Burt Lancaster and, being a star-struck junior press officer for a film company based just off London's Wardour Street, I was, to put it mildly, overawed. It was a pleasure to me that, when I got to interview him formally the first time in 1982, he remembered me. He was not just being polite, as some are when they say they remember you but really don't, because he was able to recall the event. 'Oh yeah, you're the kid who . . .'

I last interviewed him in 1986, and he still remembered me. I mention these meetings because it is from these that much of the material for this book comes. Newspaper and magazine articles are always useful to a biographer, but nothing is preferable to having first-hand material. I am fortunate, also, to have known and interviewed a number of other people over the years who have provided me with an insight into the life, work and personality of my subject. They include Richard Brooks (whom I interviewed in London in 1984); John Frankenheimer (London, 1979); Robert Aldrich (London, 1979); John Huston (whom I met and interviewed numerous times since 1972); Lee Marvin (London, 1976); Ed Lauter (London, 1984); Kirk Douglas (London, 1975 and 1989); Tony Curtis (London, 1974); Jean Simmons (on the set of *Dominique* in 1979); John Sturges (London, 1975); Shelley Winters (London, 1981); Ava Gardner (London 1969); Harry Andrews (at his home in 1988); and Denis Lawson (London 1985).

1

An Irish Temper

'I was born on a Friday or a Sunday, I'm not sure,' Burt
Lancaster told me when I first met him in London.

Vagueness seems to be a part of the early history of Burt
Lancaster. Perhaps it's simply that it was so many years ago, in
1913, or just because Lancaster never bothered to make a
mental note of what day it was. But there are other blurred
facts that make the early life of Burt Lancaster something of a
mystery. The name of his mother, for instance, seems unknown
in all the references, and yet it is known she was of Irish-Welsh
descent. It's also known that she inherited her father's large
house, number 209 East 106th Street in New York. It's an area
now known as East Harlem but was then a middle-class area
populated largely by Italians and Puerto Ricans.

The house was a three-storey tenement, next to the railway.
Mrs Lancaster's husband was James H Lancaster, a supervisor
at the Madison Square Mail Office for 48 dollars a week. His
own family background is also vague. He told people he could
trace his ancestry back to the royal House of Lancaster. He
was, in fact, Irish.

The tenement housed a number or paying tenants. 'The
house was really a series of small apartments, and everybody
shared a bathroom on each floor,' Burt Lancaster remembered.
'But my parents were not wealthy. We just about scraped by,

the same as most, although there were many more who were worse off than us.'

Before Burt came along, the Lancasters had three children: Jane, James Jr and William. Burton Stephen Lancaster was born on 2 November 1913 (a Sunday) in the Lancaster house. A second girl was born later, but she did not survive infancy. Like the rest of the family, Burt had light brown hair; the Italian residents were convinced the family were German although, for reasons never at all clear Burt was nicknamed 'Dutch' by the residents and neighbours.

He was a short, somewhat tubby boy, but very handsome. 'Both my parents were extremely good looking,' he said and he was lucky enough to inherit their looks. He also inherited something else from his mother – her quick Irish temper. Because he was small, he had to learn how to take care of himself.

Said Lancaster, 'When I was a kid, you learned quickly about life on the streets. I remember my mother used to tell us, if you want to learn about love, stay home, but if you want to learn about life, go out on the streets.'

When he was three he made his acting debut – in a Nativity play, playing a shepherd. 'I didn't have any lines to say and I quickly got bored with standing around,' he recalled, 'so I began to fidget and discovered I had chewing gum on my shoe. I said, "How the hell did that get there?" out loud and brought the reverent proceedings to a sudden stop.'

Young Burt discovered movies early in life, and became a great fan of Douglas Fairbanks. He took himself off to see *The Mark of Zorro* at the local movie theatre, arriving at eleven in the morning and staying until around eleven in the evening. When he got home late that evening his parents were frantic. He began imitating Fairbanks by leaping over the furniture in the house, climbing up lamp posts in the street, and developing a keen athletic prowess.

He was, he said, 'a dreamer. I'd go off into a world of my own and not hear a thing anyone said to me. I guess that's the mark of a potential actor, although it never occurred to me I might one day want to become an actor. I was too interested in this whole idea of leaping over balconies like Fairbanks and I guess what really fired my imagination then was the acrobatics.'

He knew how to use his fists by the age of eight. When he got picked on he could give as good as he got. He had already developed quite a temper and, when bullies, alone or in groups, attempted to beat him up, he flew into a rage that was often enough to send them running for cover.

'You had to learn to take care of yourself,' he said. 'When I got into a fight, it was always to win. So I grew up tough. I guess that's when I developed my compulsion to assert myself. I had to be on top, to win, to not let anyone push me around.'

His violent streak was not exclusively reserved for bullies. Once, during an argument with his older brother James, or Jim as he was called, Burt flew into a rage and hit big brother on the head with a baseball bat.

He said that his background was not an affluent one, 'but we didn't go without. I've heard Kirk [Douglas] talk of his childhood and of the abject poverty he suffered and how lucky he was if he found a potato lying in the gutter – my life was never like that. We managed, and we had a whole lot of love. It wasn't really that tough on the streets, although I used to get picked on a helluva lot because I was just a small kid.'

On warm summer evenings, James Lancaster Senior would strum away on his guitar, sitting on the front porch, singing an Irish ditty. The neighbours would gather around. Burt recalled, 'There was one night when I joined in the song. My dad stopped singing. I was giving a solo performance. I came to the end of the song. My audience applauded. It was my very first applause. I never forgot it.'

Two blocks down the road from the Lancaster home was the Union Settlement House where young Burt used to practise his gymnastics. He also liked to play basketball, and took time out to study art, languages and even a little drama, which he considered a 'sissy' subject. A professional theatre company, the American Laboratory Theatre, used to visit the various settlement houses to teach drama, and it was from this group that Burt Lancaster received his first training as an actor. He even took part in a number of productions directed by the company that recreated some of the Broadway successes. But he did it, he said, because it got him extra marks, and when he had enough marks, he was sent off to summer camp.

'Summer camp was like going to heaven when you were a kid from East Harlem,' he said. 'You looked forward to it all year round. It was at summer camp that I met Nick Cravat.'

Pint-sized Nick Cravat would later be Lancaster's acrobatic partner in several films. Burt was just nine when he met Nick, who was two years older and came from Italian stock. They taught themselves various hand-balancing acrobatics and, if one got into a fight, the other joined in to help.

'Nick was my first really close friend,' said Lancaster. 'I guess he's always been my best friend. He was a real rascal, a lovable rogue whose mother was forever lighting candles for his soul.'

Lancaster seemed in no hurry to gain his eventual height of six-foot-two-inches. At the age of eleven he was the shortest boy in his class at school. It was also the age at which he was very nearly 'discovered' as an actor.

He was appearing in a play, *Three Pills in a Bottle*, at the Settlement House, playing a terminally ill boy in a wheelchair. He was thoroughly embarrassed at having to be in the play but his teacher gave him no choice in the matter. He said, 'I thought acting was real sissy stuff, not the sort of thing any red-blooded male did.' Two talent scouts saw him and went to the Lancaster house on East 106th Street to offer him an acting scholarship. He hid on the fire escape while they spoke to his mother. When the men went away, he went back inside where his mother explained about the scholarship, but he told her he would have nothing to do with the scholarship, or with acting.

Of his parents, his mother seems to have been the strongest influence in his life. While he recalled his father as being a 'kind, gentle, warm sort of man, very even tempered, in fact I don't think I saw him ever get mad,' he remembered his mother being the one who 'did all the punishing and gave me an understanding of the real values of life.

'She had great strength and a wonderful capacity for love. At times she seemed like a bit of a dictator with us kids. But she was honest and she insisted on honesty, truth and loyalty.'

The family did not attend church with any great passion although Burt sang in the choir. His mother believed it was her task, not the church's, to teach her children good Christian values, as well as the hard facts of life. Local 'bums' were always knocking at the Lancaster front door; she gave them a severe talking to for not getting their lives in order and she gave them food. She never let them go without.

She once gave Burt a stinging backhand when he came home having drunk a quart of the milk she had sent him out to buy. But it wasn't for drinking the milk that he was punished; it was for not noticing that the milkman had given him five cents *too much* in change. She sent him back to repay the excess change.

By the age of twelve, Burt was part of a gang and getting into trouble on the streets. 'We fought only with our fists or stones and sticks,' he said, 'although some of the kids on our block carried knives.'

He was in a gang of three; himself, Vincent Franzone and a boy they called Moby Dick. They used to dive into the river and swim a quarter of a mile to Ward's Island, then on the way home they'd pass through the farmers' market and steal apples. The pedlars would usually give chase and the boys ran the rest of the way home. 'I was a good swimmer as a kid,' Lancaster said. 'But those long swims to Ward's Island were just a little reckless, and after doing it a few times I started to get a bit scared; like, what if I don't make it this time? I think I became hydrophobic through that experience, and for years as an adult I avoided swimming.'

One day a policeman caught him throwing beer bottles from a warehouse roof. The cop dragged Burt home and asked James Lancaster Senior, 'Do you keep your kids off the street, or do we?'

James promised to see to it that Burt stayed out of trouble. But there was no way he was going to be able to keep his son in the house for ever. Before long, Burt was back on the streets.

Third Avenue was where he played stickball and stoopball. In all he was hit by cars eight times during games. He finally got the message that it was safer to play in Central Park, or at the Union Settlement House where there was an indoor baseball field.

At the age of fourteen he discovered girls:

My first girlfriend was a beautiful Jewish girl. I was eager to experiment as adolescent boys tend to do, but she lived by a strict moral code and I learned to have great respect for Jewish morality. But there were other girls; some charged a quarter. I sometimes tried to save up. These were not hookers, you understand. Just teenage girls who discovered they could earn some easy money, and we boys were very grateful.

I suppose I was what you could call permissive from an early age. We all were, but in those days you didn't bring it out into the open. Sex was a sin, and if you sinned you had to tell the priest about it in the confessional. So I didn't tell the priest. I didn't go to church except to sing in the choir – until my voice broke. My mother never pushed religion down our throats, so I never had that kind of upbringing. So I could go out sinning and not have to confess.

Although he wanted nothing to do with the 'sissy' art of acting, he did have some secret yearnings for culture. Some evenings he slipped off quietly to the Settlement House to attend art classes and piano lessons. He tried for three months to learn to play the piano, but was disappointed not to become proficient at it. He discovered the New York Public Library and became an avid reader.

He also loved to sing and for a while decided he would become an opera singer:

My mother had a collection of John McCormack recordings which I played on our Victrola. Yes, the big horn and the dog's face listening. I had learned Irish songs and I'd sing them in the street. I was a boy soprano – quite a good voice. When I sang women would bring me glasses of milk and pieces of cake. One of my pals had very little education but he loved opera. His mother had some Caruso records and we listened to them all the time.

Our neighbourhood was full of opera singers – some were professional, most were amateurs. Everyone liked to sing opera, or just to listen. I used to sneak into the opera house by waiting outside until the interval, then walk in and try to find an empty seat. I usually did. I saw the opera quite a bit, and never paid for a ticket.

Then, when he was fifteen, his voice broke. 'My soprano voice was gone and I spent the rest of my life searching for it!'

When Burt was sixteen, his mother fell ill and died. Her sense of honesty and morality had a lasting effect on him. He recalled a day when he went into a bank and found a twenty-dollar bill. 'I don't suppose I'd ever had a single dollar I could call my own. I was going to take the money and run, but an old woman came rushing in, looking for her twenty-dollar bill. She was so upset I felt crushed, and I could almost hear my mother telling me to give it back. So I did.'

Not only did Burt retain his mother's integrity, he still had her temper and from time to time it came to the surface. One evening, while on 'locker room duty' at the Settlement House, he came across two fifteen-year-old boys and ordered them to get out. Burt was older by a year or two and, although they were doing nothing wrong, he told them, 'You're getting in my hair.'

They refused to budge, and soon Lancaster was laying into them with punches. During the fight, one of the boys produced a pocket knife. Lancaster tried to punch the boy but missed and the knife went into his thigh.

Lancaster was taken to Lennox Hill Hospital and admitted for three days. His sister Jane said, 'He was a scrapper all right. He'd fight anyone for a principle and he usually came out on top.'

'I am a violent man,' he admitted to me. 'There has always been a whole lot of violence inside of me. It's part of what makes me who I am, what I am. I make no apology for it. I have learned to keep it in check. But when I was just a kid, a teenager, and we were in the middle of the depression, I was rebelling – as was every other kid.'

He graduated from DeWitt Clinton High School in 1930 and won a basketball scholarship at New York University. His brothers had also gone there; James Jr was captain of the basketball team.

During the summer break between graduating from high school and going to university, Lancaster and Nick Cravat went regularly to the Union Settlement House where Burt coached the kids in basketball. There, one day, they saw Australian gymnast Charles 'Curly' Bent, practising on the horizontal bars which had been installed as part of a 15,000-dollar refurbishment. Lancaster and Cravat were fascinated by Bent's ability to perform on the bar and they begged him to teach them how to do it. Before long Lancaster and Cravat were able to perform kick-ups and somersaults-away.

They asked the director of the Settlement House, Helen Harris, if they could drill holes in the gymnasium floor and build a second set of bars. She turned them down.

They came back the following day and made the same request. Again, she said no. They returned each day for a week until, tired of the same argument, Helen Harris said, 'All right, drill your blasted holes.' She later explained, 'I was getting a sore neck and I couldn't get any work done.'

By the time Burt began attending university he had lost all interest in drama and literature. His ambition to become an opera singer also having vanished some years previously, he had set his sights on becoming a physical education instructor. Now, however, he began to have other ideas.

He built a further set of bars in the back yard of the house where he and Cravat continued to train. By the age of eighteen, Nick Cravat had earned some success as a professional boxer with 16 fights to his credit. He only weighed 126 pounds but he had a powerful right hand. 'He could sink his fist into a lath-and-plaster wall,' recalled Lancaster. 'We called him "Little Dempsey".'

Lancaster did not enjoy university. 'It wasn't that I didn't want to study; I did. I've always wanted to improve my mind. But there weren't enough teachers and we had up to a 150 students in some classes, with the lessons being given out over a loudspeaker. You couldn't ask questions, you couldn't respond to anything so, one day in 1931, I walked out of class and didn't go back.'

He and Cravat continued to practise until, in 1932, they had what amounted to a fledgeling acrobatic act. In the spring of that year they began looking for work as professional acrobats. They called themselves Lang and Cravat.

In the trade newspaper *Billboard* they read that the Kay Brothers' Circus was heading for Petersburg in Virginia from its winter quarters in Florida. They wrote to the circus asking for a chance to work but they never received a reply.

Cravat decided to leave the ring and they bought an old car for 90 dollars. With only 30 dollars between them, they headed south to Petersburg.

They arrived the night before the opening of the Kay Brothers' Circus and found the owner. Lancaster recalled:

We quickly discovered it was a buyer's market and we had to beg him to give us a chance. We took our own double bars with us, although the circus used a triple bar. I was nervous as hell and screwed up my first jump-up and hit my knees and fell off. I used to hit my knees from time to time even though I was proficient on the bars and I began having trouble with them and had operations on one knee over the years. I've had trouble with my knee ever since and in the end it gave me arthritis.

I got up, tried it again, missed the bar and tore my tights. I got up and tried again and this time my timing was perfect. Nick did his routine, and we were hired at three dollars a week. I don't think I was ever nervous again of

anything after that. Or I learned not to show I was
nervous. That's the trick in life; whatever you have to do,
don't show that you're nervous.

The resident bar veteran with the circus began teaching
'Lang and Cravat' how to use the triple bar with new tricks. It
was the beginning of their circus life and they loved it:

Everyone in the circus had to do their bit to advertise the
circus, to get the tent up, carry banners in the street
parades, hand out some free tickets, feed the animals. We
felt like stars of the big top, although this was only a small
circus with a single ring.

It was like every child's dream come true; running away
to join the circus, although we didn't exactly run away.
We lived in our car, washed our own clothes, cooked our
own food, trained every day – it was all worth it just to
hear that applause. They talk about having sawdust in
your blood. My veins were full of it. After a month we got
a raise – five dollars a week!

We were with Kay Brothers for six months and would
have stayed longer but Nick fell badly one night and broke
his nose so he had to go back to New York. I stayed on
and worked solo but then the owner came to me and said,
'We're going to put you to work with another act.'

I said, 'But Nick'll be back as soon as he's recovered.'

He said, 'Forget Nick Cravat. We can't wait for him.
You're getting some new partners.'

I said, 'The hell I am. I quit.'

Lancaster headed back for New York and, when Cravat's
nose was healed, the pair found an agent who took them on
and found them bookings with various carnivals and small
circuses such as the Cole Brothers and the Gorman Brothers.

They taught themselves new tricks, including a perch-pole
act which had Cravat balancing a pole on his head with
Lancaster balancing on his hands on the top.

The next few months were a whirlwind of engagements. During 1935, while performing in one of the small circuses, Lancaster met June Ernst. She was, according to Lancaster, 'the only woman in America who could do horizontal bar tricks. As far as women were concerned it was pretty much a lost art, and nobody appreciated it.' Nobody but Burt. He worked out with her on the bars, began taking her out for dinner, and for hours they would talk about their bar tricks:

We mistook our interest in our work and our admiration for each other's work for love. True, we were attracted to each other. She was a beautiful woman with a superb body. You had to be in good shape to work those bars, and I guess she thought the same of me. So we got married. It was a big mistake. We toured together although we didn't work in the same act – I still had Nick for a partner. But we were working together all the time and I guess we just got tired of each other before the year was out. That's all there was to it. No fights, no arguments – well, some arguments – but we had no real interest in each other, and we just agreed that we had made a mistake.

Her mother was a trapeze artiste and I worked with her for a while, and I learned a bit about the trapeze. That was a happy side-effect to my first marriage. I came to love the trapeze although I was never quite good enough to take it up full-time, so Nick and I stuck to the bars – but I never gave up on the trapeze.

My wife? We got divorced eventually – after about three years I guess. But we were only together a year.

All the small-time circus work finally paid off when Lancaster and Cravat were hired by the Ringling Brothers Circus in 1935, at the staggering salary of 300 dollars a week. But by this time Lancaster was growing tired of being on the road constantly. He began to think his blood was not quite so thick with sawdust after all, so he returned to New York where he worked with the Federal Theatre Project, a part of the

Works Projects Administration which had been established by
President Franklin D Roosevelt during the depression to ease
unemployment. He was an actor again for the first time since
the Union Settlement House days.

He also found a new interest – attending the theatre. He had a
friend who worked in the box office and used to get Lancaster
into the second balcony for free. He recalled seeing Lillian
Hellman's *The Children's Hour* in 1935. 'The whole audience
stood up and hissed that little girl at the end of the second act.
A year later I saw John Gielgud's *Hamlet*.'

But he began to feel the sawdust in his veins again and he
rejoined Nick Cravat on the circuit. This time they managed to
get bookings in vaudeville and toured on the Poli vaudeville
circuit. But the pay was lousy – just 15 dollars a week between
them. Their perch-pole speciality act had to be cut from many
of the venues because the pole was too tall for most of the
stages. In some theatres they were dropped altogether because
managers objected to having holes drilled into their stages. So
Burt invented and built a folding bar frame that could be rolled
out quickly onto the stage without having to be fixed. He
worked on the frame for a year until it was as good as it could
be but, while the lightweight and smaller Cravat could work
these bars with ease, Lancaster's larger frame made them lift off
the floor every time he hit them. They decided to go back to the
circus and fair circuit.

They remained on the road, sleeping out of suitcases,
working often for very little pay, but they were not able to get
back into the big time with the Ringling Brothers. In 1939 they
arrived in Los Angeles to perform at the Orpheum Theatre.
Lancaster began wondering once more about that 'sissy' craft –
acting. He went from studio to studio, 'out of curiosity more
than anything', he said, trying to get to see the casting directors.

'Everywhere I went it was the same story,' he said. 'They
weren't interested in anyone without professional experience in
the theatre and they were especially not interested in
acrobatics.'

They went to Hammond, Indiana, playing in a fair where

they seemed to prove hugely successful. But after three weeks interest in their act waned and they ended up playing in a Kansas City burlesque house.

Cravat remained optimistic about their future. 'We can't miss this time,' he kept saying.

Lancaster told him, 'Look, Nick, we *are* missing. I'm not a kid any more. I'm twenty-eight and it's time I tried something else.'

The day finally came when he knew he had to leave.

We were performing in St Louis where I tore a finger in my right hand and was warned that the finger would have to be amputated if I continued performing. So Nick found himself a new partner – a woman, by the way, whom he later married – and I headed for Chicago wearing the one suit I had and with about 20 dollars to my name.

I knew a circus family there, the Smileatas, and they put me up for several months while I worked in Marshall Field's department store as a floorwalker in the ladies' lingerie. I really knew how to get those ladies to spend their money. Of course it was all an act. I was acting even then, telling the ugliest women how beautiful they looked in the worst kind of clothing. They paid me 25 dollars a week for doing that. I got so bored with it that one day I went walking around the department on my hands, thinking that it would get me fired. It didn't, so I quit.

Then I worked for a while for a company that supplied refrigeration and steam to meat-packing plants. There were around 70 coolers at different plants, and I went from plant to plant, adjusting the coolers twice each day. That job soon drove me nuts so I went to work as a salesman, selling community concerts to civic leaders all around the country. What I had to do was to sell package deals so they'd get two star concerts but they also had to have three unknowns.

I was damned good at that job too. So good that Columbia Broadcasting gave me a job with the Concert

Bureau in New York with a salary of 6,000 dollars a year. So I arrived in York [in July 1942] only to get drafted. That was the end of my career as a pedlar of culture.

2

Sometimes a Sergeant

Lancaster did not go straight into the army; he had about four months to wait, so he went to work in the meantime as a singing waiter in a Union City night club. As well as singing standards such as 'Old Man River', he was also required to play stooge to the club's Master of Ceremonies.

In November 1942, Lancaster reported to Fort Riley in Kansas. He hoped to get into the Engineers, thinking his rigging experience in the circus would qualify him but the army decided that having come from what they considered a show-business background, he was assigned to the Special Services Branch of the Fifth Army, to perform and produce shows for the troops on base.

As in the First World War, the job of boosting morale in the ranks fell to the entertainers who would visit military bases at home and at the front. Big-name entertainers were recruited by the American Army to perform for fighting troops right at the front. Some GIs were sung to by the likes of Marlene Dietrich. Others had to make do with lesser names. The Fifth Army's biggest star was Burt Lancaster, the singing waiter and acrobat.

Around the time Lancaster arrived at Fort Riley, the Allies were landing in North Africa. The Fifth Army, including Private First Class Lancaster, followed in June 1943. Lancaster recalled, 'They made me an entertainer; I never had one heroic moment.'

But they did make him a sergeant — sometimes. He said:

We were stationed in the desert near Casablanca and the food we had was just terrible. One day my company was on guard duty at a ration dump which was nearby, and I had this idea to requisition some decent food. So I told my boys to take a truck in to the ration dump and load it with all the best food they had – bacon, hams, peaches. The lieutenant in charge came over to me and asked what I was doing. I said, 'Orders, sir.' He said, 'Okay, Sergeant, get on with it then.' So we did. I tell you, we ate like kings for weeks. I was lucky not to get caught; I would have been court-martialled.

The invasion of Sicily followed in July, and the Fifth Army, led by General Mark Clark, arrived at Salerno, on the Italian mainland, on 9 September. Less than a month later, the Fifth were in Naples, but the move on to Rome, which the Allies had expected to be a 'walk in the sun', took a further eight months. The Allies were brought to a virtual standstill when the US Fifth and British Eighth Armies were halted before the monstrous fortress of Monte Cassino at the end of 1943. There they remained until the breakthrough in May 1944.

Lancaster's job was to keep the men of the Fifth Army cheerful. It was a thankless task during the terrible months they were battling to capture Monte Cassino. More than 10,000 Americans were killed, wounded or missing.

I could sing a bit, so I sang a few Irish ditties and 'Old Man River'. Once or twice I tried to amaze them with my acrobatic skills but that didn't impress them. My other job was to turn the sheet music over for the pianist who played off the back of a truck. We were often on the front lines, performing during breaks, but we were never in any real danger.

Much of the time I was stationed either in Naples or at Caserta. I was only a private again; I'd been busted down for some minor indiscretion. Like insubordination. That was a serious crime, and I was guilty of it more than once, not without good reason, I always thought. But I was a sergeant for a while, and I knew other sergeants; that all came in handy later as an actor. I think I was a sergeant longer as an actor than I was in the army! I just kept upsetting the brass.

Like, some asshole of a lieutenant who kept telling me what I should be doing in the plays I sometimes wrote and directed. He'd had some drama training at college and thought he knew it all. Maybe he did, but I got so damned tired of him, I told him to get the hell out of my hair – which is not the sort of thing you say to an officer. I'd been due for a promotion – well, that put paid to any chance of promotion.

I didn't get on with officers. I tried to goad one into hitting me because it was a serious offence for an officer to hit an enlisted man. He didn't do it, but I felt I'd won a moral victory.

There was one captain who didn't like me at all. The USO [United Service Organization] were producing a show called *Stars and Gripes*, and I figured I'd like to get in the show. But the captain tried to keep me out and punished me by making me a 'truck jockey' which meant I had to wade up to my ass in mud, pushing and pulling at the trucks that got bogged down. I got in the show though.

While he was based at Caserta, the USO put on a show which featured an act performed by five girls, one of whom was Norma Anderson. Her husband had been killed in the war, leaving her with a one-year-old son. She had been a stenographer for a New York radio station and had found herself recruited by the USO when one of the performers fell ill. She saw this as a chance to do something positive for the war effort and, leaving her son with her parents, she went off to Europe and wound up in Caserta.

She went to see the Fifth Army show, featuring Burt

Lancaster, and was immediately attracted to him when she saw him on stage. She couldn't wait to meet him after the show, when she went backstage and introduced herself. But Lancaster was not very friendly towards her. He later said that he just was not in the mood for meeting any girl that night. So they said hello, and parted.

Not long after, while the Fifth Army was still trying to break through Monte Cassino, Lancaster met up with Norma again at a dance. This time he was more interested and asked her to dance. They spent the evening dancing and talking, and she told him about her husband and son. He told her about his life as an acrobat. They both agreed they wanted four children. They also agreed they wanted to meet up again after the war, so they exchanged addresses.

Then Monte Cassino fell in May 1944, and the Fifth Army moved on to Rome in June. Rome was a much happier place for any soldier to be during the long trek through Italy. Naples had been severely damaged by bombs but Rome still stood virtually intact. In Naples there had been far more misery and degradation among the civilian population, whereas in Rome the citizens were overjoyed to welcome the men who had once been their enemies. The girls were particularly generous to the GIs.

Lancaster recalled, 'When you've had no one but your buddies and your rifle to sleep with, it's pretty hard not to give in to a beautiful Italian girl who wants to say thank you. But I don't think I left Italy with any children wandering around who looked like me! But I did come to love Italy. It is probably my favourite country in the world, and I go there whenever I get the chance, whether it's to do with work or just pleasure.'

When a friend of his was keen to see Pope Pius XII, Burt went with him to the Vatican but, on arrival outside the Pope's audience chamber, they found a huge crowd of eager Catholics, all hoping the Pope would give them his blessing. Burt's pal became anxious and frustrated, so Burt came up with the solution: he propelled his small pal circus-style over the heads of the crowd and the GI succeeded in getting his rosary blessed.

The Fifth Army continued to push up through Northern Italy and, on 2 May 1945, the German forces in Italy surrendered. Throughout Europe, German leaders were negotiating complete surrender and on 8 May 1945, the war officially ended in Europe.

Private First Class Lancaster, who never did manage to remain a sergeant for long, was given a 45-day terminal furlough. Except for his final discharge, his army career was all but over, and he returned to New York.

There he stopped off at the Columbia Broadcasting building to find out if they were interested in having him back. They were, they said, but only after he had been fully discharged from the army.

After mooning around for three weeks, he decided to look up Norma Anderson. She had returned to her job at the RCA building, and he arranged to pick her up for lunch. He recalled:

I got in the elevator of the RCA building in the Rockefeller Center, and noticed a man staring at me. Well, this made me mad and I was all ready to bust him. But I kept my temper in check and got out at the eleventh floor. Then I saw that this guy had also got out and was still watching me. I turned to confront him and he suddenly asked, 'Are you an actor?'

I told him, 'I'm a dumb actor.' A dumb actor is a term used in the circus for a performer who doesn't speak during the act, such as acrobats.

The man introduced himself as Jack Mahlor, an associate of Broadway producer Irving Jacobs. He mistook my answer to mean that I was an actor, and he said, 'I've been looking at you, and you're exactly right physically for a part in a new play.'

He gave me an address and said to call in for an audition. I took Norma for lunch and told her what had happened. The thing was, I was unsure about whether or not I wanted to be an actor, even though I'd toyed with the idea a number of times. Norma said that if it didn't work out, she would introduce me to her boss, Ray Knight, a radio producer who she thought could help me.

Anyway, I read for the part. The play was *A Sound of Hunting* by Henry Brown and was about these GIs fighting at Monte Cassino in Italy who try to rescue one of their buddies who's got caught up between the lines. The part I read was for Sergeant Joseph Mooney. Well, I'd never made sergeant for very long, but I knew what these guys in the play were going through, and I got the part.

But first I had to get right out of the army, and to do that I was helped by an army chaplain who got my discharge papers through the separation centre just several hours before we were due to begin rehearsals. Suddenly I was an actor; I couldn't believe my luck.

I never was nervous, you know. I thought that I'd come from nowhere, so what could hurt me? If I missed a line, what could they do to me? I was there by chance, otherwise I never would have become an actor, so I had nothing to lose.

The company played for two weeks in Philadelphia and then opened on Broadway in November 1945. The critics liked the play and were especially kind to Burton Lancaster, as he was billed. Even a few Hollywood talent scouts showed interest in him:

Sam Levene, who'd appeared in a lot of films, was willing to help me and thought I could make a success of becoming a movie actor. I'd had a few offers from studios; mainly small studios offering screen tests. Sam said, 'Burt, you'll be eating in all the places you never thought you could afford, and somebody else will be picking up the tab.' I liked the sound of that. And I figured he had to know what he was talking about; he'd been in films since 1936.

But I didn't want to rush it. I was kind of half in the acting profession, half in the acrobatics profession and half in the peddling concerts business. I knew I could always make a living selling concerts, or as an acrobat, but I didn't know if I'd make any real money as an actor. But I knew I'd begun well on the stage and I knew it was time to take a gamble. So I decided to stick with acting and told Sam to go ahead and make me famous.

He began acting as my manager or agent, and he'd do all the talking and I'd just sit and listen. Then he decided he'd introduce me to Harold Hecht.

Harold Hecht had begun as an actor with the American Laboratory Theatre at the age of just 16, and over the next five years appeared in a number of classical productions on the New York stage. Then he danced with the Metropolitan Opera and Martha Graham companies, and turned his hand to directing dance sequences in films such as *Horse Feathers* and *She Done Him Wrong* in the early thirties. By 1945 he had set himself up as a Hollywood agent.

Lancaster recalled:

I had dinner with Hecht, and he levelled with me from the start, and that impressed me about him because he was honest. He didn't give any bullshit. He said, 'Look, I know everybody in the movie business, but I only have a few clients. If you sign with me, you'd be important to me because I want to eat and so I'd work hard to keep you working.'

So I agreed there and then. It was a funny thing because really I knew nothing about the film business, but I did know that I wanted to be my own boss. I admired Harold for the way he'd handled himself and built his own agency, however small it was. I told him, 'I don't know that I just want to be be an actor in movies. I want to produce movies, call the shots, make the decisions.'

And he said, 'You know, Burt, that's exactly what I'm building to do – produce my own movies. That's how you make the big bucks in Hollywood.'

The next thing you know, we're sitting there telling each other what kind of pictures we wanted to make and how in five years' time we'll be riding high, and there we were in that small restaurant with hardly a quarter between us, discussing how we were going to produce movies.

Among the talent scouts who saw Lancaster in *A Sound of Hunting* was an executive for Hal B Wallis.

Wallis was a rare kind of film producer in those days. He had worked within the usual studio system at Warner Bros but had left in 1944 to work independently at Paramount where he worked without interference. When he went to see the play, he was immediately impressed by Lancaster. 'He was excellent as the drill sergeant,' he said, 'a martinet with a striking command and attack. Looking at Burt's big shoulders and big, capable hands, I knew women would be delighted with him.'

Lancaster recalled his first meeting with Wallis:

The curtain had come down, I'd gone to my dressing room, there's a knock on the door. I open it and there stands Hal Wallis. He introduces himself, says he's a movie producer. I figure, let's play this cool, show him I'm not impressed. I don't invite him in but keep him standing there. He says he's been building up a stock company of actors and asks how would I like to sign with him.

So I say, 'Talk to my agent, Harold Hecht,' and I close the door.

He sees Hecht and proposes a two-picture-per-year contract with the right to make pictures for other companies. I'm to get a 100 dollars a week for four weeks and a first-class train ticket to the West Coast and back because first I have to pass a screen test and, if I pass, I get a flat fee of 10,000 dollars and a weekly salary of 1,250 dollars for the next seven years. I think that sounds the kind of deal I want, so I accept.

Next, I'm walking with Wallis to his lawyer's office in New York. There's a huge billboard for a picture. Wallis says, 'I produced that picture. How would you like to see it?'

I tell him, 'I already saw it – in Italy. I thought it stank.' That let him know I was no sycophant.

3

Hollywood Brains

Burt still had the play to do but, despite the good reviews, the public stayed away:

Nobody wanted to see a bitter war drama; everyone was sick of the war. They wanted something else. We closed after three weeks.

Christmas came and went. Then I got on the train and headed for California. Well, for Chicago actually where I stopped to get my two suits cleaned. Now I had two suits, so I knew I was doing better. However, the shoes I wore were borrowed and I had maybe 30 dollars in cash on me. I nearly missed my train to Los Angeles because the suits were not ready from the dry cleaners, so I had to borrow a shirt and pants and arrived in Los Angeles looking like a bum.

I got off the train and was met by Harold Hecht who looked at me and said, 'Where's your suit?'

I said, 'In Chicago with the other suit.'

He said, 'Where's your coat?'

I said, 'What do I need a coat for? This is California.'

He said, 'Yes, but this is January and it gets cold at night even in California.'

So he took me over to Robert Preston's bungalow and asked if I could borrow a jacket; a leather jacket. Then

Hecht got me over to Paramount to meet Wallis, and Wallis sent me to Byron Haskin's office; Haskin was an important director.

When I found his office I walked in and there he was reading a script, and I said, 'You Haskin?' He said he was. I said, 'I'm Burt Lancaster.' I was kind of brusque because I didn't want to show I was impressed or nervous or anything like that.

He said, 'Oh?' He was just as brusque.

I said, 'I'm supposed to read for you.'

'Is that right?'

'Yeah.'

'Well, I've no objection, Mr Lancaster.'

I decided I'd do a scene from *A Sound of Hunting* and I began to arrange the furniture in his office to create the set of a trench. I began my scene, playing the sergeant, swearing at his men, swearing at the enemy, making all sorts of noise and moving about until everyone from the nearby offices had heard the commotion and had come in to see what was going on. Pretty soon I had a whole audience and at the end of my scene they applauded. I said to Haskin, 'Well, what did you think?'

He paused, shrugged and said, 'Okay, let's give you a screen test, Mr Lancaster.' There was about a month's preparation for the screen test which was for a film called *Desert Fury* which, if I passed the screen test, would be my first picture. I was getting paid 100 dollars a week while I was given some rudimentary screen-acting lessons, and then finally we did the test, and I passed. Suddenly I was under contract and getting a flat fee of 10,000 dollars plus 1,250 dollars a week for the next seven years.

He was eager to begin his first movie but he was informed that *Desert Fury* was not scheduled to begin shooting until August. With time to spare he decided to return to New York, but before leaving he heard that somebody over at Universal was looking for an actor to play a boxer called the Swede in a film called *The Killers*.

'The Swede was a character who was confused and lacked sophistication,' said Lancaster. 'They described him as "dumb". It sounded an interesting part and I thought I'd like to take a stab at it.'

The screenplay by Anthony Veiller was based on a short story by Ernest Hemingway of whom Lancaster was a great admirer. The film was being produced by Mark Hellinger who had been a reporter and then a screen writer before Universal took him on as a producer.

The part of the Swede was originally intended for Wayne Morris but his studio, Warner Brothers, were asking for 75,000 dollars for his loan-out – too high a price for Hellinger. Universal wanted their own contract player, Sonny Tufts, to fill the role but Hellinger was not convinced Tufts had the right quality for what was quite a complex part.

Lancaster asked Marty Juroc, in Wallis's office, to sneak his screen test over to Hellinger and consequently Hellinger was sufficiently impressed to meet Lancaster.

'This guy was big, really big,' Hellinger recalled. 'His hair was tousled – no tie – his suit looked as if it hadn't been pressed since C Aubrey Smith was in short pants. But there was something about him. All the time I was talking to him, that smart guy was playing the dumb Swede for me. The Swede I had in mind was big, dumb, awkward and fumbling. The day I met him, Lancaster was all four. When you got to know him, you realized he's anything but the last three.'

Lancaster had not gone to his meeting with Hellinger ignorant of what he had to do. He purposely disguised his own personality and went into Hellinger's playing the Swede for real.

Hellinger asked Lancaster what he thought of the script. Lancaster replied, 'The first 16 pages are pure Hemingway verbatim, and after that you have a rather interesting whodunnit film, but nothing comparable to Hemingway.'

Hellinger said, 'Well, you're not really a dumb Swede after all.'

'I never thought I was.'

A screen test followed and Lancaster got the part.

Filming began in April 1946, with Robert Siodmak directing. The cast included Ava Gardner as the Swede's bad girlfriend, and Edmond O'Brien as the insurance investigator who uncovers the mystery of the Swede's murder which takes place in the first reel of the film. Thereafter, the story is told in flashback.

It was as much a break for Ava Gardner as it was for Lancaster. She had played a number of minor roles in minor films and was mainly famous for having married Mickey Rooney in 1942 and divorcing him the following year. She was currently married to musician Artie Shaw but that marriage was already heading for the rocks.

In her autobiography, *Ava, My Story*, Gardner wrote, 'Burt and Eddie and the rest of us were in the early stages of our careers, fresh kids enjoying life.'

She was clearly impressed by Lancaster who, she noted, 'had all the confidence in the world'. Although she never wrote of any relationship between them, she did once tell me that Burt Lancaster 'was not the kind of man a girl ignored. He just swept you off your feet, and I guess being young and reckless in Hollywood as we were in those days, it wasn't surprising that we enjoyed each other's company once or twice. I was married then but I never was very successful at being a wife. I think I was always a better lover.'

Back on the set, she felt that he was 'competent enough to take the whole thing over, and if Robert Siodmak hadn't been such a strong director, he might have.'

Columnist Sheilah Graham wrote in her book, *Confessions of a Hollywood Columnist*, that when she first saw him on the set of *The Killers*, 'masculinity was oozing from every pore. He was thirty-two but looked twenty-two, and what a physique! I could see the muscles rippling up and down beneath his open shirt.'

No wonder Ava Gardner was swept off her feet by him and he no doubt showed confidence in performing with her – on the set and in private – as indeed he showed confidence in all he did.

Sheilah Graham, however, noted that Lancaster was so unsure of himself that Siodmak sometimes shot up to fifteen takes of one small scene. Lancaster, said Graham, was so embarrassed that he 'apologized humbly'.

But he had to learn his craft, as indeed he had once had to learn to swing on the bars and in the process made mistakes that resulted in injuries. On his first film he was bound to make mistakes and, while he may have been brusque from time to time, he acknowledged when he had made a mistake in front of the camera.

Lancaster said that he had to learn a new way of performing for the part of the Swede. 'I didn't have to be ostentatious or theatrical, just simple because I was playing this dumb guy. This made it easy for me as a new actor, and I was lucky to be given the break in a role that didn't require any histrionics.'

He acknowledged Siodmak's direction of the film: 'He was a charming man whose strength was in *film noir* because of his inventive use of the camera. I found him very engaging and he eased me through my first film. If it went wrong, we just did it again. He didn't make any fuss. I always felt very grateful to him.'

During filming, the subject of his screen name was discussed between Hal Wallis and Mark Hellinger. He was still known as Burton Lancaster. Wallis wanted to launch him as Stuart Chase but had to scrap that idea when he was informed that Stuart Chase was a famous economist who might object.

Hellinger's secretary Myrtle came up with the solution – shorten the name to Burt and keep the Lancaster. Hellinger called Wallis and told him the suggestion. Wallis agreed. Hellinger later remarked, 'It's amazing what Hollywood brains can accomplish if they give it the works.'

The film took eight weeks to finish. Universal wanted it ready for an August release. The wait to discover if the film was a hit wasn't long. It opened to good reviews. *Variety* said, 'Seldom does a melodrama maintain the high tension that distinguishes this one,' and of Lancaster added, 'he does a strong job, serving as the central character around whom the plot revolves.' The *New York Herald Tribune* thought Lancaster 'plays a likeable fall guy in a most promising screen debut.' The London *Sunday Times*'s critic, Dilys Powell, thought Lancaster a 'husky, good-looking, straight-browed newcomer'. The *Sunday Dispatch* predicted, 'We're going to see more of Burt Lancaster . . . there is more acting done by the muscles of his face than is often done by another actor using both arms and a voice.'

The public response reflected the critical acclaim, and Oscar nominations were given to Robert Siodmak, Anthony Veiller and to Miklos Rozsa for his music score.

Hellinger recognized Lancaster's potential and signed him for two more films, the first to be called *Brute Force*, the second as yet undecided. But Hellinger had to wait because Hal Wallis was now ready to make *Desert Fury*.

Filming began in August 1946, almost as soon as *The Killers* had opened. Sensing the impact that Burt Lancaster was going to have on the screen, Wallis had shrewdly rewritten the screenplay by Robert Rossen to expand Lancaster's role to third-bill him in a major supporting role.

The star of the picture was Lizabeth Scott, an actress-model who had been discovered by Wallis and put under contract. She played the refined daughter of an Arizonian brothel-casino owner, played by Mary Astor. Lancaster was cast as the local sheriff whose job was to expose Scott's boyfriend, played by John Hodiak, as a crook. Lewis Allen, an Englishman who found himself in Hollywood under contract to Paramount, directed.

Much of the film was made on the Paramount back lot and, although there was some location shooting in Arizona, the result was a typical studio-bound melodrama.

During only his second film, Burt Lancaster was already finding himself inspired to want to do more than just act. One day Wallis came onto the set and asked Lancaster how he was doing.

'Okay, I guess,' Lancaster replied, 'but I won't be doing this much longer. I'll soon be directing.'

Sheilah Graham noted the big change that had come over Lancaster. She wrote, 'It is a pleasure being with a future star at the beginning. He is always so friendly, so eager to please. He makes a hit and is a different man.'

However, it is clear that from then on, Burt Lancaster was never a favourite leading man of Graham's. He later reflected on what she wrote of him and told me:

> I *was* different. You can't stand still. I wasn't going to be the same man I started out as. I've always wanted to get ahead – it's the compulsion to be a winner. Not just for winning's sake, but for the sake of doing the best you can, being the best you can. Okay, on my second or third film I began to speak up, tell the director if I had ideas; I call that growing. So Sheilah didn't think I was such a nice guy any more; she didn't love me any more. Those columnists were leeches, blood suckers; that's why I made *Sweet Smell of Success* [a few years later]. And that's why I've never been the darling of the newspapers.
>
> Sure, I lost my temper sometimes on the set. I ended up producing my own films with James Hill and Harold Hecht, so I had a right to blow my stack when somebody screwed up. But in those early films, I don't think it's true that I flew at anyone. I probably said a few things that were frank, and I may have been wrong even sometimes; but I was never going to remain the same man – no.

At last Lancaster brought Norma and her son James Stephen out to California. On 28 December 1946, they were married in Yuma, Arizona, and moved into a rented house at Malibu beach for a short period. Then, with fame and fortune staring Lancaster in the face, he bought a huge house in Bel-Air, into which moved his father, now his manager, and brother Jim who, during the years when Burt was at college, helped keep the family maintained on his salary as a policeman. Now he was working for younger brother Burt, dealing with his legal affairs. (Burt's other brother, William Henry, had died; the cause of his death remains as vague as many other aspects of Lancaster's early life.) Now Burt was making his movie stardom a family business. He bought himself a car, and one for Jim.

He installed a gymnasium with double horizontal bars, and he brought Nick Cravat out to Bel-Air to become his trainer. They practised flyovers three days a week. Lancaster wanted to maintain his trim build which, it was clear, was part of his fortune. He also smoked heavily.

Paramount decided to hold back *Desert Fury* while Lancaster went back to Universal in early 1947 to make *Brute Force* for Mark Hellinger. This time he got top billing over Charles Bickford, Hume Cronyn, Ella Raines, Yvonne de Carlo and Ann Blyth. The film featured five interwoven tales of convicts who eventually revolt against a sadistic warden and try to escape. Lancaster, one of the five convicts, wants only to be with his girlfriend, played by Ann Blyth, while she undergoes a cancer operation.

The screenplay was by Richard Brooks whose first book, *The Brick Foxhole*, was liked by Mark Hellinger so much that he looked for an opportunity to hire Brooks as a screen writer. In fact, Brooks wrote a number of screenplays for B-pictures, then got to work for Hellinger by doing some uncredited work on *The Killers*. Hellinger then put him to work writing *Brute Force*.

During filming, Brooks revealed to Lancaster his hopes of making a movie from Sinclair Lewis's novel *Elmer Gantry*. 'I got to know Richard Brooks fairly well back in 1947 when we first discussed *Elmer Gantry*,' said Lancaster. 'He came to me and said, "Have you read the Sinclair Lewis book, *Elmer Gantry*?" I said I was familiar with it. He said, "You know, I think I'm going to buy this property and write it as a screenplay." And I told him that was a wonderful idea. Then we went our separate ways, but I always hoped we'd maybe get to do the film one day.'

Jules Dassin directed *Brute Force* and found in Lancaster an actor frustrated by the limitations of his job. Sheilah Graham put it bluntly, 'Lancaster was already telling the director how to direct.' Burt didn't see it that way:

> Jules Dassin was an extraordinarily gifted director. I knew immediately that I was working with someone who knew how to excite an actor and who wanted to help in creating new ideas in playing the part. I never told him how to direct. But already I had ideas about directing and I talked to him about these ideas. If he was annoyed with me, he didn't show it. He was willing to listen, and I was willing to listen to him. I wanted to be a good director, but you don't become a good director on your own. You need the experience of others, and who better to learn from than a fine director like Dassin.

Lancaster was excited also by the social comment in the film. 'Today we recognize the fallibility of the penal system and that it fails to do little good other than put bad men away, off the streets.'

His temper was occasionally sparked on the set, mainly by his own inadequacy to get a take right. In one scene he kept getting one simple line wrong and after more than twenty takes, he felt so nervous, embarrassed and just plain angry with himself that he picked up a chair and smashed it against the wall.

The critics generally liked the film. *Variety* noted how 'the bristling, biting dialogue by Richard Brooks paints broad cameos as each character takes shape under existing prison life.' The *Herald Tribune* noted, 'Jules Dassin's staging has called for a great many close-ups of Lancaster looking steely-eyed and unshaven, but these do not become monotonous within Lancaster's brooding, effective perform-ance.' But Lancaster could do nothing to please Bosley Crowther of the *New York Times* who merely thought that 'big-framed, expressionless Burt Lancaster gives the chief convict a heroic mould.'

The film was well liked by Lancaster. 'It could have been just another romantic film of men in prison dreaming about their girls outside, because that's the way it was written, but Dassin turned it into a *film noir* with his visual style. It's such a potent film for its time.'

Paramount released *Desert Fury* in August 1947 to poor reviews but average business, which did nothing to harm Lancaster's growing reputation from his two Hellinger films. In retrospect, he said, he was glad that he did not make *Desert Fury* first, 'or I might never have been heard of again'.

Life was definitely going the way he wanted it to, in his career and in his private life – Norma was expecting their first child.

By the time *Brute Force* was finished, Burt Lancaster had come to consider Mark Hellinger as a close friend. He admired the producer for his ability to deal with stories of quality and they discussed plans for their next film, as yet untitled but which now had a storyline. It was to be about a group of men who plan a complicated hold-up of a Hollywood racetrack.

Lancaster was already considered to be more than just a supporting player, and Paramount put him alongside Lizabeth Scott in their all-star musical *Variety Girl* which opened in October 1947. It was little more than an excuse for a filmed tour of the Paramount studios featuring all the contract players, including those signed to Hal Wallis, who did featured bits. The slim plot was about a girl who arrives in Hollywood hoping to become a star. Lancaster played a cowboy star who is supposed to shoot a cigarette out of Lizabeth Scott's mouth. It was a short gag in which the stunt goes wrong and Lancaster is seen advertising for another girl assistant.

On 17 November 1947, Norma gave birth to William Henry, named after Burt's late brother. With his family increasing, Lancaster purchased the plots surrounding their house.

Towards the end of 1947 he began to wonder why he never seemed to be able to keep much of the money he earned. He talked it over with Hellinger who told him, 'You'll owe the government a great deal of money in taxes so you'll be broke for a long time.'

'But I don't see how. After all, I lead a fairly moderate life.'

'Look, Burt, you have your father out here, you have your brother out here as your lawyer, you bought a car for him, and one for yourself, and you've just bought a house. Well, if you keep that up, you're going to be broke.'

It was good advice from a good friend. Shortly after, Mark Hellinger died from a heart attack, aged 44.

4

Work Hard, Play Hard

In 1948, Lancaster worked on setting up his own production company, with the legal matters in Jim's capable hands. In the meantime he continued to work under contract for Hal Wallis, making *I Walk Alone* at Paramount. It was based on an unsuccessful play, *Beggars Are Coming to Town* by Theodore Reeves but, despite its failure, Wallis saw it as the perfect vehicle for a whole host of his stock players; namely Burt Lancaster, Lizabeth Scott, Wendell Corey and Kirk Douglas.

Wallis wanted to get the most out of his contract players for as little as possible. Lancaster said, 'Wallis didn't like to spend money. Once he was producing his own films, he kept them on a shoestring, but he knew how to make them look slick. He didn't really know how to deal with stories that had a literary quality as did Mark Hellinger.'

For the first time Lancaster and Douglas co-starred, playing gangsters running bootleg liquor during Prohibition. Douglas frames Lancaster who ends up doing a 14-year stretch, then comes back for his revenge.

'That's where our friendship began,' said Lancaster of Douglas. 'We both came from sort of humble beginnings. We were both young, brash, cocky, arrogant. We knew everything, were highly opinionated. We were invincible. Nobody liked us.'

The two actors actually hated their roles; Douglas recalled

Wallis's eyes widening in shock when he told him that the film's ending was dull. Douglas told me:

> The original ending had the police coming in to the restaurant, they take me away, Burt kisses Liz, end of picture. I suggested to Wallis that when the police come in for me, I say, 'Do you mind if I have one farewell drink?' I go behind the bar, pull out a gun, shoot the cop who let me have the drink in the first place, get into a dramatic confrontation with Burt, then I'm subdued and led away.
>
> Hal's eyes got bigger and bigger at the audacity of this upstart actor telling him how the last scene should be written. He hated any actor interfering but the scene was shot as I suggested.

Director Byron Haskin, who had given Lancaster his screen test, had to listen to both Douglas and Lancaster telling him how he should shoot the movie. And Wallis had to put up with them complaining not only about the script and their roles, but also that they were grossly underpaid. Sheilah Graham, always seemingly on hand to report on Lancaster's progress, dubbed the duo 'The Terrible-Tempered Twins'.

But their close friendship was not immediate. On the set of *I Walk Alone* they certainly liked each other but, after the day's work, they went their respective ways: Douglas home to his wife Diana, and Lancaster back to Norma.

The film was a success despite its mixed critical response. Bosley Crowther of the *New York Times* said that Lancaster played his part 'with the blank-faced aplomb of Tarzan'. *Variety*, however, thought 'Lancaster belts over his assignment as the former jailbird', and named Kirk Douglas as 'a standout'.

In those pre-television and video days, films were recreated for radio, and Lancaster, Douglas and Lizabeth Scott repeated their roles in *I Walk Alone* for Lux Radio Theatre in May 1948.

Lancaster thought the film, like *Desert Fury*, was

lightweight, and he looked around for something with weight to it. He discovered that over at Universal, Chester Erskine was going to produce *All My Sons*, based on the play by Arthur Miller, which had run for nine months on Broadway under the direction of Elia Kazan. Erskine himself had adapted the screenplay and had çast Edward G Robinson as the factory owner who, it turns out, had knowingly provided faulty cylinder blocks to an aircraft manufacturer during the war, resulting in the deaths of 21 pilots, including one of his own sons.

Lancaster was desperate for the role of the son who learns the truth and forces his father to take the responsibility and accept the guilt. Hal Wallis thought Lancaster should have nothing to do with the film and tried to dissuade him but Lancaster kept up the pressure until he wore Wallis down into giving his permission.

At Universal, Chester Erskine informed Lancaster that he would have to take a cut in salary for this low-budget picture; this time Lancaster had no complaints about being underpaid. He agreed to anything to get the part, including accepting second billing to Edward G Robinson.

It was not a difficult part for Lancaster to play. He said, 'I wanted the part because he had the courage to make his father realize that he was as responsible for the deaths of servicemen as if he had murdered them and, as I had been in the army during the war, I had no trouble duplicating those feelings.'

Robinson was immediately impressed with Lancaster's 'animal vitality and suppressed volcano inside that inevitably made him a star'. Lancaster knew better than to get into any arguments with Robinson who was known as 'One-Take Eddie' because he rarely had to repeat a scene. This meant that Lancaster had to be good in the first take in every scene he was in with Robinson whose 'passion imbued the whole cast', as Robinson himself put it.

This meant that the director, Irving Reis, had an easier time of it with Lancaster than many other directors. Reis had the difficult task of opening up the stagebound play into a filmable story. The *Daily Mail* thought he succeeded: 'A thoughtful, dramatic, meaty film, well performed by Edward G Robinson and Burt Lancaster.' *Variety* said, 'Burt Lancaster, as the war-embittered son, shades the assignment with just the right amount of intensity.' *Time and Tide*, however, thought Lancaster 'the blot on the film'.

The film opened midway through 1948 but was not a huge success. Lancaster was not disappointed. 'We took a chance. We tried. I'd still be a punk kid if I was too afraid to take a chance.'

He repeated his performance alongside Robinson on NBC's Cameo Screen Guild Players' radio recreation of the film in November.

Around this time word had reached Elia Kazan and Tennesse Williams in New York that Burt Lancaster was an exciting actor, and they decided they wanted him to star in their Broadway production, *A Streetcar Named Desire*. Lancaster later said that he could not accept the play because of film commitments but some sources state that he turned the play down because he was already a major movie star. Marlon Brando got the part instead, and Lancaster would comment, 'I don't know that I would have done it any better than Marlon, but I do think I would have been very good in it.'

By now he was worth 200,000 dollars a picture, although most of the money actually went to Hal Wallis. Lancaster was taking steps to ensure his independence in future years, as his brother Jim continued to work away at the technicalities of setting up a production company in partnership with his agent Harold Hecht. Burt was determined that when his seven-year contract with Wallis was over, he would never work for anyone else again.

Not that he was always at odds with Wallis. Indeed, they occasionally went fishing together. On one such trip during 1948 Wallis was relating his dilemma about who should play the weak husband in *Sorry, Wrong Number*.

'I wanted Lee Bowman,' Wallis told him, 'but he isn't available. I need someone who specializes in weak parts.'

'Why not let me play it,' suggested Lancaster.

Wallis answered, 'You can't play it. You're much too strong for it.'

'That's the whole idea; you'd have a strong-looking guy who's on the threshold of his life who allows a woman to buy him and then he suffers for it. All of his character has been drained out of him. People will see me at the beginning of the film and think I'm strong, and then the contrast will be really dramatic and exciting.'

Wallis turned the idea over in his mind and later, back at the studio, discussed it with his director, Anatole Litvak. Litvak thought it was a great idea.

Barbara Stanwyck played the rich invalid who marries the younger Lancaster. When his gambling lands him in heavy debt, he decides to have his wife killed and claim on her insurance. In the end he has to battle with his conscience.

Lancaster 'really sweated bullets' on the set, trying to achieve a performance that contained none of the movements or characteristics that identified his usual image. He also gave Barbara Stanwyck full support because he knew that she was the real star of the film. She was known for her professional and temperament-free approach to her work and Lancaster duly behaved himself.

By now Norma was pregnant again. But by this time she was beginning to feel like a Hollywood widow. She had known that she would have to sacrifice all for the sake of her husband's career but she was finding the going difficult. It may have helped that she had her father-in-law and brother-in-law constantly around to support her – or it may have been a burden. The truth was that Norma was unhappy. As Shelley Winters would later say, 'I learned myself that being married to a movie star is an almost untenable position for any intelligent, self-respecting woman.'

Norma loved Burt, and she was, as everyone knew, very patient. Burt was not a model of fidelity.

He told me, 'When you're young and you have the world in your hands, you have power. I worked damned hard in those

days, and when you work hard, you kinda play hard. There
were a lot of women around who didn't care if a man was
married, just so long as he had power. I was no angel, but you
know – everybody knows – that's not unusual in Hollywood
for anyone. It's no excuse, but that's the way it is.'

Whether or not Lancaster had remained faithful to Norma
during the marriage so far, he would not say. But he did
recognize that already his marriage was in trouble. And, when
he went to a party at the home of new Wallis contract player
Mickey Knox in 1948, he was having trouble keeping his eyes
off Shelley Winters. She, too, was attracted to him. At just 26,
the young actress from Broadway was on the verge of a
breakthrough in her new five-year-old movie career.

Burt's marriage to Norma was becoming a rollercoaster.
According to Shelley Winters, Norma was an alcoholic;
whether at this time or later is undetermined. Burt's production
company was ready to go ahead at last. And perhaps in the
hope that it might have some magic effect on his marriage,
Lancaster and Harold Hecht named the company Norma.
Actually, they had decided on the name of the company from
the outset before the marriage began to suffer.

He announced, 'Marriage has steadied me down. My wife
has good sound judgement and has the unbelievable wisdom of
waiting until she is asked for an opinion.' This was, in fact, a
clue to his rather domineering approach to being a husband.
It's an attitude that may well have driven her to drink. He
added, 'She is interested in all my ambitions, so much so that I
have named my company, Norma Productions, after her.'

It was now late 1948, and Lancaster began filming his first
production, *Kiss the Blood Off My Hands*. He had been happy
at Universal, and he and Hecht made a deal with that studio to
release the film. As far as the screen credits were concerned,
Harold Hecht was the producer, but Lancaster had his hands
firmly on the reins too. He was the first actor, since the advent
of sound, to run his own production company. Others followed
his example; John Wayne, Kirk Douglas, Charlton Heston and
Clint Eastwood were just a few among the more successful.

The film was based on a book by Gerald Butler and directed by Norman Foster, in which Lancaster played a Canadian merchant marine whose temper leads him to stab a drunk in a London pub. Robert Newton co-starred as a Cockney black marketeer who blackmails Lancaster into taking part in a hijacking. Joan Fontaine supplied the romantic interest as a nurse who manages to save Lancaster by killing Newton.

Although set in London, the whole thing was shot at Universal Studios. Lancaster and Hecht had borrowed the money to finance the film and were under the gun to get the film made within a 45-day schedule. Not all went according to plan and the pressures of producing a film began to weigh on the shoulders of Lancaster and Hecht.

Joan Fontaine, who was in the early stages of pregnancy, became unwell and had to take time off. The producers worked with their director to rearrange the schedule but this seemed to throw Robert Newton into confusion. The fact that he drank heavily probably did not help, but he was relieved, as were the producers, when Fontaine returned to work.

But then she caught a cold and had to take another break, of twelve days. Schedules were changed again, and Newton was once more thrown into confusion. Or perhaps he was suffering the effects of long binges.

It looked as though the film might never get made at all, especially when unrelenting rain held up exterior shooting. Miraculously, the film was finished within budget and only three days over schedule.

The film was rushed out to a lukewarm reception by the press. But it made money at the box office. In fact, Lancaster's name on the marquee of any cinema was now reckoned to add a million dollars to the overall take.

Lancaster knew his first film as a producer was not particularly good but he had done what he set out to do – be his own boss – and he intended to do a lot better the next time.

Meanwhile, he had an obligation to Universal to make *Criss Cross*, the film he had been going to make for Mark Hellinger. The studio were intent on the film proceeding with Lancaster as part of his contract with Hellinger.

The script was rewritten – or 'rehashed', as Lancaster described it – and Robert Siodmak set to direct. In fact, neither Lancaster nor Siodmak had the heart to do the film now with Hellinger gone but they could not get out of it.

During production, early in 1949, Lancaster came on to the set one day to watch his leading lady, Yvonne de Carlo, filming a scene, and saw a young, dark-haired man dancing with her. His name was Anthony Curtis, a young, relatively inexperienced contract player just signed up by Universal. Whether or not Lancaster was immediately impressed by the brief movie debut of Tony Curtis is not on record but in just a few years' time, he would give Curtis his first important film, *Trapeze*, followed by one of the very best films either he or Curtis ever made, *Sweet Smell of Success*.

Criss Cross won mixed reviews, ranging from *Variety*'s praise for 'Siodmak's knowing direction', and Lancaster's 'made-to-order part of a two-fisted square-shooter', to a panning by James S Barstow in the *Herald Tribune*: 'Lancaster is almost forced into a near parody of his previous dumb-brute portrayals.'

The film found an audience. Back at Paramount Studios, Hal Wallis cast Lancaster in *Rope of Sand*, a fairly blatant attempt to cash in on the success of *Casablanca* by featuring Paul Henried and Claude Rains almost repeating their villainous roles from the earlier film, helped out by Peter Lorre. The script called for Lancaster to go in search of a cache of diamonds in the South African desert. It was a script that baffled Lancaster and he was desperately unhappy making the film.

He behaved as if he didn't care about it. When powerful columnist Sheilah Graham came on the set to interview him, he led her to the large communal lunch table for cast and crew and loudly repeated each and every question she asked him.

He was testing to see how far he could go to prove that he did not need the kind of publicity the studio always arranged. He even told Hedda Hooper, one of the most powerful Hollywood columnists, 'Let's get one thing straight. I don't frighten easily, and you don't scare me at all. I see right through you. I understand you perfectly well, because you're exactly like my mother.'

Apparently she took this to be a compliment but he didn't mean that at all because he had often described his mother as 'a bit of a tyrant'.

He told the studio press agent, 'Don't bother me with any of these creepy newspaper people.'

He made a big effort to keep his family life looking as normal and as happy as possible; he often had Norma and the children on the set to watch him work, or had lunch with them at the studio commissary.

In July 1949, Norma gave birth to Susan Elizabeth. Lancaster was typically proud of his new daughter and for a while it seemed that the marriage would survive.

5

Some Enchanted Evening

From time to time, Lancaster needed to get away from the intense business of making movies and so he erected a twelve-foot-high trapeze in the back of his bungalow at Universal Studios. Most days he and Nick Cravat practised on it and he began to feel the pull of the circus once again. He decided to put Hollywood and movies behind him for a while and take to the road with Nick Cravat for a series of personal appearances with Cole Brothers' Circus.

He and Cravat were a sensation in Chicago, Milwaukee and New York, performing for 11,000 dollars a week. Cole Brothers provided a private railroad car that had been fitted out at a cost of 65,000 dollars and came complete with its own full-time chef. But Lancaster could not stand all that comfort and rich food, so he left Cravat on the train while he borrowed the manager's car and drove from city to city.

In New York he stayed at the Gotham Hotel and managed to obtain two tickets to see *South Pacific* on Broadway. Cravat did not want to go, so Lancaster got into his suit and caught the hotel elevator. On the way down it stopped and in walked Shelley Winters. The doors closed and the elevator continued on down.

Lancaster casually mentioned that he had two tickets for the fifth row centre to see *South Pacific*. Winters was also on her way to see the show but she only had a ticket for the back row.

'Why not go with me,' he said.

He was, she said, 'so handsome, so charming, and he was just so graceful that he was the most graceful man ever, and almost a physical pleasure to watch.'

He had a limousine waiting outside. She climbed in with him and when they arrived at the theatre a fan saw them and begged for an autograph. Lancaster took Shelley's back-row ticket and handed it to the fan. It was only the second night of the show and photographers were there to snap the arriving celebrities.

Inside, after they had sat down, Shelley told him that she felt uneasy about them being photographed together.

'Yes,' he said, 'but my wife and I are not getting along. We're discussing a separation.'

The lights went down, the curtain went up, and the show began. During the number 'Some Enchanted Evening', Lancaster took Shelley's hand and asked, 'Do you remember meeting me at a party at Mickey Knox's house?'

She lied that she could just remember the party but could not exactly recall him.

She told me, 'It was all so corny, you know, all that romantic music playing and we were having such a happy time and getting caught up in it all, it really was an enchanted evening. During the curtain calls, I yelled so much I got hoarse. Burt just suddenly picked me up and carried me to a horse carriage outside, and we went for a drive through Central Park. It was all so corny but we were just both so carried away.'

Later they had champagne and caviar for supper at Le Pavillon. Norman Mailer joined them at their booth and began a sales pitch to Lancaster to buy the screen rights to his war book, *The Naked and the Dead*. Shelley did not want to talk about the book and, when Lancaster left the booth to find out if there were any messages for him, Mailer said to her, 'Thanks, Shelley. Here am I making a quarter-of-a-million-dollar sale on my book and you keep trying to sit on Lancaster's lap.'

She told him that he was managing to louse up a very romantic evening. When Lancaster returned, Mailer stood up, kissed Shelley on the cheek and said, 'You're on a fast track, kid.'

Lancaster agreed to meet Mailer the following morning. Then, after Mailer left, Lancaster told Shelley the story of his life. Later, they walked – or rather sang and danced – back to the hotel. The streets were empty as they ran along Fifth Avenue.

He saw her to her room but at the door she realized she had left the key at the desk. He told her, 'I'm one flight up – and my key's in my pocket.' With his arm around her, he led her up to his room. She kept saying, 'We're just going to listen to records.'

'Right,' he said.

'And then I'm going down to get my key.'

'Right.'

'After all, you're married.'

'I am.'

'And I've this girlfriend who had a very unhappy love affair with a married man.'

'Poor girl.'

They reached his room where he put on a record and opened the window. He poured brandy for each of them and then, as she described it, 'the fresh smell of spring and the music and the brandy and us dancing all led to the inevitable – on a thick white rug on the living room floor. And that's how it began with me and Burt.'

Burt awoke first in the morning and ordered breakfast but by this time Shelley had had second thoughts. She told me:

> In the morning, all I wanted to do was get dressed, get out, and get away. It was guilt, confusion, a sudden coming down to earth with a bump, because he was a married man with kids, and I asked myself what the hell I was doing there. But he was just so charming, I caved in and stayed a bit longer. And when I did leave, it was after arranging to meet him that evening to go to the theatre. Unfortunately, I was clumsy enough to get myself knocked down by a car that day. Someone called an ambulance and I refused to get in, and they said I needed to get my nose X-rayed because it was bleeding.
>
> Anyway, the point is, I made it back to the hotel and

when Burt saw me he and Norman Mailer – they were continuing their discussion of Mailer's book – rushed me to an orthopaedic specialist who X-rayed me and told me to get to hospital because if the studio found out, they would never let me go to New York again without a chaperone. So Burt got me back to my room – in fact, he carried me to my room and he just really took care of me. He was just so kind and he bought me flowers and presents and made me laugh with his funny stories. He blamed himself for whatever reason and, when the end of the week came, and he had to go back to Hollywood, he promised me he'd get in touch when I was back there too.

Then, one day, having heard that Shelley Winters was back in LA, he decided he would take son William over to the house where she lived with her parents, and found her by the swimming pool.

She was shocked, to say the least, and the sight him carrying William quashed her into silence. Around William's leg was a bandage; he had undergone an operation after contracting polio. Burt had built a swimming pool of his own because William needed the therapeutic benefits of swimming. Burt did not use the pool much himself; he still suffered a mild form of hydrophobia. But William loved swimming and when he saw the swimming pool at the home of Shelley Winters, he tried to jump in.

Burt introduced William to Shelley who was still so speechless that she simply nodded to a series of questions which Lancaster asked her. William said, 'Daddy, hasn't Shelley Winters learned to talk yet?'

Lancaster introduced himself to Shelley's parents; her father, disapproving of the whole affair, refused to speak to him. Shortly after, Lancaster was approached by the lifeguard who informed him that children under the age of eight were not allowed by the pool; Burt knew he was being persuaded to leave, and he did so without argument.

Determined to enjoy her love affair without parental

interference, Shelley moved out of the family home and spent a week sleeping in a bungalow at Universal Studios – often with Burt. He was now trying to get Norma to agree to a legal separation but she refused to allow such a thing because of the effect on their children. Finally, Burt managed to get Shelley her own apartment.

By now, desperate to get out of his contract with Wallis, he began exploring legal loopholes and succeeded in cutting down the number of films he had to make for Wallis from the seven originally agreed. In between balancing his affair with Shelley and maintaining an image of marital bliss, he was about to enter the most powerful stage of his professional career.

In his bid to become more independent as a film producer, Lancaster went to Columbia where studio boss Harry Cohn had expressed an interest. Burt had a script by Waldo Salt called *The Flame and the Arrow*, which was loosely based on the story of William Tell.

Cohn told him, 'No, no, we want you to do a gangster picture, like *Brute Force*.' But Burt didn't want to do another gangster picture and he left Cohn's office.

Some time later he and Hecht were negotiating with Warner Brothers for a contract whereby their company, now called Hecht-Norma Productions, would make three films for the studio over three years. When Lancaster mentioned to Jack Warner that he had a script based on the William Tell story, Warner had his script department read it and told Lancaster, 'Let's do this film first because we've got all the sets from *Robin Hood* still standing and we can use them.'

The Flame and the Arrow went into production at the Burbank Studio with Jacques Tourneur directing. Lancaster had the role of Dardo, an Italian daredevil in the mould of William Tell and Robin Hood, and Virginia Mayo was his fair maiden in distress. Lancaster wanted to give his partner and friend, Nick Cravat, a part so that they could exploit their amazing acrobatic skills on screen. Cravat was not an experienced actor, so Lancaster invented a part for him, that of a deaf-mute sidekick.

When Jack Warner saw some of the early rushes, he threw his hands up in horror at the over-the-top and rather camp humour. 'What the fuck is this, *A Midsummer Night's Dream*?' he cried.

Because of his athletic prowess, Lancaster was able to perform most of his own stunts, especially in scenes in which Lancaster and Cravat performed high-bar walking and high-pole balancing.

During production, Lancaster divided his time between the Warner Brothers studio, being at home at certain times of the day and night, and spending the rest of the time with Shelley Winters.

'I believe that Burt really did care for me,' Shelley Winters reflected many years later. 'He would come to my apartment on Sunday mornings for breakfast.' To him, she was a breath of fresh air in his life. She was sexy, funny and very beautiful, if not in the conventional Hollywood way. 'Burt tried to get a legal separation from Norma,' said Shelley, 'but I think he ended up agreeing with her that they would never separate in her lifetime.'

Shelley never met Norma – she made a point of avoiding her at all costs. Shelley wrote, 'I'm sure she loved him, and everything I ever heard about her made me know that she was a patient wife and a wonderful mother.'

All she heard about Norma, she heard after the event. At the time of her affair with Burt, she avoided hearing anything about Norma, and 'with this magical thinking, in a way, she didn't exist'. The daily ritual of Burt's affair with Shelley usually had him home by eight o'clock in the evening, and then he was back with Shelley in the morning for breakfast.

Norma was clearly unhappy in her marriage, hence the drinking, but she was also dedicated to staying married, whatever the personal cost. But it could not have been for love of Burt alone that she refused him a separation. Shelley Winters believed that Norma was 'ambivalent [about a divorce] because of their small children'. Actor Farley Granger told Shelley, 'I'm sure you're not the first extra-marital fling in Burt's life, and I bet his wife grits her teeth and waits.'

Twenty years after they married, Norma was to accuse Burt of cruelty. What this cruelty entailed was never made public but clearly she felt he made her life unbearable enough to eventually grant him a divorce. Burt never wanted to hear any unasked for opinions from his wife; he clearly felt her role in his life was to play the subservient wife and mother. He once said, 'After we married she said she'd had her professional fling and was quite happy to sit on the sidelines while I had mine.' The thing was, Burt's professional fling was obviously going to be lifelong.

His temper would not have helped matters. There is no evidence that he was ever physically violent with her but he was known to be verbally violent and he once told me, 'Of course we argued. Every couple argues. Ours may have been louder than most other couples' but that's because I can argue louder than most men.' He was talking tongue-in-cheek at the time, but I am sure the point was valid.

What he never told me was what really went wrong with his marriage – a subject he was always careful to keep strictly private. But he did say that he was 'a restless man with the women. I have often said to reporters, "I know what you've heard about me; that I'm always difficult and grab all the broads. It's not true. I'm difficult only some of the time and grab only some of the broads." That's what I tell 'em because that's the truth.'

To have sought Norma's consent to a separation surely meant that he was seriously in love with Shelley Winters and must have felt desperate to find a way to be with her permanently.

He became frantic one week when he tried in vain to get in touch with her. He called Universal several times, tried calling at her apartment and even phoned her parents' home; her mother hung up on him.

Shelley was extremely busy but she was also in some doubt about her feelings for Burt. In fact, she was torn between him and Farley Granger. Lancaster had seen reports in movie fan magazines that Granger and she were an item but he chose to believe that her relationship with Granger was purely platonic.

It wasn't. They were certainly good friends but they were also occasional lovers. For a while, she was confused about which man she loved the most.

To her complete horror and surprise, Lancaster turned up at her place one evening at eight o'clock – a time she least expected ever to see him – right in the middle of a cosy dinner she had made for Farley Granger. Burt politely asked Granger to 'go ride around the block for a while', and as soon as Granger had gone, Burt grabbed Shelley and kissed her. Any doubts she had had about which of the two men she loved the most vanished; she wanted Burt. But she complained about his treatment of Granger and then told him that she was about to go to Lake Tahoe to film scenes for *A Place in the Sun*. He wanted to visit her but she persuaded him to stay away because of the risk of the press finding out about them. He told her he would be over in the morning but when he left her apartment, he came across Farley Granger, now with writer Arthur Laurents, in the garage block. Burt ignored them and drove off.

Shelley, meanwhile, had been reading the script of her new film and drinking not only Granger's champagne but also Lancaster's brandy, and had become very melancholy, refusing to open the door to Granger. She later realized that she had become affected by thoughts of the girl she was to play; a poor pregnant girl whose situation reminded her of her own hopeless situation with Burt who, she now knew, was never going to leave his wife.

Granger furiously kicked the door open and Shelley became hysterical and threw up. Granger wanted to go and find Lancaster to beat him up but Laurents calmed him down.

The following morning, Lancaster arrived at Shelley's at five o'clock. The two men were still there and they gave him a detailed account of the condition he had left her in. He was frightened by what he thought he had done to her yet she found it impossible to explain her feelings.

Lancaster tried not to be jealous of Shelley's friendship with Granger and never pried into what went on between them. But he was obviously suspicious. One Sunday morning when he was about to leave her apartment, Granger arrived to take her fishing. Lancaster wanted to go with them, but she reminded him that he had to be back in his own home by eleven. She recalled, 'He left hurriedly with a very suspicious look in his eye.'

The Flame and the Arrow, released late in 1950, received critical acclaim. Margaret Hinxman, in the British publication *Time and Tide*, wrote that the film contained, 'a surprising number of good things; among them the discovery that Burt Lancaster's greatest skill lies not in glumly defying the minions of the Hollywood underworld, but in performing perilous acrobatics; a rollicking, riotous banqueting scene; and a gay air of inconsequence which defies criticism.'

Even Bosley Crowther of the *New York Times* was impressed for once: 'Not since Douglas Fairbanks was leaping from the castle walls and vaulting over the rooftops of storybook towns has the screen had such a reckless and acrobatic young man to display these same inclinations as it has in Mr Lancaster.'

Warner Brothers rashly offered a reward of a million dollars to anyone who could prove that Lancaster did not do his own stunts. To their horror, an extra in the film, Don Turner, came forward and said that Lancaster did not do all his own stunts. Lancaster was not delighted at the way Warners had handled this, especially when he had to go to court to prove that he had performed his own stunts.

He was very suspicious of the whole thing and told me, 'I hadn't realized this before we went to court but, of course, Warner Brothers wasn't going to risk a million dollars so they used a little legal trickery and had me state that I did all the stunts myself, but that there were times when I had to be elsewhere when some long shots were needed, and a stand-in was then used. I had to show that these long shots did not constitute stunt work as I had already filmed the same stunts in close-up. It was all very suspicious and the judge told us that we were all very naughty but I think he was amused by it all. So the extra never got his million bucks.'

Harry Cohn then called to say that Columbia was once again interested in the Hecht-Norma company. By this time Lancaster had developed a story about a returning serviceman's attitude towards his newly arrived baby.

Cohn told him, 'No, no, you don't understand. We want you to do a movie like *The Flame and the Arrow*.' Lancaster left Cohn's office.

Hal Wallis wanted to reunite Lancaster with Lizabeth Scott in *Dark City*, but Twentieth Century-Fox made a lucrative offer for the loan of Lancaster and Wallis accepted. So instead of Lancaster starring in *Dark City*, Wallis cast his discovery, Charlton Heston, who had first been brought to Wallis's attention when one of his scouts saw Heston in a Broadway production. The scout told Wallis, 'He's another Burt Lancaster.' Wallis replied, 'Yes, but do we need another Burt Lancaster?'

To Wallis's relief, Heston was nothing like Lancaster in either temperament or style. Meanwhile Lancaster went over to Fox to make *Mister 880* playing a US Treasury agent on the hunt for an old man making rather bad counterfeit one-dollar bills. Edmund Gwenn played the not-too-successful crook and, in Lancaster's words, the film was 'a small picture, kind of sweet little film with Dorothy McGuire and Edmund Gwenn'.

Around this time Lancaster became involved with a group of prominent movie people who were in opposition to the so-called Hollywood witch-hunt. They had begun in 1947 when the House Un-American Activities Committee – HUAC – selected the film industry as its first major target. HUAC had begun seeking out communists in the United States in 1938, although it was then little more than a back-street operation. But in 1948, under the direction of such men as chairman J Parnell Thomas and congressman Richard Nixon, the committee had become an awesome and fearful organization with access to the so-called Attorney-General's List which named organizations suspected of holding totalitarian, communist or 'any other subversive' ideas.

In 1950, Senator Joseph McCarthy added his strength to

HUAC and the Hollywood witch-hunt began to take its toll on the movie industry with a number of alleged subversives rounded up, including Dalton Trumbo, Robert Rossen and Clifford Odets. Hysteria swept through the industry and many, in an effort to save their own careers, became 'friendly' witnesses by providing to the committee names of people who might be communists. Anyone found guilty of subverting the film industry was blacklisted.

When Burt Lancaster became aware of this intensification in the witch-hunt, he agreed to join a group calling themselves the Committee for the First Amendment which included John Huston, William Wyler, Edward G Robinson, Gene Kelly, Humphrey Bogart, Billy Wilder, Philip Dunne and Judy Garland.

They met at the home of the Gershwins where they drew up plans to buy space in the trade papers to deplore the congressional investigations which, they said, would endanger the livelihood of many Americans and throw the motion-picture industry into disrepute. They also stated that the committee was in violation of the Bill of Rights, with charges being made that were equivalent to criminal accusations while the accused persons were denied the right of trial. They stated their own opposition to communism but deplored the hysterical manner in which it was being pursued.

Many others agreed with the group's anti-HUAC campaign and when it decided that a formal petition be drawn up and sent to Washington, more than 500 signatures were added. Finally, a group from the Committee for the First Amendment agreed to go to Washington, among them John Huston, Humphrey Bogart and Lauren Bacall. Lancaster was unable to join them due to work commitments, but he gave them his whole-hearted support.

In the event, nothing could be done to stop the blacklisting of the 'Unfriendly Ten', which consisted of actors, writers and directors who were forced to leave America or work under assumed names. It was a shameful episode in Hollywood's history.

6

Shelley's Regret

Lancaster maintained dressing rooms at both Universal and Paramount and so he and Shelley Winters were able to meet privately whenever their shooting schedules permitted, either in his bungalow or hers. When she was shooting night interiors for *A Place in the Sun* at Paramount, he made sure he saw her at lunch time. They would make love in her dressing room and Shelley's director, George Stevens, did not fail to notice that on some afternoons her skin and eyes seemed to glow, and he wondered what had happened to her over lunch.

On a day when Lancaster knew he had to shoot nights, he phoned the Paramount operator, disguised his voice, and left a message for Shelley Winters that 'Mr Richards' had called, asking Miss Winters to have dinner with him. Richards was his code-name. That evening, Shelley rushed to his dressing room but he was late because of filming. When he arrived he was bubbling over with talk about the communist witch-hunt the film industry was engaged in, and of his opposition to the campaign and how self-destructive he felt the studios were in their support of it all.

Shelley listened to 'his erudite discourse', but finally had to interrupt with, 'Burt, I have to get up awfully early so could you please make love to me fast so I can go home?'

Lancaster was so surprised, he fell about with laughter until tears were rolling down his cheeks. He duly obliged with some hurried love-making and she went home.

Whenever Burt wanted to go out in public with Shelley, it helped if a friend came along so that the couple were not quite so conspicuous. One night, Lancaster successfully broke curfew so that he and Welsh actor Hugh Griffith could take Shelley to the Players Nightclub where the two men were informed they could not be let in without ties. They duly put on two rented ties and removed their trousers on the basis that there was no rule about having to wear trousers. Shelley joined in the spirit of things by removing her skirt and sitting at their table in stockings and a pink satin chemise.

Burt and Shelley danced a rumba in their state of undress while Griffith got drunk, fell down and had to be taken away on a stretcher. Eventually a Universal publicity man, who had been alerted by the maître d', arrived before the cops and persuaded Burt and Shelley to get dressed and leave. As she wrote in her autobiography, 'Burt and I were young and full of fun.' What Burt did not tell her was that Norma was pregnant again. Not that Shelley harboured any further hopes that he would actually leave his wife. She had already decided that she really did not want to sit on the sidelines while he got on with his career and she played the part of Mrs Lancaster III. She was also a little more enlightened, with the help of Farley Granger, who told her he was sure Norma knew about it all. He told her, 'Not every love affair has to be for ever. Just enjoy it, and it will help you grow.'

She took his advice. Intent on having fun, she allowed Burt to teach her to fly on the trapeze. After a couple of weeks training on the trapeze he'd had erected outside his bungalow at Universal, they had something of an act; Lancaster, swinging by his legs, threw Shelley who did a half-somersault before being caught by Nick Cravat. They decided that they would try to persuade Universal to make a circus picture featuring them as trapeze artists.

But William Goetz, the head of the studio, was mortified when he came across Shelley and Lancaster up on the 12-foot trapeze while he was accompanying the New York bosses around the back lot. Quietly he told her to come down and Lancaster carefully lowered her. Goetz grabbed her wrist and began yelling, 'Are you all such idiots that you don't realize you are putting millions of dollars in jeopardy?'

Lancaster and Cravat responded by performing triple somersaults and pretending to fall. Goetz was so furious that he ordered the trapeze to be dismantled and removed from the studio.

That act did not endear Lancaster to Goetz and he was only too pleased to move over to Metro-Goldwyn-Mayer to make his first western, *Vengeance Valley*. It was now early 1951 and Lancaster enjoyed the opportunity to film on location in the Rocky Mountains in Colorado. He played a good guy with a bad brother who gets the blame for his brother's misdeeds. Joanne Dru provided the romantic interest and Robert Walker played the troublesome brother.

MGM director Richard Thorpe helmed this one, and before long he was locking horns with Lancaster who had all sorts of ideas on how to improve this, his first horse opera. Thorpe was more concerned that Lancaster should learn to ride a horse, or at least look as if he could. Lancaster, never one to back off from a challenge, spent a few weeks learning how to ride for the first time in his life. Veteran stunt man Gil Perkins recalled that, in his first western, Lancaster was 'fairly weak' at horse riding, although within a decade Lancaster learned to ride as well as the best cowboy stars.

Around this time an item by columnist Mike Connolly appeared in the *Hollywood Reporter*: Burt Lancaster and his wife were expecting a child. Shelley Winters read this while sitting in Schwab's drug store waiting for a prescription. She was stunned, and went straight to a bar on Sunset Boulevard and ordered a triple gin martini. Then another. Then, when she was joined by Marlon Brando, she rushed to the ladies' room and burst into tears. She knew then that whatever she and Burt had going between them was over.

Brando came in to see what was wrong. She showed him the item in the *Reporter*, and he said, 'Mike Connolly never gets anything straight.'

But Shelley was convinced. She told Brando, 'I know in my heart it's true. That bastard is fucking his wife.'

Brando took Shelley home where, she told me, they made love all night. 'I was in need of comfort and he was happy to give it.'

Lancaster had seen the item too and was worried what effect it would have on Shelley. He went to her apartment the following morning around five and knocked on the door. Shelley told me:

I knew it was Burt and I virtually pushed Marlon out of bed and told him get his clothes and get up on the roof. By now Burt was pounding on the door. Then he went down the stairs and called me from a phone booth.

I put on a sleepy voice and said that I had taken sleeping pills and did not want to see him but he wanted to come in because he was worried about me. He hung up and I raced around the apartment trying to clear up. It sounds very funny now but at the time I was terrified. He knocked on the door again and this time I opened it, and he came charging in, his face white with worry.

I just behaved calm and sleepy. And then he went into my bedroom and I followed, and I saw one of Marlon's shoes on the floor. So I quickly kicked it under the bed and, then out of the bedroom window I saw Marlon limping down the street with one shoe on.

Burt wanted to know who'd been with me and deciding that the best defence was offence, I yelled, 'You've been fucking your wife all this time, haven't you?'

He sort of mumbled, 'Yeah, I guess so.'

I said, 'What do you mean, you guess so? Is your baby an immaculate conception?'

Then I began to laugh and cry at the same time because, I suppose, I had been so tense and now I knew that my relationship with Burt was really, finally over. That was the end of my love affair with Burt Lancaster.

It was all so traumatic for her that she was admitted into Cedars Hospital for a few days with nervous and emotional exhaustion. During her stay, Lancaster bribed a floor nurse to allow him up to see her in the middle of the night. He brought her roses and 3,000 dollars in cash. She told him, 'You can keep the roses. I'll keep the cash.'

It was the last time he saw her for several years. She later said, 'One of the things I regret in my life is that I did not continue the relationship with Burt, or that it couldn't continue. I regret that I ended that relationship so abruptly.'

Burt seemed to accept Shelley's decision meekly, perhaps because he felt there was little point in fighting for a relationship that had no future. They had both enjoyed it while it lasted, had some fun, and now he got back to being a full-time husband. In July 1951, Norma gave birth to another daughter, Joanna.

For a while Burt had been looking for a film that had some social comment to it and in 1951 he found it in *Jim Thorpe, All-American* This was the true story of an American Indian who won two gold medals in the 1912 Stockholm Olympic Games, for the pentathlon and the decathlon. When it was revealed that he had previously played professional baseball, his amateur status was compromised and he was stripped of his medals. He took to drink and, after his son died, drifted in and out of various jobs, turning up as a spectator at the Los Angeles Olympics in 1932 where he was applauded enthusiastically. In 1940 he arrived in Hollywood as an extra, usually playing Indians. When he wrote his autobiography, Warner Brothers bought the screen rights.

Warners offered Lancaster the role of Thorpe and he accepted eagerly because not only was it an acting challenge to portray an Indian, but it was also a chance to explore his athletic abilities.

Thorpe was hired as technical adviser although Lancaster only met him once during production, when Thorpe came onto the stadium field to teach Burt how to do drop-kicks. 'It was sort of touching,' said Lancaster. 'His life had gone to pot. He

was at the time in pretty dire financial straits. His wife had
opened a bar during filming and the producers went crazy and
bought her out.'

Warners did, however, try to get Thorpe back his medals,
mainly because they thought it would make a great ending to
their film. They failed.

The weakness of the film lay not in the direction of Michael
Curtiz or the performance of Lancaster or any of the
supporting cast, which included Charles Bickford as Thorpe's
coach and Phyllis Thaxter as Thorpe's wife (Thorpe actually
had three but they were merged into one for the film); it lay in
the failure to convince the viewers that Lancaster was actually
performing all the sports himself. Paul Dehn of the *Sunday
Chronicle* was not fooled by a scene in which Lancaster, in
performing a high-jump, was interposed with 'a shot of
someone quite different clearing the bar at six feet'.

Burt had hoped that he would have a chance to make a story
that tackled the issue of racial prejudice and exploitation but
the script had to be toned down so as not to cause offence.
Later, Lancaster conceded that the film generally avoided the
racial problem, saying defensively, 'We didn't beat people over
the head with the Indian problem. Thorpe had his bad breaks
but they weren't due to the fact that he was an Indian. As he
realized in later life, his downfall as an athlete was largely
brought on by weaknesses in his own nature – a feeling that the
world was against him, unreasonable stubbornness, and the
failure to understand the necessity of working as a member of a
team.'

He would get his chance to tackle the Indian problem later.
But he was next able to come to an agreement with Harry Cohn
at Columbia for a film that had nothing to do with gangsters or
William Tell-type characters. It was *Ten Tall Men*, to be
produced by Hecht-Norma Productions in collaboration with
Columbia.

Lancaster accepted it on the condition that Columbia
released what he hoped would be his first production that did
not also feature him as the star, *The First Time*, a tale of a baby

who tells of his problems with his parents. The same idea was used again more than 30 years later in *Look Who's Talking*. Burt was constantly on the search for the kind of deals that allowed him to produce his own films in return for making commercial hits for major studios. He had a number of projects he needed the backing for, including *The Naked and the Dead*, which he had bought from Norman Mailer, Theodore Dreiser's *St Columba and the River* and *Advance Man*, about a circus press agent.

Cohn was not enthusiastic about the baby comedy but he had to accept it if he was to have Lancaster in *Ten Tall Men*, an action-packed, tongue-in-cheek yarn about the French Foreign Legion. In its approach it had much in common with *The Flame and the Arrow*. Wallis Goldbeck, a noted screen writer who had directed a number of films, wrote the screenplay and brought it to the attention of Lancaster who liked the idea of doing a humorous Saharan swashbuckler. Harry Cohn simply liked the idea of having Burt Lancaster in what would undoubtedly be a profitable and commercial picture.

It was a light story, about a Foreign Legion squad assigned to thwart an expected attack on a garrison by the Riffs. The Sahara Desert was recreated on the Columbia sound stages and Burt romped in great style across the sets, battling warring Arab tribes, facing ferocious sandstorms and kidnapping the Arab chief's daughter, played by Jody Lawrance.

In a sense, the film was the forerunner to pictures like *The Magnificent Seven* and *The Dirty Dozen*, and featured a strong supporting cast, which included Keiron Moore, Gilbert Roland, George Tobias and John Dehner. Curiously, *Variety* had trouble understanding the tongue-in-cheek approach, noting that the film 'at times achieves an almost satiric effect. Whether that was intentional or not is tough to determine.'

The film made pots of money but it was not shown in France where it was assumed that its humour in sending up their Foreign Legion would not be appreciated.

During the filming, people could not help but notice that Lancaster seemed to spend a lot of time with Jody Lawrance, who had made only a couple of pictures previously. Rumours of a fling were dampened by Lancaster explaining that he was simply helping her with her acting. 'If I feel that a scene is going wrong,' he said, 'I want to do everything in my power to correct it, even if it means an argument with the director. Not my ego, but the picture is involved. In *Ten Tall Men* I worked with a girl relatively new to the screen. I'm sure many people couldn't understand why I spent so much time helping her to do the best possible job. I wasn't particularly concerned with her as a person or with her career. I simply knew that if she looked bad, the scenes would fall flat.'

In the end, he stopped denying that he ever had affairs or even one-night stands and said, in relation to the film *The Leopard*, 'All [my fans] said the same thing – "Burt, I thought you were going to screw the girl." I guess I'm the guy who always screwed the girl – even if it was only after the movie had finished.'

That he did play around is confirmed by his admission to me but whether Jody Lawrance was among those he 'screwed . . . after the movie had finished', he would not say. But there were others, like Ava Gardner and Shelley Winters. And a few more.

7

Caricature of a He-Man

Lancaster told me, 'Of course it was important to make films that made money because I also wanted to do films that allowed for me as an actor, and for the time when I wouldn't be able to jump around with such agility. That's why I decided to make *The Crimson Pirate*.'

Warner Brothers were eager for a film that followed the same style of action and humour as *The Flame and the Arrow* and at first Burt resisted all such attempts.

He said, 'After *The Flame and the Arrow* was such a success, I had a helluva time avoiding making the same film again. Yet before that, all any studio wanted me to do were gangster pictures. In the end, I decided that the kind of fun we had in *The Flame and the Arrow* could be taken to greater extremes in *The Crimson Pirate*, and I thought that here I could have a chance to finally have a go at directing some of the scenes myself.'

He had once told Wallis that he would soon be directing films. Warner Brothers were not convinced that he could direct all of *The Crimson Pirate*, and so Lancaster assigned Robert Siodmak to direct on the understanding that Burt himself would direct the action scenes and some of the comedy. Siodmak accepted the assignment, little knowing the tough time Lancaster was about to give him.

The screenplay, by Roland Kibbee, was fashioned to exploit

the acrobatic talents of Lancaster and Nick Cravat who, once more, played his deaf-mute sidekick. The story followed a gang of pirates, led by Lancaster, through a series of adventures which required very little solid plot but plenty of action and comic set pieces.

For the first time, Lancaster went to Europe to film location sequences, such was the high budget for this film from which Warners expected to earn a fortune at the box office. Some scenes were filmed in London, a city Burt found was a breath of fresh air after the smell of the communist witch-hunt in Los Angeles.

'When I came here [in 1951], I walked through Hyde Park and saw people shouting "Down with the king" and so forth and so on, and threatening to shoot people – and nobody paid attention. People sat in their chairs and children played and bobbies yawned, and I thought to myself, how marvellous.'

He had found himself at Speaker's Corner, an area of Hyde Park where people were – and still are – free to stand on a soap box and speak their minds without fear of being arrested. He knew that if anyone did that in any area of Los Angeles, they would be arrested immediately and hauled before the House Un-American Activities Committee.

Most of the film's spectacular exteriors were shot in Italy off the small island of Ischia in the Bay of Naples. Never before had Lancaster been so intense on the set. As co-producer with Harold Hecht, he was concerned about every aspect and his temper was on a short fuse. He refused to allow Robert Siodmak to get on and make the film his own way. Lancaster defended his actions by saying, 'I like to find out how the camera works, then I can try for the best effect in what I'm doing. I want to know the director's angle on things as well. I know it's difficult, but I'm like that; restless and strung up inside when I'm working.'

Tension between Lancaster and Siodmak on the set was high from time to time. There were a number of outbursts. Once Lancaster yelled at Siodmak and called him 'a has-been' in front of the cast and crew. Siodmak was embarrassed and humiliated; he was relieved when he was able to go to London to shoot scenes that did not involve Lancaster.

With Siodmak gone, Lancaster and writer Roland Kibbee co-directed the film's final scenes which included a complicated and lengthy fight on board a ship. The sequence ran for 18 minutes on the screen and Lancaster was delighted with the results.

Even Nick Cravat found himself on the receiving end of a bawling out by Lancaster. Cravat may not have had any lines to say in the film but he had plenty to tell Lancaster in terms that turned the air blue. But their quarrel was not enough to destroy their friendship and the most incredible thing of all was that none of this tension was reflected in the film that reached the screen in early 1952.

The *New York Times* said, 'Burt Lancaster is truly a picture pirate. A blond, smiling, muscular and agile athlete, he leads the climactic fight with the bounce and elan of a tumbler at an opening night under the Big Top . . . As his mute lieutenant, Nick Cravat needs no lines to add enough comic pantomime bits to earn his share of the laughs.'

Variety wrote, 'Lancaster and his deaf-mute pal, Nick Cravat, sock the acrobatics required of hero and partner under Robert Siodmak's rugged but tongue-in-cheek direction.'

Siodmak may well have felt justified in feeling that little of what was eventually shown was the result of his own work and, thoroughly dispirited with Hollywood and its stars, especially Burt Lancaster, he left America for good and spent the rest of his life making films in Germany, France and Spain.

The film firmly established Lancaster and Hecht as formidable movie producers and, to celebrate, Hecht had his home elaborately and expensively decorated. He decided to throw a party to show off his new interior and of course invited Burt Lancaster. But Lancaster declined. Hecht wanted to know why.

Burt told him, 'Look, you know I don't go in for all that Hollywood party stuff.'

'But I'm your partner.'

'So?'

'So it would look pretty bad if you did not show up. You know what this town is like. The columnists would have a field day writing how we're not really friends because we don't go to each other's parties.'

Lancaster relented and attended the party. But he was in dour spirits, having felt compelled to attend a Hollywood function he had no wish to be at. He just had a couple of drinks; he never got drunk. He was careful about maintaining his physique, even though he smoked.

When he asked, 'Where's the can?' and nobody answered him, he ranted, 'How do you like this? He builds this dump with my money and I don't even know where the can is.'

Hecht hurriedly led him to the bathroom and words were exchanged which no one was privy too, least of all Sheilah Graham, who was at the party and who later wrote of the incident in her book. She wrote, 'Fifteen minutes later, Burt was laughing and joking as if nothing had happened.'

Hecht, it seems, wanted to stand as tall as Lancaster, if only in status. Burt was a tall gentile with golden hair. Hecht was Jewish and short. Each man had his own talent; Burt was creative, perhaps even artistic, Harold was a businessman with little talent for creativity. In an effort to even things out, Hecht offered journalist Hollis Alpert vast amounts of money to write him clever one-liners in the style of Sam Goldwyn which he could spout cleverly at every opportunity. Alpert asked a mutual friend why he thought Hecht had made such an offer, and the friend replied, 'He wants you to make him into a tall gentile.'

When Cecil B De Mille announced his intention to make his big circus epic, *The Greatest Show on Earth*, Lancaster wanted to be in it. But for some reason he just could not land the role he wanted, that of the trapeze star ultimately played by Cornel Wilde. It may have had something to do with complications in negotiating contracts due to Wallis having already loaned out Charlton Heston whom De Mille was anxious to have playing the circus manager. Or it could have been that Lancaster's reputation for being difficult with directors was enough to dismiss any thought from De Mille's mind of casting Lancaster.

De Mille's style of working was to work out the exact blocking of actors and camera and then to have his actors simply step into shot. He gave his actors very little direction as he often cast to type and expected them to know their jobs. What he did not need on an expensive picture like this one was to have an actor like Burt Lancaster who would question every set-up, every motivation, and probably even argue with the director. It is therefore likely that Lancaster's own reputation prevented him from being in one of the few films he really had set his heart on.

So Burt turned his attention to a project that Hal Wallis was producing, *Come Back Little Sheba*, based on the Broadway play by William Inge. Lancaster was always looking for something that had some literary value and this was such a project.

Shirley Booth, repeating her role from Broadway, was to play the slatternly Lola who is unable to perceive that her cloying love and craving for affection is destroying her weak and ageing husband. Lancaster wanted to play the husband, but according to an interview he did with the *New York Times* in 1953, he himself was not confident he could fill the role and that it was Michael Curtiz who encouraged him. But Burt had had to persuade Wallis.

'You're not right for it; you're too young,' Wallis told him. 'You're right,' Lancaster replied. 'I am too young. But I understand this character. He is the most human, if imperfect, kind of guy ever written into a play, and I can play it. Now we both know that Shirley is the star – it's her film. But I can do a respectable job on it and I'll lend some weight to the box office for you.'

That last part of the argument persuaded Wallis.

Lancaster did not actually see or read the play; he only ever read the screenplay. And already he had decided on how he would play the part without even consulting the director, Daniel Mann. Lancaster saw the part, not as of a weak man, but of someone who was undermined by the love of his repellent wife.

When he informed his agent he was going to do the film, his agent said, 'What for? The role is secondary and you're a star now. And this guy is older, he's a drunk. You're not right for it.'

Lancaster would not be dissuaded. 'I think you're right. But I understand this man and it's an opportunity to broaden myself as an actor.'

On the set, Lancaster was highly respectful of Shirley Booth's talent and noted how she worked hard to adapt her role for the motion-picture screen which, he said, 'is anything but easy when you've grown to play a character in a certain way over months of constant association.'

For a change, he listened when someone else gave him advice. He always said he did not want a woman to give advice he did not ask for but he respected Shirley Booth enough to listen when she said, 'You know, Burt, once in a while you hit a note of truth and you can hear a bell ring. But most of the time I can see the wheels turning and your brain working.'

This is a much used quote by writers on the subject of Burt Lancaster but there seems to be some confusion over its meaning. However, that is because most writers are not actors. One writer thought the advice given by Booth to be 'somewhat ambiguous'. It was in fact sound advice, for Booth was trying to get him to stop concerning himself with the mechanics of the role, especially since he had to play someone older, and just feel for what is true, and that only comes from the inside. Lancaster said:

> I learned gradually that what goes on inside is more important than the little bits of trickery, such as flashing my famous teeth which I get accused of. But that's what critics fail to understand; it's all to do with feeling the part from inside – and wearing the clothes of the character always helps – but then the rest of it comes from my own physical attributes and personality. I can't help but grin

this way – it's me. But if I'm grinning like this [grins] and inside I'm thinking, 'What's for dinner tonight?' instead of thinking what the character is thinking, it comes out dead on the screen. It's even better if you can be deadpan but keep it working inside because then it shows through the eyes. It's no great secret – any actor will tell you that.

Booth's criticism is true of much of Lancaster's early work and would from time to time apply to his later work. Whatever the flaws in his performance in *Come Back Little Sheba*, he still won some of the best reviews to date. Even Bosley Crowther of the *New York Times*, who was not Lancaster's greatest admirer in those early years, said that 'the excellence of Mr Lancaster as the frustrated, inarticulate spouse, weak-willed and sweetly passive, should not be overlooked.'

Lancaster was delighted with his personal reviews. 'The tendency of the reviewer is to regard you in the image you had before. In other words, I was the leading man or the swashbuckler, blah, blah, blah, and suddenly they were beginning to think of me as a serious actor. So that was a progression in my career.'

The film won Shirley Booth an Oscar as Best Actress. 'Shirley Booth is the finest actress I have ever worked with,' said Burt.

He was now fast approaching the age of 40 and he began to seriously consider his future as an actor.

'As I approach 40,' he said at the time, 'I'm beginning to ask, is being a movie star at that age worth all the trouble? I don't think it is. It seems that I've spent all my life in gyms. I've grown to hate training. I can't go on being the caricature of a he-man.'

He said he was working his way into production more. 'I asked myself what happens to people when they have nothing to do. They become a lonely burden to themselves and others.' But he would continue to blow hot and cold on the subject of retiring from acting for the rest of his life.

While he was making *The Crimson Pirate*, *The First Time* went into production at Columbia Studios in 1952 with

Barbara Hale and Robert Cummings as the parents. Frank Tashlin, who wrote the screenplay with three other screen writers, directed. Harold Hecht had virtual control as producer although this was clearly a Hecht-Norma production. It was the first of a handful of films produced by Lancaster and Hecht in which Burt did not appear and, like the films that followed, this one was a modest film which had simply appealed to Lancaster.

Under the agreement he had made with Warner Brothers, he had to make a couple of other films for them of their choice. They chose to put him in *South Sea Woman*. He told me, 'Films like *South Sea Woman* are the price you have to pay the piper. I was lucky not to have got into films earlier because I might have found myself shackled to a studio contract. As it was I could hustle my way through those early years in my career, agreeing to do this or that in exchange for making the films I wanted to do. As for *South Sea Woman*, I tried like hell to get them to change their minds. But they wanted it, so I did it as quickly as I could.'

Once again he was a sergeant, this time in the marines, who is court-martialled for desertion in pre-war Honolulu. The reason for his desertion, it transpires, is the woman of the title, played by Virginia Mayo, Burt's leading lady in *The Crimson Pirate*.

By now the love affair between Warner Brothers and Burt Lancaster had definitely turned sour and he persuaded them to release him from all further obligations in return for allowing them to make *South Sea Woman* without any interference. Hence, director Arthur Lubin was able to make the film without any arguments from Lancaster.

However, Warner Brothers did tie him down to a small appearance in their musical, *Three Sailors and a Girl*, which was being made almost at the same time as *South Sea Woman*. He did not even have to change his uniform, working for precisely four hours on the set of the Gordon Macrae-Jane Powell musical. His brief appearance came during the film's finale when he appears backstage at a show and tells Sam

Levene, his friend from *A Sound of Hunting*, 'You'll never make it in show business, kid.'

His chore done, he returned to finish *South Sea Woman* thus ending his obligation to Warners. But he still had one more film to make with them which fortunately would be a production of his own. It was called *His Majesty O 'Keefe*, another swashbuckler. Still in pre-production stage at this time in 1953, it had a screenplay by Borden Chase and James Hill. Hill had literally started at the bottom at NBC, turning his hand to writing scripts and landing on his feet with this assignment from Hecht-Norma Productions. Hill would play a more significant role in Lancaster's film production company later.

8

Kissing in the Sea

While the script for *His Majesty O'Keefe* was still being polished, another more important screenplay had been commissioned by Harry Cohn to provide Lancaster with his biggest break yet – *From Here to Eternity*. As well as giving Lancaster a role that would lead to the best notices of his career so far and put him at the very top of his league, it was also his introduction to the world of film-ensemble playing, whereby a relatively large star cast would be called upon to work together. It would also result in a certain amount of egotistic tantrums.

James Jones had been given the task of turning his own bestseller, *From Here to Eternity*, into a screenplay. His story of brutalities in a US Army unit based in Honolulu before, during and after the attack on Pearl Harbor, was largely based on Jones's own military experience, including his time in prison where sadistic officers had inmates humiliated and tortured – even killed. The book was a tough, uncompromising anti-military exposé with plenty of sex and four-letter words.

Jones's first screenplay draft accurately reflected the elements of his book that made it so compelling and controversial. But Cohn knew that to make the film well he needed the co-operation of the US Army and that with this script he would not get it. So he asked Daniel Taradash to clean it up, to Jones's chagrin. As Jones put it, 'Columbia pictures ass-kissed the Army so they could shoot the exteriors of the film at Schofield

Barracks in Hawaii without being bothered.'

To play the young boxer, Prewitt, who refuses to fight in the ring for the army because he had previously blinded an opponent, Cohn chose a Columbia contract player. When the film's director, Fred Zinnemann, heard about this, he told Cohn, 'I don't think he's right.'

Cohn asked, 'Who is it you want?'

Zinnemann replied, 'Montgomery Clift.'

Cohn grew angry and told Zinnemann that Clift was no soldier or boxer and that he was suspected of being a homosexual. Zinnemann told him that the first paragraph in the book described Prewitt as a 'deceptive slim young man', and that was the exact quality Zinnemann wanted to see in the part; Clift would give the role that quality. Zinnemann told Cohn if he could not cast who he wanted in the film, then Cohn had better find another director. Cohn ranted, 'I'm the president of Columbia. You can't give me ultimatums.'

The next day Cohn sent the script to Montgomery Clift.

When Zinnemann was considering who should play the part of Karen, a captain's adulterous wife, an agent suggested one of his clients, Deborah Kerr. Up to this point Kerr was known in Hollywood as 'class' because she only ever played upright young ladies. Early in the film, a corporal says of Karen, 'She sleeps with every soldier on the post.' Zinnemann was excited at the prospect of the audience hearing this line and, knowing a 'class' lady was to play the part, wondering how events would develop. So he decided that casting Kerr *against* type was the *perfect* casting.

But when it came to finding someone perfect to play the tough but sympathetic master sergeant, Zinnemann wanted to cast to type: he chose Burt Lancaster. 'Not only did he have the right authority and weight,' said Zinnemann, 'but more importantly there was a chemistry between him and Deborah, and the combination worked out well.'

To get Lancaster, Columbia had to deal with Hal Wallis who made them pay for the privilege, demanding and receiving a 150,000-dollar loan-out fee for the use of Burt, who received

120,000 dollars of it, and getting Cohn to use two more Wallis stars, Charlton Heston and Lizabeth Scott, in the Columbia picture *Bad for Each Other*.

The choice for Sergeant Warden had, in fact, been between Lancaster and Robert Mitchum. Zinnemann explained:

> I'd seen Burt in *The Killers*, and I could see he made his mark. He was someone, so he was very much the front runner. Mitchum wasn't available at the time, but fortunately Burt was, to my great delight because, personally, I couldn't have imagined anyone better.
>
> Warden was a very forthright character and actually had less dimension than some of the other people. He was not as neurotic as Prewitt or Karen so I didn't call on Burt to analyse and project in the same way as Monty and Deborah had to. His ambition was to be a good soldier and, in a sense, he was the catalyst, the commentator on the whole situation. He was a very straight man, very gung-ho, and he knew all the tactics for keeping alive and getting along. He was a survivor, but he was very compassionate towards Prewitt, a victim who was determined to stick to his guns even if it killed him, as it eventually was bound to do.

The other important roles were that of Lorene, a small-town girl from Iowa who works in a Hawaiian brothel, and Maggio, Prewitt's rebellious army friend, who gets thrown in the stockade and eventually beaten to death by a sadistic sergeant (played by Ernest Borgnine).

Cohn wanted Donna Reed to play Lorene. Said Zinnemann, 'Donna was not my first choice, but one could not forever say "no" to Cohn. She got the part, and played it so well that an Oscar was her reward.'

For Maggio, Zinnemann tried to get Eli Wallach but Wallach had agreed to work for Elia Kazan on Broadway. Frank Sinatra began bombarding the offices of Cohn, Zinnemann and producer Buddy Adler with cables, signing himself 'Maggio'.

Sinatra's career was in the doldrums and he needed a part like Maggio to get back on top again. Cohn agreed to give him a test, and subsequently Sinatra got the part.

Zinnemann's principal cast was complete. Filming began at the Columbia Studios on 2 March 1953. The ensemble cast started off in high spirits. Said Zinnemann, 'We had a lot of fun. We'd have dinner together every night – Deborah Kerr, Burt Lancaster, Frank Sinatra and Monty. Frank tried to phone Nairobi where his wife, Ava Gardner, was making a movie, and we'd kid him about being jealous of Clark Gable, Ava's co-star.'

Clift became completely immersed in his work, carrying round a copy of the book which he referred to as a character guide. Said Deborah Kerr, 'If we had dinner, we'd start discussing something other than the movie and then Monty would slip back into talking about Prewitt.'

Clift would ask his fellow actors, 'Do you think I should move that way? How do you suppose Prewitt feels about this?'

Said Kerr, 'His concentration was positively violent. We had only one scene together. I walked behind him and Monty was supposed to say to Burt, "Who's that?" He spent two days figuring out how to say, "Who's that?" '

Clift and Sinatra became firm friends, despite their different approaches to acting. Clift used each take as a rehearsal while Sinatra was always at his best in the first or second take. Said Zinnemann, 'It was an interesting problem when they did a scene together; how to get the best performance from them both in the same take.'

In this sort of ensemble playing, the chemistry between actors in different groups – Sinatra and Clift, Kerr and Lancaster, Lancaster and Clift – was crucial to the success of each scene.

Lancaster had great respect for Clift: 'He approached the script like a scientist. I've never seen anyone so meticulous. I'll never forget when we shot our first scene together. It was the only time that I could not stop my knees from shaking because he had such power. His concentration was enormous. Just as well the camera was only shooting me above my waist or the world would have seen my knees knocking.'

In April, the entire company flew out to Hawaii. The script called for a love scene between Lancaster and Deborah Kerr: the famous beach scene in which they kiss while the waves roll over them. Harry Cohn had told Zinnemann that the scene was to be shot as soon as the cast arrived following their night flight. Zinnemann ignored the order. When he felt Lancaster and Kerr were suitably rested for the seemingly easy but in reality difficult task of embracing in the surf, Zinnemann had his crew assemble on the beach near Diamond Head.

'That damned scene was no picnic to do, even if I did get to kiss Deborah over and over,' Lancaster told me. 'You know, kissing in the sea may look like fun, but when you get this big wave suddenly rolling over you and you get all this salt water in your mouth and up your nose and in your ass, and you do it over and over again until your skin is all wrinkled, it ain't that sexy.'

'The challenge,' explained Zinnemann, 'was timing the scene with the incoming waves so that they would break over the couple at the right instant.'

In those days the Breen Office, the official censor in Hollywood, had to approve all scripts and any censorship would usually be done on the script so that cutting from a finished film was usually unnecessary. The Breen Office had a number of things they wanted changed in the script of *From Here to Eternity* and so Zinnemann had to shoot from what was basically a censored script. The beach scene had been written so that it satisfied the censor but even after it was completed, the Breen Office insisted on four seconds being cut.

Black and white photographs of the scene taken for publicity and advertising purposes, were forbidden publication by the Breen Office, who said that their objection to the pictures was 'the water'.

'That scene, regarded as sensational and extremely provocative, seems harmless and friendly by today's standards,' said Zinnemann.

'It's hard to believe that scene should have been thought so provocative and corrupting all those years ago,' Lancaster told me.

Lancaster, who had to learn to control his anger in real life, used this aspect of his character to good effect during the scene in which Ernest Borgnine pulls a knife on him. 'I break a bottle and stand there, facing him,' recalled Burt. 'It would have been easy just to snarl, "All right, you son-of-a-bitch." But I didn't do it that way. I just said quietly, "Come on. Come on." And it was much more effective. Monty had been watching this scene and when it was over he came over and put his arms round me. He was such an emotional man and he thought the scene was just great. It was certainly one of my most effective moments in the film.'

He had no time for the long nights of drinking that Clift, Sinatra and author James Jones shared on Hawaii. Nevertheless, he was always there to help the drunken actors into bed. 'Monty and Frank would get roaring drunk every night and I had to carry them to their rooms every night, undress them and put them to bed. Frank took to calling me "mom", and still does. Every year he calls me and says, "Happy birthday, mom." '

Lancaster had always been good friends with Sinatra and he thought he got on well with Clift. He said, 'Monty and I became good friends. Mind you, he was a very complicated man.'

In fact, Lancaster seemed unaware of what Clift was saying behind his back. Clift regularly phoned his actress friend, Pat Collinge, to discuss the nuances of Prewitt. In her biography of Clift, she said, 'He would be making superb actor's sense, and then out of the blue he would start ranting against Burt Lancaster. "He gets top billing, he doesn't deserve to!" he'd yell. "He is a terrible actor. He thinks he's a dynamo; he's nothing but a big bag of wind, the most unctuous man I've ever met!" and then he'd drop the subject and go back to talking about Prewitt.'

The fun that marked the beginning of the group's work

together was fading in the final weeks. Even Zinnemann, one of
the most patient of directors, felt the strain, especially from
Lancaster. 'I can't say that Burt was easy, but then neither was
Monty and neither was anybody, except Deborah and Donna.
The men were always a bit highly strung, shall we say. It's
understandable because it is nerve-racking to be there
exposing yourself emotionally, as it were, before a bunch of
strangers. It takes a colossal amount of concentration. I
imagine it must be harder for men than women.'

But Zinnemann had no complaints about Lancaster's
performance. He had cast him to type and Burt delivered the
goods. 'Burt had a very impressive way of putting across that
sympathy in the reverse as it were. By being tough, he was able
to project a great deal of actual tenderness and a feeling of
comradeship. To me it was a very moving performance.'

Zinnemann found himself on the receiving end of hostility in
the last week of filming. He had rehearsed Clift and Sinatra
through the scene in which Prewitt and Maggio get blind drunk
in the park. MPs arrive and Maggio, feeling harassed, jumps up
to berate the two towering MPs.

When Cohn heard about it, he became worried about how
the army would react and told Zinnemann to tone it down by
asking Sinatra to sit down to deliver his provocative speech.
Zinnemann argued against it but realized that the objection
had obviously come from an army source. Since he was filming
on army territory, he had no choice but to tell Sinatra to do the
scene sitting.

Sinatra was furious and blamed Zinnemann for the decision.
Thereafter, Sinatra refused to speak to the director.

By the time the film was finished in May, no one was having
fun.

While *From Here to Eternity* was being edited and scored,
Lancaster, after a brief holiday to get over the rigours of
filming, went back to work at Warner Brothers to make *His
Majesty O'Keefe*.

For this picture, which Warners hoped would be a successful
follow-up to *The Crimson Pirate*, the cast and crew spent four

months filming on the Fiji island of Viti Levu. Byron Haskin, who had given Lancaster his first screen test and directed him in *I Walk Alone*, also directed this swashbuckler, which told of an enterprising Yankee freebooter (Lancaster), who is cast adrift by his mutinous crew in the South Seas in the 1870s. He reaches an island where he meets and marries a beautiful Polynesian, played by British starlet Joan Rice, overthrows the German traders and slave dealers and becomes the islanders' king.

For an exotic location, filming on Fiji was relatively cheap but Lancaster soon discovered that it was a far from ideal climate for making movies. He said, 'It was so tough working in the humidity that one day I actually watched fungus grow on my clothes.'

Norma and the children came with him on this location. Since his break-up with Shelley Winters, Burt and Norma had managed to find some form of framework to hold their marriage together.

Back in the United States, when Harry Cohn had a completed print of *From Here to Eternity*, he arranged for a preview for two hundred people. Their response indicated that Columbia had their biggest hit ever.

From Here to Eternity opened in August 1953. Cohn came up with a seemingly reckless idea to promote the film which some, including Zinnemann, thought was bound to backfire. Instead of giving the film a lavish, star-studded Hollywood première, Cohn opened the film in New York at the Capitol Theater. New York in August, often unbearably hot and humid, was considered the worst time to open a major film because cinemas had no air conditioning then. Harry Cohn had decided that there would be no publicity except for a full page ad in the *New York Times* in which he personally urged people to see the film. Zinnemann, in Los Angeles that night, was convinced the film was destined for disaster.

Then he received a call from Marlene Dietrich in New York saying that the Capitol Theater was 'bulging' and people were still queuing around the block so an extra performance had been scheduled for the early hours of the morning.

'How is that possible?' asked Zinnemann. 'There has been no publicity.'

'They smell it,' Dietrich replied.

Burt eagerly scoured the press reviews. He was not disappointed. *Variety* thought the film 'rates as one of the all-time greats in the ranks of motion pictures having an armed forces background. Burt Lancaster, whose presence adds measurably to the marquee weight of the strong cast, wallops the character of Top Sergeant Milton Warden. It is a performance which he gives a depth of character as well as the muscles which have gained marquee importance for his name.'

British critic Leonard Mosley, in the *Daily Express*, did not like the film much but said, 'Miss Kerr and Burt Lancaster succeed in conveying with some skill the ecstasy and despair of an illicit affair they know can't work out.' Bosley Crowther wrote in the *New York Times* that the film was 'almost as towering and persuasive as its source . . . It captures the essential spirit of the James Jones study . . . It stands as a shining example of truly professional movie making.'

Early in 1954, news came that Burt had been nominated as Best Actor by the American Academy of Motion Pictures Arts and Sciences. Clift had also been nominated. It is generally agreed that the fact that they were both nominated for the same movie cancelled out each other's chance of winning, and that year the Best Actor award went to William Holden for *Stalag 17. From Here to Eternity* had thirteen nominations in all, including one for Deborah Kerr. It ultimately won Oscars for Best Picture, Screenplay, Direction, Black and White Photography (to Burnett Guffey), Best Supporting Actor (to Frank Sinatra) and Best Supporting Actress (to Donna Reed).

As a consolation to Burt, he won the New York Critics award as the year's best actor. He was well satisfied. 'It was an enormous turning point for me,' he said. He hoped his films would now take him in new directions and he decided that *His Majesty O'Keefe* was to be his last swashbuckler.

9

Being God

In 1954, Burt at last seemed to be settling down. Norma was expecting their fourth child and, with the accolades that he had received, he could afford to indulge his love of art and music. He bought various works of art – by Renoir, Vlaminck, Chagall and Utrillo – and he spent lavishly on expanding his Bel-Air house to incorporate a full-sized baseball pitch complete with floodlights, where he coached his children.

He rarely went out except to go to the opera, when he usually dressed in a blue suit, black shirt and white tie. Norma often wore a white mink and diamanté model sleeves. They were considered a couple with garish dress sense.

He maintained a small circle of close friends, few of whom were in the film business. They were a mixture of doctors, lawyers and businessmen, with whom he played bridge, setting up the Savoy Club. After an incident in which he complained about a lady's bidding, followed by a heated exchange during which she threw her cards in his face, he took to playing at home where he had two bridge tables: should he have a disagreement at one table, he was able to move to the second and continue playing. Some guests, who were on the receiving end of his verbal outbursts, refused to return to play again. His regular bridge partner, Nick Cravat, was among those whom Lancaster berated but he did return after each argument.

Around this time, Burt discovered golf which he began to

play virtually every day.

He was devoted to his children, which may have been the prime motivation for sustaining his marriage and he tried to make sure they had all they needed to keep them entertained and interested within the confines of their home. In fact, because he and Norma had decided that the children should be free to express themselves without limitations, the children tended to run wild.

'Where we live,' he once said, 'there is nothing for the kids to do but go to a movie, and then we have to drive them because it's too far to go on foot and there is no safe place for them to walk. So it really isn't as good as it might seem.' William had progressed well since the first of his several operations on his leg, but at the age of just six, he walked with a limp. Perhaps to help William, Burt taught all his children how to walk on their hands.

In July 1954, Sighle-Ann (pronounced Sheilah-Ann) was born to Burt and Norma. The movie fan magazines reported on the couple's happy event and called them one of Hollywood's happiest couples. But Norma was not the happiest of women. She had developed a slight eye twitch due to a somewhat nervous disposition. She had learned to cope with Lancaster's bursts of temper by waiting silently for the storm to abate.

Perhaps it was his struggle with his temper that kept him smoking most of his life; he loved untipped Camels. Nevertheless, he trained most days, despite the fact that he said he hated having to do it, and ran around the UCLA track early each morning. Perhaps his obsession with remaining fit and healthy was in part ignited by the sight of his ailing father who was now confined to a wheelchair. He continued to train on the horizontal bars and the trapeze with Nick Cravat, and he maintained a strict diet. Each evening he ate a plain steak with green salad and never drank more than two Scotches.

He underwent an extreme form of dental treatment, costing in the region of 10,000 dollars, to have his teeth fixed to prevent them from grinding against each other when chewing. This was a brand-new dental technique, pioneered in

California, and after Burt had it done, Harold Hecht followed suit.

The Hecht-Norma Production company went through a change of name and became the Hecht-Lancaster Company. Perhaps Burt had decided that his name meant more than his wife's, or perhaps he simply did not feel enough about her to include her name in his business.

Lancaster and Hecht signed a new deal with the recently restructured United Artists company. United Artists had its offices at the Samuel Goldwyn Studio but because it had no studio facilities of its own to maintain, its overhead charges to independent producers, like Hecht-Lancaster, were considerably lower than those of major film companies. United Artists also offered their directors and producers a considerable measure of autonomy during filming. So now Hecht-Lancaster had more independence than ever before.

When they moved into their new offices at 202 North Cannon Drive, Burt's flair for visual opulence was manifest in his huge kidney-shaped desk, which was covered entirely with white leather. He also had a small pool, complete with electric waterfall and artificial tree, installed in his office. Impressionist paintings hung on the white walls and the corridor outside was a gallery of original Rouaults. He also liked to practise golf in his office.

Even at work Lancaster needed to maintain strict discipline to preserve his physique. Every day his secretary prepared him a lunch of hard-boiled eggs, cottage cheese and crackers.

Frustrated by their failure to examine civil rights and the Indian problem in *Jim Thorpe, All-American*, Burt and Hecht produced *Apache* in 1954. Based on a book by Paul I Wellman, it was a true story which, probably for the first time in Hollywood, was told from the Indian point of view. Said Lancaster, who played the part of Massai, the Apache of the title:

It was all based on truth. Massai fought in the wars with the White Man when the Apache nation was led by

Geronimo, but when Geronimo surrendered, Massai just kept on, waging his own war against the United States government. He was a very fierce warrior who hated the white man, and we didn't try to hide that, although we fictionalized the story a little because we didn't want him to come over as too unrelenting and therefore one dimensional. We had to see Massai as more than just a savage Indian, and we had to see the white men in shades of grey rather being all good or all bad. This meant we needed to invent some of the story but it had to be done with honesty, otherwise it becomes just another cowboy and Injun picture.

Robert Aldrich directed, his first of several films with Burt Lancaster. He told me:

I found Burt wasn't the easiest man to get along with, but then he was the boss. He was the one putting up the 900,000 dollars – or getting United Artists to put it up – to make the film, and he had worked long and hard with James Webb on the screenplay. But the thing I found with Burt was that he would respond to you if you responded to him. I think the trouble is there are some directors who feel threatened by him and actors like him, because those actors get to know quite a bit about making movies. So they tell you what they think and in Burt's case, he told you because he was also the producer.

Sometimes I just had to tell him, 'Burt, you're a pain in the ass,' but I didn't want to argue with him. Arguing doesn't achieve anything creative, only disharmony. We didn't agree on everything, but I had to tell him once or twice that I was the director, and if he wanted me to do my job, butt out. I think the fact that we made four pictures together over many years says a lot about the way we work together.

Making one of his early screen appearances was Charles

Bronson, then called Charles Buchinski. Jean Peters co-starred as the Indian wife who gives birth to Lancaster's child at the end of the film; a scene which was an alternative to the original ending, imposed by United Artists in one of the company's few acts of interference. The scene, as filmed, had Lancaster hearing his baby's cry and, instead of going down fighting, he surrenders to the cavalry. Aldrich told me:

> In the final scene Bronson was supposed to kill Lancaster. It was a good scene as written and kept the story honest. There was Massai outnumbered by the cavalry and in the original ending he died fighting them. But United Artists told us, 'You can't have Burt Lancaster getting killed.' We argued with them on that, but then the exhibitors started up with, 'Burt's fans don't want to see him die.' Burt hated the idea of changing the scene. I hated the idea. But we had no choice. The film just wouldn't have got shown, so we shot an alternative, happier ending. It worked anyway because the film made lots of money.

It made 6,000,000 dollars, in fact. Lancaster said of the changed ending of the film, 'As I have done many times before, I sold my soul to the devil.'

Although the public flocked to see the film – which is what counts in the end – the critics did not warm to it. Howard Thompson of the *New York Times* wrote that Hecht-Lancaster had come up with its first 'clinker'.

Britain's *Monthly Film Bulletin* was of the opinion, 'We remain conscious that these are two actors [Lancaster and Jean Peters] doing a very decent best in an impossible task. The strangeness is missing; Indians are not just white Americans with a different-coloured skin and a simplified vocabulary.'

Lancaster and Aldrich immediately agreed to work again, on *Vera Cruz*. Again the film was produced by Hecht-Lancaster and told of two American adventurers who escort a French countess from Mexico to the port of Vera Cruz. She is carrying a cache of gold to finance troops for the Emperor Maximilian and the trio become involved in plenty of double cross. It was an unusual western for its time in that the two men were neither all good, nor all bad. The one who becomes the villain has a satirical touch to him, while the other is the good guy, but with various shades of grey about him. Said Aldrich, 'It was the forerunner to those spaghetti westerns Sergio Leone made with Clint Eastwood, no doubt about it.'

Lancaster wanted to play the hero, and thought it would be a sensational piece of casting if he could persuade Cary Grant to play the villain. He heard that Grant was visiting Grace Kelly on the set of a Hitchcock film, and went along to see him with the script. But Grant did not want to read it. He told Burt, 'I never go near horses. I can't stand horses.'

Lancaster told him, 'But, Cary, this would be such a departure for you. It's a good script written in a mocking vein; it's a *Gunga-Din* type of thing. You'll be the villain and it'll be a lot of fun to play. I'll be your straight man. What do you say?'

Grant could not be persuaded. So it was decided to send the script to Gary Cooper, who immediately agreed to play the straight man. So now Lancaster had the role of the villain. He did not complain. 'Mine was the entertaining part,' he said. 'It was fun, playing that kind of character.'

Burt even accepted second billing, below Cooper, but still succeeded in stealing the film in a performance that was very much over the top.

'The problem with directing Burt in that film,' Aldrich told me, 'was that when it came down to it, Burt would not be directed by me. What he really wanted to do was direct the film himself, and he was a bigger pain in the ass than he was on *Apache*. He got a bit hammy in his role and in the end I couldn't stop him but to an extent it worked nicely because there was Coop underplaying as he always did, and there was Burt overplaying, and in the end when Coop shoots him, you're kind of relieved.'

The role of the French countess fell to Denise Darcel. Among the actresses who tested for the role was Bruce Cabot's wife,

The friendship between Lancaster and Nick Cravat began in childhood and developed into an acrobatic partnership, first in the circus, then in movies.

Lancaster with friend and producer Mark Hellinger who made Burt's earliest successes, *The Killers* and *Brute Force*.

In his first film, *The Killers*, Burt co-starred with the sultry Ava Gardner. She said that away from the set 'he swept me off my feet'.

Lancaster brought his brother Jim to Hollywood to handle his legal affairs.

Francesca de Scaffa. She later claimed that when she came to a studio in Santa Monica to test for Lancaster, he hit her. What is not at all clear is whether he was actually violent with her, or was using a scene in which he has to slap the heroine around the face as her test. Whatever the reason, it was a scandal that would surface later.

On the set Cooper always kept out of the arguments between Lancaster and Aldrich. Cooper had been paid to learn his lines and play the part as directed by Aldrich and that is what he did. But he seemed to bear no ill will towards Lancaster. Burt told me, 'I really liked Coop. He had that great quality of being liked by the camera. He did not look too great by then and he was kind of gaunt and lanky and looked old – he was probably not well, I guess, by then – but he was a true movie star. I figured I had to play it big against him, and that's what made the movie fun to watch.'

Shot on location in Mexico, it was also a violent film for its time with scenes of men being mown down by gunfire, and Lancaster roughing up Denise Darcel.

The producer of *Vera Cruz* was James Hill who had co-written *His Majesty O'Keefe*. He was also Hecht-Lancaster's story editor. Hill's position was becoming vital to the partnership to the point that he found himself in the middle of the jealousies between Lancaster and Hecht. In contrast to the burly physique of Lancaster, Hecht was a small man. Burt nicknamed him 'The Mole', or sometimes 'Lord Mole'. Mrs Hecht he called 'Ladybird Legs', because she had such slender legs. Hecht objected to what Lancaster intended as a harmless joke.

Burt conceded that Hecht was 'the best executive [he] ever saw and an exceptional critic'. But, said Lancaster, 'he's not creative.' James Hill, however, was, in Burt's estimation, a wonderful addition to the company. 'Good material is the life and breath of this business,' said Lancaster. 'No actor can make a bad story good.'

In return for his work in finding material that Lancaster liked, Hill's reward was to be made producer of *Vera Cruz*, which opened in time for Christmas 1954. The critics slated it. 'Guns are more important in this shambles than Mr Cooper or Mr Lancaster,' said Bosley Crowther of the *New York Times*. 'In short, there is nothing to redeem this film – not even the spirit of the season . . . [Lancaster] is a mess as a villain who displays his meanness by frequent diabolic laughs.' Some critics balked at the film's violence, such as Campbell Dixon on the *Daily Telegraph*: 'In a life-time's film-going, I have never seen a film quite so bloodthirsty and brutal.'

Despite the critical backlash, the public loved it and it earned 11,000,000 dollars at the box office, having cost 1,700,000 dollars. Next, Lancaster felt it was time to flex his muscles as a director. He also wanted to find something that, as an actor, would stretch him still further and, as a producer, make a film that would be something different and thought-provoking.

The latter type of picture was *Marty*, based on the TV play by Paddy Chayevsky, about a man and a woman, both plain looking – in fact, quite unattractive – who brighten their dull and gloomy lives when they fall in love against the odds.

Lancaster liked the story and the whole idea of filming a love story about two people who were certainly not attractive by conventional Hollywood standards. But, he later admitted, he did not think the film could make much money and it would be valuable right now to stand as a tax-loss.

He had admired Ernest Borgnine, who had a major supporting role in *From Here to Eternity*, and gave him the title role. Lancaster's involvement in producing *Marty* was mainly in setting it up with Hecht. From then on Hecht was the only credited producer. But getting United Artists to agree to making the film was not easy.

'Who wants to see a film about two ugly people?' they asked.

Lancaster told them that they ought to underwrite young talent like Paddy Chayevsky. He reminded them that they had made money from *Apache* and *Vera Cruz* and should be willing to gamble by encouraging new writers and new ideas.

That did not persuade the directors of United Artists. So

Lancaster gave them an ultimatum: make the picture or he would make every effort to get out of his contract with them and go elsewhere. That was argument enough and they agreed.

Since finishing *Vera Cruz*, Lancaster had been looking for something to flex his acting muscles. So when he heard that Hal Wallis had bought the rights to Tennessee Williams's play *The Rose Tattoo*, he asked for the male lead role.

The play had been written by Williams specifically for Italian actress Anna Magnani whom he had met in Italy. When he sold the film rights to Wallis, it was on the understanding that only Magnani could play the part. She had not been able to play it in the theatre because of her poor English, so the Broadway role of the woman who longs for her dead husband and settles for a slow-witted driver who resembles her departed one, went to Maureen Stapleton.

Lancaster asked Wallis if he could play the driver, and this time Wallis, recognizing Lancaster's box-office pull, had no arguments. But first, Burt was to achieve his long-held ambition – to direct. His choice for this task was *The Kentuckian*, based on the book *The Gabriel Horn* by Felix Holt. Lancaster not only directed but also starred as an 1820s widower who takes his son away from their home in Kentucky to head for Texas. He cast Diana Lynn as the school teacher who falls in love with him, and chose Walter Matthau, then a newcomer, to play the sadistic villain who bullwhips Lancaster.

As an actor, Burt may have plagued his directors with his own ideas but, on the set of this film on location in Kentucky and Indiana in early 1955, he could not quite live up to his own expectations as a full-time director. Because he hardly cared too much about making films for the masses, he chose this story to cut his director's teeth on. Although it was a western – his third in a row – it was hardly an action-packed adventure. The only action in the film was the fight with Matthau, which occurs 80 minutes into the picture.

Unable to leave the screenplay alone, Burt constantly changed it even though he hardly had time to do so. Each day he had to rise at five to get to the location to make sure all was ready for the other actors' arrival. Since he appeared in virtually every scene, his concentration was constantly shifting from directing to acting. Late each evening, he viewed the day's rushes, then finally crawled into bed at midnight.

I quickly discovered that directing is the hardest job of all. But it's also the best job in movies because you're God when you're director.

But I was on my own, really. No one to help me except Ernest Laszlo who was a really fine lighting cameraman, but he wasn't the kind of guy to lock horns with me, which is something I need. I need that edge when someone argues with me. He was just a nice, quiet guy; very artistic, but maybe he was intimidated by me. Who can blame him?

But it's no life being a director, and I realized I didn't want to be a director full time after that. In fact, I thought I might never direct again because I had no life. You never let up because the work doesn't finish until it is in the can. I wore myself out on that one, so it was a long, long time before I directed again.

During filming, he applied for membership of the Screen Directors Guild. He received the reply that his application had been denied because he had 'publicly expressed opinions of contempt for our members in the newspapers and over TV'. It was an act of revenge by many of the directors to whom Lancaster had given such a hard time.

Making the film was a long, arduous task for Lancaster. It could not have been painless for him to read the reviews. Even *Variety* was unimpressed: 'The footage is often long and slow, with the really high spots of action rather scattered . . . [Lancaster] does a fairly competent first-job of handling most every one but himself . . . a bit too self-conscious, as though the director and the actor couldn't quite agree.'

Bosley Crowther wrote, 'There is no excuse for letting the whole thing run wild in mood and tempo with no sense of dramatic focus or control.'

Lancaster had some consolation. He said, '*Time* and *Life* wrote some very nice things about my work as a director.' But he knew that he had taken on too many jobs at once – acting, directing and producing. He would not make the same mistake again, although he referred to *The Kentuckian* as 'a very pleasant little film' and added, 'that's about all that could be said for it.'

At the Goldwyn Studio, Delbert Mann had been having a much better time directing *Marty*. The film was made on a shoestring budget of less than a third of a million dollars. When it was released in 1955, the critics loved it. Influential critic Gavin Lambert described it as 'something rare in the American cinema today; a subtle, ironic and compassionate study of ordinary human relationships'.

Lancaster was not surprised. But he was amazed when *Marty* showed a profit. It took 5,500,000 dollars, not what he had expected at all. He said, 'I was groaning all the way to the bank!'

As if the failure of *The Kentuckian* was not enough to cope with in 1955, he and Harold Hecht were landed with a lawsuit, brought by Ernest Borgnine who claimed he had only received 10,000 of the 50,000 dollars for his part in *Marty*. The case was eventually settled out of court and Borgnine, when asked what he thought of Lancaster, replied, 'He is a very tough hombre.'

Then the spectre of the scandal sheet called *Confidential* reared its tacky head. Its publisher, Robert Harrison, had come up with the idea for the magazine after watching the daily televised investigation into organized crime by the Kefauver Committee. It became obvious that the public relished stories about vice, crime and prostitution.

Harrison, who had worked for the respectable *Motion Picture Herald*, had previously been a junior in the offices of *Daily Graphic*, an earlier scandal rag. He chose the great stars of Hollywood as his target for *Confidential* which, at its peak in the mid-fifties, had 4,000,000 readers. In 1955, Harrison published the story that Francesca de Scaffa had been roughed up by Burt during her test for *Vera Cruz*. To further corroborate the story that Lancaster was an 'habitual abuser of women', the magazine named Zina Rachevasky, the playgirl daughter of a banking magnate, as another of Lancaster's victims.

According to the story, Lancaster had picked up the habit as a youth and had 'been handing out lumps ever since. Not a few of these have been collected by some of the world's best-known beauties.'

There were some Hollywood stars who agreed to 'purchase' evidence, such as photos and tape recordings that incriminated them, thus preventing their scandalous goings-on from being printed. Some refused to pay, including Burt Lancaster.

Whether or not he ever actually played rough with women remains a matter of speculation. That he had trouble containing his temper was without question. A story reported by Sheilah Graham told of an evening when Burt and Norma invited a couple over to watch a film in Lancaster's private theatre. The couple, not named, apparently worked for Hecht-Lancaster.

Before the film rolled, Burt and the female guest got into an argument about pre-marital sex. He was for it, she against it. They quietened down, the lights dimmed, and the film began. But for almost the entire film, Lancaster was seething and finally he could no longer contain his anger. He got to his feet, pointed at the woman and yelled, 'Get out of here and don't ever come back.'

He marched the couple out of his house to their car and kicked their car door closed. Throughout it all, Norma had said nothing, having learned long ago not to get involved in Burt's arguments or to express opinions of her own. It was not long before the other couple were friends again and made welcome at the Lancaster house. No doubt, the couple, whose livelihood depended on Lancaster, accepted the fact that anyone who socialized or worked with Burt would inevitably find themselves on the receiving end of his violence.

His temper would get him into more trouble in the future.

10

Back on the Trapeze

Shortly after finishing *The Kentuckian*, Lancaster was on board a train bound for Kansas, accompanied by James Hill and Burt's personal make-up man, Bob Schiffer. Lancaster still had the long, golden locks of *The Kentuckian*.

They were eating in the restaurant car where Hill began picking olives out of his pie. Lancaster sat next to him, eating his soup and Schiffer sat opposite them. Burt did not see Hill flicking his olives over Schiffer's shoulder; one landed in the cleavage of a woman in a low-cut dress sitting behind Schiffer. The woman's furious husband stood up, walked over to where Lancaster stood and loomed over him. Burt just kept on eating his soup. The man threatened to punch him. Lancaster put down his spoon, stood up and, as Schiffer described it, 'the next minute all hell was let loose'.

The conductor arrived to break up the brawl. Schiffer was already trying to stop the fight but the conductor started fighting with him. Hill said nothing and just sat there eating. Eventually the fight broke up. Schiffer, fed up with Hill for causing the trouble and with Lancaster for throwing the first punch, sat down and fumed silently.

Lancaster started talking about his next film, *The Rose Tattoo*. Schiffer said gruffly, 'You can't play it with all that long hair.'

'Then you'd better cut it,' said Lancaster.

'But I've only got my nail scissors,' Schiffer protested.

'They cut, don't they?'

So Bob Schiffer gave Lancaster a close crop with a pair of nail scissors on board a train bound for Kansas.

The Rose Tattoo was shot partly on location in Key West in Florida, almost next to Tennessee Williams's home, in 1955.

Anna Magnani had to travel from Naples to Hollywood but was so terrified of aeroplanes that she refused to fly. Tennessee Williams sailed with her from Italy to New York – a two-week journey – then went by train to California where the interiors were shot at Paramount. Throughout the journey Williams coached her English. When the cast and crew flew to the location in Florida, she again went by train.

She was extremely attracted to Lancaster and made every effort to seduce him. 'He was just her type of big, broad-shouldered he-man,' said Hal Wallis. But she was not his type. 'She got nowhere and gallantly settled for friendship.' Wallis said that both stars had enormous egos but, 'were unselfish in their playing, and respected each other's talent'.

Daniel Mann, who had directed *Come Back Little Sheba* and *Marty*, tried to persuade Lancaster not to use an Italian accent but he insisted and subsequently failed to win over the critics with his performance. He had not yet learned the lesson that Shirley Booth taught him. 'He attacks the part with zest and intelligence,' wrote Arthur Knight in *Saturday Review*. 'But one is always aware that he is acting, that he is playing a part that fits him physically, but is beyond his emotional depths. His strong-toothed grin, his cropped, slicked-back hair, his bent-kneed walk are, like his precarious Italian accent, mannerisms and devices carefully acquired for the occasions and barely more than skin deep. The earnestness of his effort only serves to highlight Magnani's own complete submergence in her role.'

Variety wrote, 'The characters inspire little sympathy. Magnani has animalistic drive and no beauty. Burt Lancaster, as the village idiot by inheritance, is called upon to take on a role bordering on the absurd.'

In Britain, the *Sunday Times's* Dilys Powell had a more sympathetic opinion: 'He seems to me to have not the clown's mug which the widow sees, but the face of a good-looking wolf. All the same, Mr Lancaster, a much better actor than a few years ago one had any reason to suppose, contributes much of the boobyish sympathy and gentleness which the role needs. Indeed the whole film is finely acted.'

It did fairly well at the box office in 1956 – nobody really expected the movie-going public to flock to a filmed Tennessee Williams play – and, having got it out of his system, Lancaster set about producing a labour of love – *Trapeze*.

The partnership was now newly refurbished as Hecht-Hill-Lancaster, James Hill having been made a full partner. The new company called itself Susan Productions for reasons that probably have more to do with the American tax system than anything else. But James Hill was the credited producer and once more the company was working in collaboration with United Artists. To add extra prestige to the production, Carol Reed was assigned to direct.

Lancaster had had the idea for doing a circus picture when he was involved with Shelley Winters. Except that now he did not have Shelley to be his leading lady. He had, apparently, tried to get the exciting new Italian star, Sophia Loren, but instead he got Gina Lollobrigida, an arguably more beautiful if less charismatic Italian lady. Better still, he recalled the young actor he had been so impressed with on the set of *Criss Cross*. That young man, Tony Curtis, had become a leading light at Universal. But apart from a relatively superior production at Paramount, *Houdini*, Curtis had not managed to climb out of the low-budget Universal programming pit.

So when Lancaster offered him the role of a young trapeze artist, Curtis jumped at the chance. Universal tried to talk him out of doing the film and predicted all sorts of calamities for Burt Lancaster and his circus film.

Tony Curtis told me, 'In Hollywood they all tell you you're making a mistake, whatever you do. As you usually are, they're onto a safe bet. But I did *Trapeze*. And I thought that at the time, acting with real professionals like Burt and Carol Reed, that if I was still working when it came out, I'd got it made.' Curtis received 150,000 dollars to do the film, the most he'd been paid for any film.

Lancaster worked hard to get the script right. James R Webb was credited with writing the screenplay, based on *The Killing Frost* by Max Catto. But other writers were brought in to polish the final draft, including James Jones, Ernest Lehman, Sam Taylor and Ruth and Augustus Goetz. 'We spent 100,000 dollars for the writing on *Trapeze*,' explained Lancaster. 'A lot of money to spend before you ever get into production.'

Filming began in Paris shortly before Christmas 1955. Like Anna Magnani, Curtis was terrified of flying. 'Anywhere I went was by boat, train or pack mule,' he said. 'I never got 40 feet off the ground. It was written into every contract that I would not fly to a location. So if a studio wanted me bad enough, they'd take me without flying.'

Lancaster really wanted him and so Curtis was allowed to take a cruise to France at United Artists' and Hecht-Hill-Lancaster's expense.

Despite his fear of flying, Curtis had no fear of working on the trapeze. He and Gina Lollobrigida were trained by Eddie Ward, who knew Lancaster from their days with the Gorman Brothers' Circus in 1935, and Fay Alexander at the Cirque d'Hiver. Both Ward and Fay Alexander now worked for Ringling Brothers' Circus. Lancaster did not want to use doubles any more than was necessary and he knew he could manage many of his own trapeze stunts.

'Tony really put everything into learning how to fly on the trapeze,' Lancaster told me. 'When his wife, Janet Leigh, saw him for the first time standing up on the bars, she screamed. He just got onto the rope and descended like a real circus veteran. His dedication helped make that film possible.'

One of the highlights of filming was when the cast had to join the big circus parade down the Champs-Elysées. Dressed in dazzling costumes, Lancaster, Curtis, Lollobrigida and Katy Jurado rode down the boulevards of Paris, followed by the animals and the chariots.

Curtis quickly progressed to flying without a safety belt. He was what they called a 'yugo', because as an apprentice flyer, he stood on the platform catching the bars and waiting for the command from Lancaster, 'Now next time, you go!'

When Gina Lollobrigida and her husband threw a formal dinner at the exclusive Laurent restaurant, Burt broke his usual rule about parties and took Norma to it. Curtis and Janet Leigh were also there. For Curtis, the location work in Paris was harder than it was for Lancaster because Janet Leigh could only be there for a week as she was in the middle of filming in Africa and London.

When Reed got down to the real meat of the film – shooting the actors flying on the trapeze – he was able to film important close-ups of them because each was capable of performing a certain amount without the use of stand-ins. Lancaster, as the veteran trying to teach the young Curtis how to do a triple, did the majority of his stunts, except for the extremely dangerous shots when Eddie Ward doubled for him.

Of Carol Reed, Lancaster said:

He was marvellous, a real gentleman who was brilliant in the way he used the camera; he could find original ways to use it, and I was just in awe of his talent for that. When we got Carol Reed we also got class. And the reason we were able to afford him – because he did not come cheap – was because he agreed to take a percentage of the profits, so we did not have to pay an enormous fee outright. And what happens with people who work for a percentage is that they feel they own a piece of the film – and they do – so they give it that extra effort to make it work.

My only criticism about Carol is that when it came to talking about what the story was about – as he saw it – he was not very articulate. He couldn't really pin down exactly what he wanted to say.

Nevertheless, *Trapeze* was a huge commercial hit. It was, of course, the perfect star vehicle for Lancaster to display his acrobatic skills, even though his character was partially crippled. It also established Tony Curtis as a major star who was liked and admired so much by Lancaster that he and Curtis would soon co-star together again.

When Oscar-nomination time came around in early 1956, Lancaster could feel justifiably proud that two films he was involved in were prominent in the nomination lists. *Marty* received several nominations and went on to win Best Picture, Screenplay (adapted), Director and Best Actor (Ernest Borgnine). The nominations it did not win were for Best Actress (Betsy Blair), Black and White Photography and Best Supporting Actor (Joe Mantell).

The other film was *The Rose Tattoo* which won, not surprisingly, Best Actress for Anna Magnani and Best Colour Photography for James Wong Howe. Its other nominations were for Best Picture, Music Score (Alex North) and Supporting Actress (Marisa Pavan).

Perhaps Burt just wanted to jump for joy, or maybe it was pure exuberance but, during a flight to Boston, he suddenly performed a back-flip in the aisle and landed in the lap of Artur Schnabel, the pianist. Schnabel did not share Lancaster's amusement at having his precious hands sat upon by the hard-muscled actor and expressed concern that his hands might be damaged: they weren't. On arrival in Boston, Lancaster spotted a reception committee of reporters and, wishing to avoid them at all costs, vaulted over a ten-foot wire perimeter fence.

If there was one thing that Lancaster loathed, it was the press. Especially when they were lined up waiting for him at places like airports. Woe betide any reporter who asked what Lancaster considered a 'dumb question'. He even threw one magazine reporter out of his New York hotel suite.

Later the same reporter turned up on a film location, accompanied by a photographer. When Lancaster recognized him, he said, 'You guys are all assholes. You ask people to do things and you do nothing in return. You waste our time and there is no guarantee that the story will appear. I can go into a market and buy a can of beans and I pay for it. That's good business. But you guys . . !'

To which the reporter replied, 'You're spending all this money on advertising in our magazine. Wouldn't it be a good investment to give us 30 minutes of your time and you'd have several pages of free publicity?'

'Absolutely not. I don't care what you do. You can take pictures of me picking my nose or scratching my ass but I won't give you any of my time.'

Consequently, Lancaster gave very few interviews in his life. I got to interview him twice at length (as well as meet him on a separate occasion) and, when I asked him why he avoided interviews but allowed me to question him twice, he replied, 'Because you obviously know about films and don't ask the kind of dumb question the tabloids go after. Like, "Tell me, Mr Lancaster, what would you say irritates you the most?" to which I would respond with, "You, asking me such a stupid question." '

However, he did, in the first interview, refuse to talk about his friendship with Kirk Douglas because, he said, 'This interview isn't about Kirk Douglas. It's about me. All anyone ever wants to know is what it is like working with Kirk. Well, ask Kirk. He can talk about himself better than anyone.' And he finished the answer with his charming grin so you couldn't be offended by him.

When I spoke to him the next time, when *Tough Guys*, his last film with Douglas was on release, he did talk about Kirk Douglas and, when I reminded him that he had previously refused to talk about his friend, he said, 'But now I'm talking about our new film together, so I'm promoting the film, me and Kirk.'

The film that really established the friendship between Lancaster and Douglas was *Gunfight at the OK Corral*. Hal Wallis had bought a story outline from ex-newspaperman Stuart Lake, who had been a friend of Marshal Wyatt Earp's and had written the biography of the legendary lawman. Wallis commissioned novelist Leon Uris to write the screenplay and

John Sturges to direct. Although Burt Lancaster was no longer under contract to Wallis, the producer nevertheless wanted to cast him in the role of Marshal Wyatt Earp. And he wanted Kirk Douglas to play Doc Holliday.

Kirk Douglas (who was happy to talk about Burt Lancaster) told me, 'Hal was trying to set up *Gunfight at the OK Corral*. They sent the script to me and I turned it down. Then they sent it to Burt Lancaster and he turned it down. Then I reread the script and I thought, wait a minute; if Burt and I played in it I think we could make this a fun picture. So I said to Burt, "If you play the part of Wyatt Earp then I'll play the part of Doc Holliday," and he said, "Okay." So we made *Gunfight at the OK Corral*.'

Actually, it was not quite that simple from Lancaster's point of view. He told me:

Wallis had this script written by Leon Uris about Wyatt Earp and Doc Holliday and he wanted me and Kirk to play the roles. I was a bit surprised since I thought that he had had enough of the two of us when we made *I Walk Alone*, but the thing about Hal was he recognized the pulling power of the two of us, and so he sent me a script, and Kirk a script. I did not want to do it really, but Kirk seemed enthusiastic and so he said that if I agreed to do it, he would too.

At that time I was trying to get Wallis to cast me as Starbuck in *The Rainmaker*. Now that was a part that really interested me. Starbuck was a con man who could spin a yarn a mile long. He was a colourful man with persuasive ways, a brash salesman who promises that he can make the rains fall for a fee of a hundred bucks. That really appealed to me; this guy who can sell anything, including rain! So I told Hal that I would do *Gunfight at the OK Corral* if he would let me do *The Rainmaker*. That made good business sense to Hal, so we made a deal.

The Rainmaker was another stage hit that Wallis purchased

the screen rights to. Katharine Hepburn had agreed to play the part of Lizzie Curry, the spinster who runs the family farm which suffers, like all the other farms, from drought. William Holden was Paramount's choice for the role of Starbuck, the so-called Rainmaker but, after Lancaster made Wallis an offer that was hard to turn down, Holden was passed over for Burt.

Shooting at Paramount Studios, director Joseph Anthony had no chance to film on location to capture the authenticity of the dust-bowl setting. But then, being adapted from N Richard Nash's play by Nash himself, the film relied more on the sparks that fly between the two leading players. And the sparks did fly, not only for the cameras.

On the first day of shooting Lancaster was late on the set and Hepburn, furious at his tardiness, stormed onto the centre of the sound stage and announced, 'I'm here, all these people are here, and if you're not going to be here on time we can't work.' He was never late again.

But Hepburn, who was making a comeback after being away from the screen for four years, was annoyed at the way Lancaster insisted on last-minute script changes almost every day. She thought him 'sloppy and unprofessional'. He disliked her for what he considered her 'affected ways'.

Despite their animosity, the film worked for the *Daily Herald* critic, who wrote, '*The Rainmaker* is much better than the play, mainly because of the magical combination of Lancaster and Hepburn. He has never done anything as good as this. She is at the height of her talent. Together, they push the film to greatness and hold it there.' *Variety* called the film 'solid screen entertainment with Burt Lancaster turning in perhaps his most colourful peformance'.

But Dilys Powell of the *Sunday Times* felt that Lancaster's 'gestures and poses are a shade athletic, and once or twice I had the fancy that he was still impersonating the Crimson Pirate . . . But when it is needed, he brings a hint of uncertainty to the part and the result is a very likeable pathos.'

The Rainmaker opened in 1956. Katharine Hepburn was nominated as Best Actress but lost to Ingrid Bergman in

Anastasia.

While *The Rainmaker* was in production, the Hecht-Hill-Lancaster partnership was producing *The Bachelor Party*, under the banner of Norma Productions with United Artists. This was a Paddy Chayevsky screenplay, from his own TV play, about New York book-keepers who throw a stag party for one of their colleagues. It is largely seen through the eyes of a reluctant married guest, played by Don Murray. As the party becomes more lewd, he gets sexually involved with a good-time girl, played by Carolyn Jones. It was a shrewd, bitter-sweet comedy full of detailed observation and wry comment.

Carolyn Jones was nominated for an Oscar. But the film was held up for release until 1957 and was not a great success at the box office, which disappointed United Artists who had hoped for a similar success to *Marty*, especially as Delbert Mann was directing again.

From time to time Burt heard from Richard Brooks, the screen writer on *Brute Force*. He had not given up his hope of turning *Elmer Gantry* into a film and had met the author, Sinclair Lewis, who told Brooks, 'If you ever get around to making it, do yourself a favour. For God's sake, make it a *movie*. Don't be afraid of the book.' Lewis agreed to sell the option to Brooks who then spent years working on the massive screenplay.

During the mid-1950s he ran into Lancaster in a restaurant and announced, 'I've got the property. We've got to do the movie some day.'

Lancaster did not take Brooks too seriously: 'Fine. Let me know when you've written it.'

Brooks left his employment at MGM and went off to Europe, writing his script on a barge on the canals of Belgium. At last, in 1956, he had ready his first draft of *Elmer Gantry*, which he sent to Lancaster to read. Burt recalled:

I did not like it then, not because it was badly written – it was very well written, but it was too damn long. So I phoned him and told him and we got into a big argument.

I said to him, 'Look, Dick, if you really want to do this, then so would I. But don't start the movie with me as a twenty-year-old kid in some seminary. Start the film further into the book.'

He was pretty upset with me after all his hard work and wouldn't talk to me for a while, but then his agent called and got us talking again and Dick said, 'I hear you like to play golf.' I thought he was going to challenge me to a game but instead he said, 'Well, there's no time for that. No more golf. I want you to come over to the studio every day and work on this script with me.'

We moved into a small apartment and got to work. In all we worked for seven months until he had a script he believed in, and I believed in. It was the fifth draft he had produced, and it was brilliant.

Burt's job was to try and persuade United Artists to let him produce it, and in time they agreed. But it was to be four more years before *Elmer Gantry* could start production and then it was to be with another studio.

11

Smell of Success

Towards the end of 1956, Lancaster and Kirk Douglas converged on Tuscon in Arizona to begin filming *Gunfight at the OK Corral*. According to Sheilah Graham, the two stars were this time 'in the driver's seat and they made sure Wallis knew it'.

John Sturges, the director, told me:

I had been warned by Hal Wallis about these two men, and true to form they each told me that they were producers as well as actors, and Burt had also directed. I told them that if I needed their help, I would ask for it. I did not ask, but they obviously felt I needed their help and each night they hid away in their hotel room and rewrote their dialogue. I told them that the scenes would be shot as written; Hal told them the scenes would be shot as written. They refused to budge.

Finally Burt just threw a tantrum on the set, demanding he be allowed to speak the lines he had stayed up half the night rewriting. I said, 'Let's have a look at what you've written.' I took a look and said, 'This has nothing to do with the action.' He just threw his weight around and I thought he would walk off the set, so I decided to humour him and let him do the scene as he wrote it. What I did not tell him was that we did not have any film in the camera.

He was all over the set, shouting his lines until he was hoarse, and sort of got it out of his system.

No wonder Sheilah Graham called the Lancaster-Douglas team, 'The Terrible-Tempered Twins'. Curiously, neither star recalls behaving that way on the set. Douglas told me, 'I've enjoyed working with Burt. He's fun. He's aggressive. Sparks fly. I like that. It's fun, exciting. We always had fun. *Loud* fun. We were together a lot after the day's shooting. We'd have dinner and we'd talk until three or four in the morning.'

Lancaster said, 'We were out there on location without our wives, so naturally Kirk and I spent a lot of time together. Our hotel rooms were adjoining and we'd sit up most nights talking about our families and our careers, our hopes and dreams.'

According to Douglas, Hal Wallis was perplexed by their friendship and asked Kirk what he and Lancaster found to talk about all night long. Wallis, said Douglas, was not a man who could hold lengthy conversations after dinner. 'He did not know that between friends the well of conversation never runs dry. To Hal, the camaraderie between Burt and me was one of the mysteries of the universe.'

The camaraderie was not always so strong. One day, as they were walking off the set, a crowd of fans converged on Lancaster for an autograph. He told them, 'Go and ask Mr Douglas for his autograph. He's a great actor. Of course, you probably did not recognize him without his built-up shoes.' It was just a joke but Douglas was visibly upset by the remark. Some reports said he literally was weeping as he got into his car.

They enjoyed many moments of unintended hilarity. In a sequence in which Doc Holliday helps the unarmed Earp to face down a saloon full of cowboys, Earp says, 'Thanks, Doc.' Holliday replies, 'Forget it.' But the two stars fell about with hysterical laughter and were unable to say their lines. 'The ridiculousness of the scene – our great bravery, our machismo – made us howl,' recalled Douglas.

They did the scene over and over again but it made them

laugh even louder until John Sturges halted the shooting and had to 'send us home like bad boys', according to Douglas.

Lancaster was always intense in his acting and he did not mind what people thought of his technique. But he was shocked to discover how far Jo Van Fleet, who was playing Doc Holliday's hooker, was prepared to go. He came on to the set one day at the request of Kirk Douglas to watch the way the actress needed to be 'pumped up' before she went on to do a scene. She had been asking Douglas to slap her. He did, and she went on to do her next scene. It happened each time she had to go on the set.

So Kirk told Burt to witness this masochistic ritual. Lancaster stood with his huge jaw gaping open as Jo Van Fleet told Douglas, 'Hit me really hard.'

The gunfight was, of course, the climax of the film. The real gunfight in 1881 lasted only a few minutes but, for the film version, it had to be shot as a major action sequence.

Said Sturges:

It was a difficult scene to plan and shoot because John Ford had done it before brilliantly [in *My Darling Clementine*]. So we planned it like a piece of choreography. The last thing we wanted was for Lancaster and Douglas to play it with the kind of robust jollity they display throughout the film, so I told them to keep their expressions dead-pan while dealing out all this death. Burt said to me, 'What should I be thinking of while I'm killing these guys?' I said, 'Think, *meanwhile back at the ranch.*' He and Douglas did it just the way I asked them to.

The film today is regarded as a classic, and rightly so. It was beautifully photographed by Charles Lang who was told by Hal Wallis to give it 'the burned-out born look of a Remington'. Wallis was an avid collector of Frederic Remington paintings. It was filmed in the Paramount wide-screen VistaVision, a short-lived process because few cinemas were equipped to show it in its original big-screen form. Sadly, there is now no way to see the film as it was intended.

The supporting cast was strong in every department, from the two leading ladies, Jo Van Fleet and Rhonda Fleming to the male co-stars such as John Ireland, Frank Faylen, Earl Holliman, Lyle Bettger, Dennis Hopper and De Forrest Kelley. The whole thing is linked by a thundering musical score by Dimitri Tiomkin who came up with a spirited theme song sung by Frankie Laine.

The film was a runaway success. *Variety* reported that it was 'an absorbing yarn in action leading up to the gory gunfight . . . Both stars are excellently cast in their respective characters. Rhonda Fleming is in briefly as a femme gambler whom Lancaster romances, beautifully effective, and Jo Van Fleet, as Holliday's constant travelling companion again demonstrates her ability in dramatic characterization.'

The *New York Herald Tribune* noted that 'no single event in the movie will surprise anybody. But everything is done with an extra degree of quality.'

Bosley Crowther told the *New York Times* readers: 'It is all very obvious, but it is very active. Things happen all through the film . . . It is firmly directed by John Sturges, and it is ruggedly acted by all and sundry – of which there is quite a heap.'

As far as John Sturges was concerned, the experience of directing Burt Lancaster and Kirk Douglas had not been so awful as to put him off directing either one ever again.

He told me:

I knew I could handle those guys so when Hal Wallis asked me to do another western for him a year later – *The Last Train From Gun Hill* – I said, 'Okay, let's get Kirk and Burt back together.' He said, 'Do you think that's a good idea?' I said, 'Sure, why not? They'd be perfect for these parts; Kirk as the lawman whose Indian wife is killed by the son of his old friend, and who's his old friend but Burt Lancaster? Kirk comes to arrest Burt's son, Burt doesn't let him, they may have to kill each other. In fact, either man could play either part.'

But Burt either wasn't interested or just too busy. Kirk played the bereaved lawman, and Anthony Quinn played his one-time friend. It was a good picture. In the end we did not miss Burt, but I got to work with him again on *The Hallelujah Trail*.

Gunfight at the OK Corral established Burt Lancaster as a major star of westerns, even though he had only made one prior to this. In time he would come to accept his image as a tough-talking, straight-shooting star of cowboy films but at first he tried to fight it. What he wanted after *Gunfight at the OK Corral* was a chance to do the more offbeat films, like *The Rainmaker*. 'As long as you're making money in most of your films,' he said, 'the studio will let you do the occasional offbeat film.'

In January 1957, the screenwriters' branch of the Writers' Guild of America considered strike action against Hecht-Hill-Lancaster because the company allegedly refused to negotiate in collective bargaining. At the same time writer John van Druten sued them for 90,000 dollars for failing to pay on a contract for a rejected screenplay. The partnership settled out of court for 70,000 dollars.

Burt was determined that, from now on, he would work only for his own company. He, Harold Hecht and James Hill made a formidable team but they were often at odds with each other over the kind of product they wanted. Lancaster didn't care too much about making big commercial pictures, while Hecht was keen to avoid financial failures. James Hill, always the man in the middle, had to keep his eyes open for a good story, and leave it up to Lancaster and Hecht to fight it out as to whether it would be worth making or not. Hecht wanted to turn down the ones that did not smell of money. But Burt had little interest at the age of 43 in making more money than he already had.

Lancaster bought the rights to Terence Rattigan's play *Separate Tables* with the intention of casting Spencer Tracy as

the American writer, John Malcolm, and Laurence Olivier as
Major Pollack. The stage play, successful in London's West
End and on Broadway in New York, was written and
performed in two acts and featured Eric Portman and Margaret
Leighton, each playing two roles. Because this stage technique
would not work on film, Rattigan, who insisted he write his
own screenplay, agreed to intermingle the two acts into one
story with the four characters played by four actors. Olivier
was assigned to direct and contracts were signed in February
1957. Naturally, Olivier wanted his wife, Vivien Leigh, to be in
it, so she was promptly cast. Then Olivier made an offer to
Spencer Tracy who asked cautiously, 'Won't Burt Lancaster
want the part?

Olivier replied, 'No, he's agreed that you do it.'

So Tracy accepted and Olivier threw a party to celebrate
before flying back to London. Almost the moment he arrived
Lancaster was on the phone to say he had changed his mind
and wanted to play the part of the writer.

Olivier told him that he had already spoken to Tracy. 'Either
Tracy does it or you can't have us,' threatened Olivier, meaning
Vivien would also not be interested. Lancaster persuaded them
both to stay on.

Other problems arose for Lancaster and his partners in July
1957. They tried suing Sophia Loren for 350,000 dollars,
claiming that they had retained her services for two films (the
first being *Trapeze*) but Loren denied the accusation.

Meanwhile, Burt had *Sweet Smell of Success* to make. Ernest
Lehman was commissioned to adapt his novelette of the same
name into a screenplay. Lancaster, who had no respect for the
gossip columnists of Hollywood, was to play a New York
columnist: a powerful man who could make or break a show-
biz or political career with a few choice words in his column.

Lancaster met Lehman often to discuss the script's progress.
Burt was nothing if not blunt and to the point. Over lunch one
day he told Lehman, 'I've a good mind to beat you up.'

'Why?' asked Lehman.

'I think you could have written some of the scenes better.'

'Go ahead. Beat me up. I'd like to get my hands on some of your money.'

Dissatisfied with what Lehman had written, Lancaster brought in Clifford Odets to finish the screenplay.

Odets would later say that he never thought of Burt Lancaster as just 'one man'. He was also 'the cocksure, the wild (inexhaustible physical energy plus unreflected enthusiasm), the paternal (and slightly patronizing), the cruel (the Hyde side of Jekyll), the would-be gentleman and the con man'.

For the role of Sidney Falco, a hustling PR man virtually begging Hunsecker to write about his clients, Burt chose Tony Curtis.

'I liked working with Tony on *Trapeze* and I recognized something inside of him that was bursting to get out,' said Lancaster. 'Tony had gallons of acting talent he needed to flush out, and I figured this was just the right part for him.'

Those who watched Curtis on the set were amazed that the hero of a handful of Universal swashbuckling adventures – the guy with the famous DA haircut – was not only giving the performance of his life but he was seeming to act Lancaster off the set. In fact, once captured on film, the two performances balance out very well, with Lancaster as the cold, uncompromising newspaperman who managed to call his sister 'dear' in such a quiet, forceful way it was chilling, while Curtis was full of energy and almost exhausting to watch. For Curtis, the film was also a chance to break into the producing side. He and Janet Leigh had formed Curtleigh, and Burt agreed that Curtleigh could co-produce the film with Norma Productions.

Curtis told me:

Universal told me to steer clear of the movie because they said it would fall flat on its face because of the subject matter which wouldn't go down too well with many of their business associates in the movie and newspaper industries. Well, they said not to get involved with *Trapeze*, but it was the best move I'd made in my career up till then. Plus it was a chance to get into motion-picture production. But more than anything I had unused resources as an actor which I wanted to discover. Burt had every confidence in me, and that gave me the confidence. He never tried to steal the film or any scene. It was a partnership. I don't know who these actors are who say that Burt did this or Burt did that, and they got all upset. You treat the man with the respect he deserves and he gives you respect in return.

English director Alexander MacKendrick was perhaps the surprise choice since his background was in Ealing comedies. Lancaster found in Alexander (Sandy) MacKendrick a director whom he had difficulty arguing with because MacKendrick just got on with the job the best way he could.
Said Burt:

I respected Sandy. He was good, very good. But he could never make up his mind what he wanted. He'd spend ages setting up the shots he wanted, planning thirty camera moves on a dolly so everything had to be perfectly synchronized. We had tape all over the floor so we could hit our marks as the camera dollied around. The camera never seemed to stand still – closing in, pulling back, tracking and turning.

We rehearsed the scene all day until four in the afternoon just to get it all right technically. The crew were sweating because they knew if they missed a single mark the whole shot would be ruined. It was a six- minute scene. The kind of thing Orson Welles loved to do. And we did it. Perfect. Sandy called, 'Cut. Print.'

Then he thought for a moment and said, 'Let's do one more.' So we did, and again it was perfect. I was very pleased because I knew we had six minutes of excellent footage. In all, a good day's work. But he shook his head and said, 'I don't like it. We'll have to change it and do it again.' There was no point in arguing. In the end he made a brilliant picture.

Of Lancaster, Sandy MacKendrick said, 'He has never faltered in his career. One thing he has, that the stars had, is that he can walk into a room and there is a change in the heartbeat. If you had some instrument, you could measure it. It's like having a wild animal there suddenly. It has to do with aggression and potential violence. I think politicians have it, but no English actor has.'

MacKendrick said he was very conscious that Lancaster had an ego that was 'different to others. The stars had this, a neurosis which goes right to the edge. You somehow use this to get performances from these deep-sea monsters. There was this enormous difference between him and Tony Curtis. Tony has a fantastic vanity but no ego. He could act Burt off the screen, but he will never be a star. He hasn't this granite quality of the ego.'

Bosley Crowther found the film to reflect, 'meanness rendered fascinating'. Pauline Kael wrote in the *New Yorker*, 'A sweet slice of perversity, a study of dollar and power worship.' *Variety* said, 'James Hill's production captures the feel of Broadway and environs after dark. It's a no-holds-barred account of the sadistic fourth estater played cunningly by Burt Lancaster. Tony Curtis as the time-serving publicist comes through with an interesting performance, although somehow the character he plays is not quite all the heel as written.'

At the première, Burt threw his arms around Clifford Odets. But Harold Hecht hated the picture and said that he wished it had never been made. He thought it even more when the film failed to recoup its cost. James Hill said it failed because 'people kept waiting to see Burt jump out of a tree'.

Over the years, though, it has become a classic, and in it we see what may well be the greatest performances ever given by Burt Lancaster and Tony Curtis.

Said Burt, 'You could say *Sweet Smell of Success* is the greatest failure my company ever made. Moviegoers did not care for it in 1957. I don't think they understood the background and the incredible Clifford Odets dialogue. It's the best acting I've ever seen Tony do; he should have got an Academy Award for it. Really he should have. We may have had an expensive flop but over the years it's become such a classic. I've never read a bad critique about it. And quite right too.'

12

An Actor Like Mr Olivier

After the commercial failure of *Sweet Smell of Success*, Lancaster needed a moneymaker. He must have known that the film would not make good box-office returns because he had already spent considerable time setting up *Run Silent Run Deep*, a Second World War drama, directed by Robert Wise and set on board an American submarine. Lancaster was going to co-star with Clark Gable, his biggest co-star since Gary Cooper; Lancaster did not mind being second-billed to Gable. There were numerous films about submarines and most of them were run-of-the-mill actioners. Wise thought this one had the potential to be one above the rest. Gable had the role of a commander whose submarine had been sunk by a Japanese destroyer and whose new command just happened to be the boat that executive officer Lancaster expected to be his.

Robert Wise was frustrated by a screenplay he felt had too many weakness. He told *Film on Focus* in 1973, 'We had a lot of problems with the script when we started – getting something we could all agree on. Then, as we were shooting, there was a lot of behind-the-scenes fighting and pulling going on between the three partners [Lancaster, Hill and Hecht].

'Gable started to sense two-thirds of the way through the film what was going on with the script and, since it was Lancaster's company, he started to be concerned about what was going to happen to him. So he started to raise a little fuss

114

about wanting to know what the end of the script was going to be.'

The film needed to thrive on the uneasy relationship between the two men as well as on the action. 'The trouble with every submarine film is that they are all about firing torpedoes at surface ships and dodging depth charges,' said Lancaster. 'We had to make something of the tension and rivalry between the two men. Gable was a real pro and we got on well; he did not get involved with the problems some of us were having back then. It was hard on Robert Wise but he, I think, gave us what is a really good submarine film, much better than most, if not all, others I've seen.'

Bosley Crowther, in the *New York Times*, agreed: 'A better film about guys in the "silent service" has not been made.' *Time* did not quite agree: 'Mostly good sea fights. Otherwise it's damn the torpedoes, half speed ahead.'

In 1958, work at last began on *Separate Tables*. Olivier, as a director, wanted to get the whole film rehearsed before his cast set foot on a film set but, from day one, Lancaster argued with him. Olivier was unused to this sort of interference from an actor and he was also convinced that Burt could not give him what he, as director, wanted. It was not just a clash of egos but of artistic interpretations. In the end, Olivier felt he had no choice but to pull out and with him went Vivien Leigh.

To get things his own way, Lancaster did not mind paying Olivier a figure in the region of 300,000 dollars to settle the matter. David Niven replaced Olivier as the Major, and Rita Hayworth took over Leigh's role of Lancaster's estranged wife who follows him to the Bournemouth hotel where the film's action takes place. During filming, Rita Hayworth fell in love with James Hill and became his wife but only until 1961 when they divorced. Margaret Leighton, the star of the stage version, reputedly told Hill, 'If I could have done the part in the theatre as well as your wife did it on the screen, they'd never have had her take my place.'

Deborah Kerr played a repressed spinster who becomes attracted to Niven, a retired old major who is not what he seems. Wendy Hiller and Gladys Cooper were also in the cast.

Lancaster brought Delbert Mann in to direct. 'My first instinct,' said Mann, 'was that I was quite the wrong kind of director, and I'd never even been to Bournemouth or experienced that totally British small-hotel life; but Hecht sent me there to research it, and within half a day I'd found prototypes of all the characters that Terry had written about, all living there in retirement homes – the old schoolmaster, the little lady who played the horses, the retired army man. Terry knew them all; his mother had once lived in a private hotel just like the one he was writing about . . .'

Mann admitted to having 'great reservations about David Niven; the role of the Major was so different from anything I'd seen him do before.'

Mann changed his estimation when he watched Niven on the set, especially when he did a scene towards the end. The Major, discovered to be a charlatan who has been arrested for molesting women, is asked to leave the hotel by some of the guests. Watched by the guests, he enters the restaurant and hides his shame by burying his face in a menu. 'We shot this scene over about four days,' Mann explains, 'and finally we had to get a close-up of David registering all the emotion of that scene. There was this whole line-up of the British stage all staring at him and when he'd finished they all applauded. I think that was maybe the best moment of his whole acting career.'

The 'line-up of the British stage' outnumbered the American actors nine-to-two, according to Wendy Hiller. 'Gladys Cooper never seemed to know a line and it was all Burt Lancaster's own money that we were using up with the retakes. As soon as he and Rita Hayworth started to do any of their scenes, Gladys used to remove her glasses and fall into a deep sleep at the side of the set, which I did think was rather naughty and certainly used to unnerve Rita, a poor darling dancing girl who was already lost in the film.'

Around the third or fourth time Gladys Cooper fell asleep, her snores were beginning to drown out the dialogue between

Lancaster and Hayworth. It was all getting a bit tense, so David Niven announced, 'Lunch, I think,' and smoothed the situation over with his gentle humour.

When the film was released in 1958, Campbell Dixon of the *Daily Telegraph* thought Lancaster 'powerfully suggests the tensions and violence locked up in a man fundamentally tolerant and good'.

'The camera tells us with brutal frankness that in Burt Lancaster we have a not-so-able actor acting,' wrote Arthur Knight in *Saturday Review*.

The *Spectator*'s Isabel Quigley was not convinced by the performances of Lancaster and Hayworth 'because they don't give the air of being lonely has-beens. They are too obviously in their prime, on top of things, altogether far too competent and tough for failure and self-pity.'

The best reviews went to the British stars, particularly to David Niven and Deborah Kerr. Both were nominated for Oscars, as was Wendy Hiller as Best Supporting Actress. Hiller and Niven won. The film also received a nomination as Best Picture, which was a particular pleasure to Lancaster as one of its producers.

He told Thomas Wiseman of the *Evening Standard* in 1958:

I am terribly wealthy. I am worth three and a half million dollars, I am very happily married, I have five children. I've everything I want. What more could I possibly need? I am not moved by the desire to make more money or win fame. I've got enough of both and there comes a time when you can't get any more of either. I am just interested in doing things that interest me. When I first started in movies I was unsure of myself, and insecure. I would flare up easily. When success comes as quickly as it came to me there are bound to be problems. You ask yourself, 'How do I come to be here and have I any right to be here?' It took me a certain amount of time to adjust. Now I think I'm adjusted. I keep calm.

During 1958 Metro-Goldwyn-Mayer offered Lancaster the title role in *Ben Hur*. William Wyler was to direct and Charlton Heston was probably going to play Messala, the boyhood friend of Ben Hur. But Lancaster disapproved of the film's implication that Christianity was the one true religion, and he rejected it. Consequently, Charlton Heston swapped roles and won the Oscar for Best Actor as Ben Hur. Stephen Boyd played Messala and became a star and the film won eleven Oscars in all. On reflection, Lancaster said:

I grew up in an area of New York where we had Jews, Buddhists, Muslims, Catholics, Protestants – many creeds, many faiths. The problem with *Ben Hur* when I read the script was that it was sub-titled, 'A Tale of the Christ', and seemed to go out of its way to portray Christianity as the one true faith. I don't know if it is or isn't but I felt it was religious bigotry. But what I didn't know was that Willy Wyler, the film's director, was going to bring Christopher Fry, the playwright, onto the set in Rome to write new dialogue and tighten up the whole concept of the two friends – one a Jew and the other a Roman – who become bitter enemies. Now that part of the story fascinated me. And I would have sure liked to work with Christopher Fry. But that's the way of things; you go by your instincts and make your decisions. What could making *Ben Hur* have done for me? Made me richer still and maybe given me an Academy Award. But to be honest, I think I was too old for the part. Chuck Heston was perfect for it. He was the right age and he had that classical stage background in Shakespeare that allowed him to carry that kind of a role. It's all supposition, but I'd like to think I could have done it as well as he did. I looked younger in those days. And I'm not the one to claim I made the best decision. I mean, look what I did instead – *The Devil's Disciple*!

The question Lancaster must have forever asked himself was, why did he make *The Devil's Disciple*? Kirk Douglas had the

At the height of Lancaster's success in Hollywood he suddenly took a break to go on the road with Nick Cravat to perform their old circus stunts; that's Burt at the top of the pole.

Burt and his wife Norma presenting the happy public face of their marriage which, in private, had a very different complexion.

A quiet moment during the filming of *Ten Tall Men*.

answer. 'I said to Burt "let's do something a bit classy. Let's do George Bernard Shaw." So we did. I was willing to bring Bryna [Kirk Douglas's production company] in on things and work with Hecht-Hill-Lancaster. We thought it would be fun. Boy, oh boy, did we have problems.'

Much earlier, Lancaster had purchased the rights to the play for 60,000 dolars, but no writer they gave it to was able to furnish a satisfactory screenplay. Set during the American Revolution, Shaw's play was not, by his own admission, his best.

Originally Lancaster was going to play the part of Dick Dudgeon who gets mistaken for a preacher, who was to be played by Montgomery Clift. But Clift was undergoing some severe mental problems following a car crash which nearly killed him in 1957. He survived but was heavily scarred and had to have plastic surgery to rebuild part of his face. He reputedly drank heavily, used drugs and behaved most oddly and Lancaster found that insurance companies refused to cover Clift for a film part.

Then Kirk Douglas told Lancaster that he was interested in playing the Dick Dudgeon role and Lancaster decided he could play the preacher. It was, at first, going to be a 3,000,000 dollar colour film but, even after Douglas agreed to bring Bryna in on the deal, they decided they could only afford a million and a half and to shoot it in black and white.

The screenplay was finally finished by Roland Kibbee and John Dighton but Lancaster and Douglas worked alongside them to fashion the screenplay into a double-star vehicle for themselves, thinking to turn it into a lively neo-western.

Despite their differences at the rehearsals of *Separate Tables*, Lancaster persuaded Laurence Olivier to play General John Burgoyne, the British commander. Olivier would probably have never agreed to it had he not needed 1,500,000 dollars to produce, direct and star in his planned film of *Othello* which had met with rejection from every studio. Currently he was appearing in *The Entertainer* for £50 a week at London's Royal Court Theatre. Lancaster offered him 200,000 dollars and he accepted.

After Lancaster and Douglas had finished spicing up the
screenplay with some sex and a bit of action, they made an
appearance on the American Academy Awards Show of 1958,
doing a song and dance routine called *It's Great Not to Be
Nominated* which the celebrity audience loved. Then they
packed their bags and flew to England to film *The Devil's
Disciple*. Burt brought Norma with him. Kirk left his wife Diana
behind: they had some problems to sort out. Also trying to deal
with marital problems was Laurence Olivier, who moved his
family into a house in Shenley for the film's duration.

Vivien Leigh had developed behavioural problems, which
included having extra-marital affairs not due so much to
promiscuity but to a growing mental disorder. It was all
gradually wearing Olivier down and he had found some solace
in the company of Joan Plowright while together in *The
Entertainer*, and for a while he had been happy.

When filming began on *The Devil's Disciple* he found that
the 'heart-wrenchings, the guilt, the longing, the romantic joy
and the tortured conscience of the past few months had taken a
toll on me, which not only cowed my spirit but impaired my
efficiency.'

He may have thought himself to blame for the problems that
beset the filming from the very start. But whatever the flaws in
his performance, Lancaster was more concerned with the
manner in which Alexander MacKendrick was directing. They
had a 48-day shooting schedule but MacKendrick was already
falling behind. At the end of the first week, they had only two
days of film. Lancaster had told him in the first days of shooting
that each day he went over schedule, he and Hecht had to find
the extra money the delays cost from their own pockets. After
the first week, MacKendrick was fired and replaced by Guy
Hamilton. The British press came down hard on Lancaster and
Douglas for firing one of Britain's finest directors. Harold
Hecht told the newspapers in no uncertain terms, 'Look, we
didn't agree with how the picture was being done. I don't know
which of us is right – Hecht-Hill-Lancaster or MacKendrick.
Before we started filming, we were in agreement, but things

don't always work out, I guess. That's all there is to it.'

Actually, Lancaster ended up with the opinion that MacKendrick's two days of film were the best scenes in the finished picture.

Olivier continued to be plagued by his own personal problems. Such was his despair that he began getting names mixed up and kept calling Burt, 'Kirk'. Olivier said that Lancaster 'would look at me straight and steely-eyed and say quietly, "Burt".'

Olivier thought that after the troubles of *Separate Tables* Lancaster treated him very well. 'I really wasn't at all happy on the film,' Lord Olivier told me in 1981, 'but Burt Lancaster was very patient with me and we didn't have a single cross word. In fact, when it turned out they weren't at all happy with what I was doing, it was Harold Hecht who came to me and said, "Can you put more Mr Puff into your general please?" I think overall it was the most miserable time of my life, and I couldn't blame Mr Lancaster for that.'

Harry Andrews, however, told me he thought that Olivier was 'treated disgracefully by the producers. Larry, who was the most confident of all actors at that time, suddenly lacked confidence for the only time I can think of.'

There were attempts at socializing among the cast. Lancaster and Douglas were among a group who joined the Oliviers at a restaurant. Douglas wrote that everyone pretended there was nothing wrong with Vivien Leigh, even though they all knew she was 'not well emotionally'. In the middle of dinner she suddenly asked Olivier, 'Why don't you fuck me any more?'

Then she started flirting with Douglas, being 'very seductive', with Olivier sitting right there. On the set, as Olivier's confidence waned and he lost concentration on his lines and his character, and kept mixing Burt up with Kirk, he told Lancaster that he was very sorry and that he was having a nervous breakdown. Lancaster and Douglas understood, and no heated words were exchanged.

Kirk Douglas became a victim of producers' quarrels when, part way through filming, he was told two scenes he had shot were going to be cut because the film would be too long. So he changed his whole approach to the role only to be told a week later that the scenes were going back in.

During the production, Lancaster gave some rare interviews to the London press, taking the opportunity to argue his case for casting star names – particularly his own – to Tom Wiseman: 'In terms of popular appeal what counts is appearance and personality. Skill as an actor, that's something extra. I like to think of myself as a craftsman rather than as an artist. It is not my ambition to be a great actor like Mr Olivier, nor would I be capable of becoming one.'

Over lunch with TV personality Robert Robinson, he said, 'People go to the movies to see the star. Whatever you are playing, they come looking for *you*. The real you. The star's unique personality must never be submerged. And how to be yourself? The most difficult thing of all. The script gets in the way, so does your own lack of self-confidence. But even when I played a cripple in *Trapeze*, people came along. They came to see Burt Lancaster in those circumstances, to see how he would behave as a cripple.'

He went on to say that he enjoyed the business side of films more than the acting: 'Producing is like giving birth to a baby.'

Mid-way through production, Lancaster and Douglas were invited by the Motion Picture Relief Fund to take part in a charity performance, *The Night of a Thousand Stars*, at the London Palladium. They decided to do a song-and-dance act but were nervous at the prospect of performing before many of the giants of British theatre and variety.

Standing in the wings while American comedy duo, Sid Caesar and Imogene Coca, preceded them and metaphorically 'died' on stage, only heightened their anxiety. But it was too late to back out as the two Hollywood stars were announced. Onto the stage they came and had such an ovation before they had even sung or spoken that Kirk whispered, 'Let's get off now. It can't get any better.'

Then they sang 'Maybe It's Because I'm a Londoner' and the audience cheered as the actors did a soft-shoe shuffle which ended with Douglas climbing onto Lancaster's burly shoulders. They were a roaring success. The film, *The Devil's Disciple*, was much less so. In spite of Olivier's problems he came off with the best notices.

'The Greatest Actor of Our Day,' screamed the *Evening Standard*. 'It is a film to see, just because Laurence Olivier gives the performance of his life. And because in his superb self-confidence, he dared to take the third lead. Knowing that he would steal the film from Burt Lancaster and Kirk Douglas, the two male leads. And he does. Those two able actors look like stupid oafs who have wandered back from a Western into the American War of Independence.'

Time said, 'Lancaster glooms away Shaw's most romantic scenes as if he were lost on a Brontë moor.' The *Times* reported that 'Lancaster finds himself for long periods in charge of the screen for little discernible purpose and with nothing in particular to do. Towards the finish he is the central figure in a farcical free fight which ends with his exploding the British ammunition. From the point of view of the play as Shaw wrote it, Anderson is a dead loss – whenever the film, as it all too often does, seems to think it knows better than the author, its mistake becomes glaringly apparent.'

Back in Hollywood, another Hecht-Hill-Lancaster film had been in production, *Take a Giant Step*, based on a Broadway play that revolved around a black youth, played by Johnny Nash, who grows up in a small New England town where the populace are not used to seeing black people.

Arthur Knight of the *Saturday Review* said, 'No film to date – not even *The Defiant Ones* – has attempted to describe so explicitly what it means to be a Negro in a white man's world.' Other reviews were not as encouraging and Hecht-Hill-Lancaster had yet another box-office disaster on their hands.

The failure of both *Take a Giant Step* and *The Devil's Disciple* was almost the end for Hecht-Hill-Lancaster. But they staggered on, hoping that they would learn from their mistakes. But another was made, by John Huston, who said, 'I made the mistake of agreeing to direct a western called *The Unforgiven*.'

He told me, 'Burt Lancaster and his partners Harold Hecht
and James Hill came to me with the script by Ben Maddow
who I'd worked with on *The Asphalt Jungle*, and I thought it
was very good and had the potential for a more serious film
than either Ben or Hecht-Hill-Lancaster had intended. I had
no say in the cast – the producers had chosen them – Burt
Lancaster, Audrey Hepburn, Audie Murphy, Charles Bickford
and Lillian Gish. Well that was a helluva good cast I thought so
I decided to do it. I shouldn't have broken my own rule that a
director never undertakes to do a film that he doesn't believe in,
but that's what I did.'

The Unforgiven, made in 1959, had Audrey Hepburn as an
unlikely Kiowa Indian who has been raised as a white girl.
Lancaster was her foster brother who refuses to allow the
Indians to take her back. It was a turnabout on the traditional
theme of the white girl raised as an Indian as in John Ford's *The
Searchers*. After fighting off the Indians, Hepburn and
Lancaster are left free to marry.

As the time to shoot the picture in Durango, New Mexico
drew near, it became apparent that Huston and his producers
were in conflict over the concept of the film.

'I wanted to film it as a story of racial intolerance in a
frontier town, a comment on the real nature of community
"morality",' said Huston. 'But when I told the producers that
they disagreed with me; they wanted what I accepted when I
signed my contract – an action-packed film featuring Burt
Lancaster as a larger-than-life frontiersman. From the moment
they told me to make the film their way, the whole thing just
went sour for me.'

The heavy-duty cast were each paid 300,000 dollars, and the
budget was set at 5,000,000 dollars. Filming began in January
1959. Throughout, Burt Lancaster behaved himself, due to his
admiration for John Huston. But, said the director, 'it was as if
some celestial vengeance had been loosed upon me for infidelity
to my principles. Everything went to hell.'

He told me of this celestial vengeance:

Poor Audrey fell off her horse and fractured a vertebra in her back. She'd never ridden before the film, but had been taught well and slow and she was really a good rider in the end, but it was me who put her on that goddamned horse and I promised her she would be all right. But the damned horse bolted for some reason with her on it and some idiot tried to stop it by throwing his arms up, but all he did was make the horse rear up and Audrey fell off. I felt responsible for her accident. And it cost us three weeks of shooting.

The next catastrophe to hit was when Audie Murphy and an old pal of mine, Bill Pickens, went out duck shooting on a lake. Somehow Audie, who couldn't swim, got into deep water and Bill stayed with him, keeping him from going down. They managed to get themselves about a mile away from the shore and were only discovered because Inge Morath, who was a championship swimmer, happened to see them through the telephoto lens of her camera, and she threw off her clothes and dived near nude in to save them. She swam the full half-mile there, and back again with Murphy. When I heard about it I nearly had a coronary. I wondered what else the gods would throw my way.

Things were actually worse than Huston remembered. When Audrey Hepburn fell, she broke *two* vertebrae and four ribs. She was also pregnant at the time, it turned out. At first Huston tried to shoot around her, but then Hecht-Hill-Lancaster closed the production down while they tried to make an insurance claim. Filming resumed in late February.

All the exposed colour film, shot by Franz Planer, was flown, not to Hollywood, but to London at Huston's insistence because he believed the processing there would be of better quality. It added to the already tremendous costs.

The house in and around which most of the film's action takes place was constructed with breakaway walls which could be rolled back for interior shots; there were to be no false studio sets for the film. To make it an authentic-looking 'sod' cabin, it was built to look as though it were cut into the side of a hill, which was in fact a man-made hill covered in grass and cactus.

When the colour film was flown back to the location, Huston and his editor worked on the rushes at the back of the house, under the artificial hill, in a specially constructed room.

Huston did have one happy memory which he liked to share. Lancaster, however, was never amused by it:

> There was a new luxury golf club just outside of Durango which was opening with a tournament featuring international golfing stars. Burt Lancaster was one of the tournament sponsors; he loved golf. My old friend Billy Preston came down to visit me and when I told him about the tournament, he said, 'Let's give them all a surprise.'
>
> We bought 2,000 ping-pong balls and had wrote all sorts of disgusting, foul things like 'Go home you Yankee sons-of-bitches' and 'Fuck you dirty Mexican cabrones'. We got ourselves a small rented plane and flew over the fairway while they were playing, and dropped our cargo; 2,000 ping-pong balls all over the place. Nobody could find a single golf ball among them and it took days to clean up the whole course. The tournament was cancelled, everyone went home complaining and Burt Lancaster was furious. But I thought it was a great caper.

Of Huston, Lancaster said, 'John's a charming man, but he takes chances with the safety of his actors.'

Huston didn't like *The Unforgiven* although he conceded that it had some good performances. 'The overall tone is bombastic and over-inflated,' he wrote. 'Everybody is bigger than life.' It was released by United Artists in 1960.

Stanley Kauffmann of *The New Republic* wrote, 'That Huston could not get a good performance out of Lancaster cannot be held against him, but he has achieved what no other director has done; he has got a bad performance out of lovely Audrey Hepburn.'

Variety, however, thought 'Audrey Hepburn gives a shining performance' and that 'Burt Lancaster is fine'. It added that 'Audie Murphy is surprisingly good as Lancaster's hot-headed brother'. It was dissastified only with Lillian Gish who 'has a tendency to overreact emotionally', which no doubt was a throwback to her days as a silent screen star.

The end of Hecht-Hill-Lancaster seemed ever more certain. Burt said, 'We built a company that just grew too big for what we had wanted to do. We just couldn't afford to operate in the way we wanted to. We were spending two or three years preparing films that in the end had only limited appeal and we had by then taken on the overheads of a major studio. By the time we made – and failed with – *The Unforgiven* we knew we had just about played out. And we would have ended it there and then except we had one or two more projects that we had spent two or three years working on which we had to get out of the way.'

It therefore came as a relief to Lancaster, who only ever wanted to work for himself, to work for someone else. Richard Brooks was ready to make *Elmer Gantry*.

13

A Popular Victory

In 1960 Lancaster and Richard Brooks finally got to make *Elmer Gantry*, not for United Artists, as it turned out, because they were unable to find studio space. So the project moved to Columbia. Brooks's wife, Jean Simmons, had been cast as Sister Sharon Falconer, the evangelist who conducts revivalist meetings in a travelling tent. In the book, Gantry was an ordained minister but for the film he begins the story as a travelling salesman and former divinity student who got thrown out of the seminary for seducing a deacon's daughter. As a salesman, he can sell anything – much like the character Lancaster played in *The Rainmaker*, and not altogether unlike his real self – so, when he sees two Salvation Army women trying to collect donations from gamblers and drinkers, he gives a helping hand. When he comes across Sister Sharon's revivalist meeting, he becomes fascinated by her, charms his way into her life and proves to be a giant among evangelists, even though he does not really believe a word he is saying. He falls from grace when he is framed by a former girlfriend, now a prostitute, by which time Sister Sharon is deeply in love with him.

Sinclair Lewis had told Richard Brooks not to be afraid to adapt his book to suit the medium of film, and this he did with Lancaster's help. Said Burt:

Elmer Gantry in the book is a caricature, a one-dimension character who really had no redeeming features. He never cared about anybody, least of all his wife, but what was fascinating about the character in the book is that despite all this he fits comfortably into the world of evangelical preaching. He was excited by swaying the emotions of others.

Dick and I knew that to capture the audience's sympathy, Elmer had to have a more human touch, so we made him interested in women. He drank and gambled, and he could holler hell-fire and brimstone. He had weaknesses common with us all, and he had vanities, and he had a great gift of communication. He liked the sound of his own voice, and he liked the effect it had on people when they got all stirred up. He wanted people to like him and he was searching for something missing in his life; someone to be with him.

It was the easiest role I ever played because I was playing myself. I think that there are some parts that fit you like a glove, and Elmer Gantry was one of those parts. Actually, I partly based him on John Huston who had charm. I copied many of John's mannerisms; I don't know if he ever recognized himself, but then it wasn't an imitation. Just the inspiration for part of the chemistry that I created to play Elmer.

Just as the cameras were about to roll, Columbia received a letter from the head of Paramount asking them to cancel the production, offering them a sum of money to recoup their costs. The head of Columbia went to the apartment still rented by Brooks and Lancaster and showed them the letter. Before he could explain what he intended to do, Brooks told him, 'We have a contract. What have Paramount to do with this?'

The Columbia boss said, 'He's a Baptist and he thinks making this film would be a terrible thing. When he offered me money to recoup my investment and forget the whole thing, I said to myself, No, we've rented the space and we're going to make the picture.'

Jean Simmons thought that Lancaster 'was just a real charmer. He was a fireball of energy and he and Dick worked well together.'

Brooks said of Lancaster, 'I know all the stories about him. Directors say he is difficult because he makes suggestions. I didn't find him difficult. Burt is one of the most professional actors there is because he really knows what goes into the making of a movie. And he knows what his character is about and isn't afraid of expressing emotion. You treat Burt with respect, he gives you respect, and then you don't have him mouthing off about you. Sure we argued, but that's the way Burt works. There's nothing personal in it. It's all for the good of the picture.'

Some of the most effective moments during filming for Jean Simmons was in the travelling evangelist tents where Elmer preached, especially when Burt had the background artists singing and praying. Miss Simmons told me, 'Dick scoured Long Beach to find real Baptists who wanted to be in the movie, so all the extras were not the usual professional extras but real Baptists who knew all the songs, and they really believed they were in one of their own meeting places. It was extraordinary.'

Elmer Gantry was a much-needed success for Burt. A H Weiler in the *New York Times* wrote, 'Without the performance of Burt Lancaster, the film's overall effect would be vitiated. He is an Elmer Gantry who would have delighted the cold enquiring eye and crusading soul of Sinclair Lewis.' 'He is Elmer Gantry,' proclaimed Arthur Knight in the *Saturday Review*.

Variety said, 'Brooks honours the spirit of Lewis's cynical commentary on circus-type primitive exhortation with pictorial imagery that is always pungent. He also has written dialogue that is frank and biting . . . Burt Lancaster pulls out virtually all the stops as Gantry to create a memorable characterization. He acts with such broad and eloquent flourish that a finely balanced, more subdued performance by Jean Simmons as Sister Sharon seems pale by comparison.'

The *New York Herald Tribune*'s Robert Beckley wrote,

'Lancaster's portrayal may not be the subtlest performance of his career, but it is certainly among the strongest.'

Lancaster was voted Best Actor of 1960 by the New York Film Critics at their annual awards ceremony in 1961. He was also nominated for an Oscar, and the Film Critics Award made him a favourite to win. 'I'd like to win,' he said, although he said he preferred to win the New York Critics Award because of their 'high standards. Consequently when they give you an award of this kind, you feel that they are expressing a considered opinion. You don't have to feel that politics is involved. When Hollywood gives out its Oscars, you generally feel that there is a political manoeuvring going on. So in my opinion – and I think all Hollywood actors really feel this way – the New York Critics award is the prestige award, even though it doesn't carry the box-office weight of an Oscar.'

There are some movie actors who might argue the point with him but, nevertheless, he was glad to be in the running for an Oscar. *Elmer Gantry* was nominated for four further Oscars: for Best Picture, Best Director for Brooks, Best Supporting Actress for Shirley Jones (as the hooker who frames Gantry), and for André Previn's music. On Academy Awards night in 1961, Brooks collected his gold statuette, so did Shirley Jones. And, for the first time, Burt Lancaster picked up his Oscar.

He was pleased to have won, but underwhelmed. 'I wish I had more enthusiasm for winning it,' he said. 'Winning will represent a kind of popular victory but I doubt if it's as fair a test as it ought to be.'

He told me:

The trouble with winning Oscars is, while the nominees are undoubtedly worthy of the award, the voting system is based largely on sentimentality or politics. There is a lot of advertising that goes on around awards time. I remember when *Elmer Gantry* was up as Best Picture, United Artists was touting John Wayne's *Alamo* picture for a Best Picture Oscar as well as others. They came up with an advertising slogan that went something like, 'A vote for *The Alamo* is a vote for America.' That's bordering on emotional blackmail. If you don't vote for *The Alamo* you won't be a good American. I think that's why John Wayne lost out on a lot of Oscars because it went too far.

As for the sentimental approach, the way it works is this: if you've been nominated before and not won, then the second or third time you get nominated is the time you're likely to win. That doesn't mean that winning is not rewarding. It is, but you have to recognize that you're not necessarily being given the award for the right reasons.

On hearing that he'd won his Oscar, Shelley Winters sent him a telegram: THANK GOD YOU WON TOO. SHALL WE GO FOR TWO? CONGRATULATIONS SHELLEY.

Perhaps it was the sudden remembrance of his former flame sparked by the telegram but Burt Lancaster decided he wanted Shelley Winters to be in his next film, *The Young Savages*. This was one of just a couple of remaining Hecht-Hill-Lancaster deals waiting to be completed before the partnership finally dissolved. They had tried to salvage their business by going into television, making the pilot for a programme called *The Office*, based on *The Bachelor Party*. But not a single network picked it up, possibly because the film had not exactly been a runaway success. They decided to forget about going into TV.

Despite the jealousies that had grown between Hecht and Lancaster, James Hill admired both men. Of Hecht, he said, 'Among Harold's many talents, the one that particularly interested me was his ability to pull the rug out from under a person. It was the subtlety with which he managed this that was impressive, because he invariably won the admiration of the other party even as they were picking themselves up off the floor.'

Hill was positively in awe of some of Lancaster's more intimidating talents. He recalled a time when he and Lancaster were playing golf with two others at the Riviera Golf Club. Hill had taken his first drive, sending his ball into the trees, then found himself getting deeper into the woods and into a trap that was 'so high,' he said, 'there was no way to see over it or into it.' It took him three more strokes to get out of there, a further stroke to get back on the green, and then he finished with a 50-foot putt that amazed even him.

Lancaster came up to him and asked, 'What did you take?'

Hill was trying to figure out how many strokes he could shave off his score when Burt looked at him 'with the steely blue-eyed gaze, the one that could empty out any bar, even the OK Corral.' Before he could answer, Lancaster said, 'You took an eight.'

Burt then ticked off each of the eight shots Hill had supposedly made in front of their opposing players and then he told the other players how many strokes they had each taken. Said Hill, 'It never entered my mind to question where he found the time to hit his own ball. Nor did I ever think to question his score.'

The Young Savages was the topical story of juvenile delinquency in the New York area of Spanish Harlem where Burt himself lived as a boy. Lancaster was to play an assistant district attorney investigating the murder of a boy from a Puerto Rican gang. In the process he puts his own life and that of his wife in danger. Dina Merrill was cast as the wife and, as the girl Lancaster used to love, he wanted Shelley Winters.

To direct, Burt wanted John Frankenheimer, fresh from the medium of live television. 'I don't think anybody is better with the camera than John Frankenheimer,' Lancaster said. 'Those early *Playhouse 90s* that he directed weren't just interesting plays; they were shot uniquely, were sometimes even crazy and bizarre.'

Frankenheimer had only made one previous film, *The Young Stranger*. When he read the screenplay of *The Young Savages* by Edward Anhalt, he thought it was 'pretty bad', so he and his friend J P Miller rewrote it.

Harold Hecht held the reins as the main producer but often his job was to do what Burt wanted him to. And he wanted Hecht to get Shelley for the film. Hecht got in touch with her and she told him that she must have equal co-star billing with

Burt and demanded a salary of 100,000 dollars. Hecht checked with Lancaster and called back. 'The salary is okay but Burt gets billing alone above the title.'

Shelley said, 'Good for him. I pass,' and hung up.

The role went instead to Lee Grant and, with the casting complete, the film went before the cameras. Frankenheimer managed to get clearance to film some of the scenes on location in Manhattan but, because New York was such an expensive place to shoot, most of the film was made in Hollywood.

The film got off to a bad start with the Manhattan location. Four scenes were scheduled that involved Lee Grant and Lancaster. But from the beginning Lancaster was telling Frankenheimer what to do. Lancaster put the blame on his director for the problems. 'At the outset John and I had some problems. I felt his approach to his work did not get the best results because of his attitude. He was touchy and arrogant and terribly demanding on the set, sometimes to his own detriment. After we settled our personal problems we got along great; became great friends. I did five movies with him.'

During the second scheduled scene which called for an argument between Lee Grant and Lancaster, fiction turned into fact when the two really flew at each other verbally. They swore and yelled and called each other names and then Lee walked off the film.

Lancaster ordered that she was not to be persuaded back and told Hecht to offer the role to Shelley Winters once more. So Hecht phoned Shelley, who only ten minutes earlier had had a tearful Lee Grant on the phone saying, 'Burt is impossible to work with,' and now Hecht was saying, 'Burt wants you to do this film.'

Shelley told him that she still wanted co-star billing. To complicate matters she was in the middle of rehearsals for *Two for the Seesaw* which she was soon to take to six theatres around the country, so Hecht would have to arrange the shooting schedule around her.

'We'll try to do what you ask,' he said. 'The script is on its way to you. We won't be reshooting the scenes in New York,

so we'll make your hair dark to match Lee's so all we have to
do is shoot your close-ups in Hollywood. Then we'll dub your
voice over the back of Lee's head in the long shots.'

'Do your best,' Shelley told him, and he did.

Lancaster arranged for the entire set of *Two for the Seesaw*
to be built exactly to specifications on Sound Stage 27 at
Twentieth Century-Fox Studios, right next to *The Young
Savages* stage. In between filming, Shelley went to Stage 27 to
rehearse her play under the direction of Sydney Pollack who
was Frankenheimer's dialogue director. His main job was to
coach the young actors in the film but he suddenly found
himself directing Shelley Winters with stand-in actors while on
the East Coast the rest of her cast was rehearsing with an
actress standing in for her. After a week of this, she flew east to
open the play and then returned to Hollywood to continue
filming.

She began to suspect that the reason Burt wanted her in the
role was because, as a former lover, it was easier for him to
relate to her. This certainly made for some effective acting
when the cameras were on them but, after each scene, they
hardly spoke. 'We were just sitting around the sound stage,
waiting for them to light scenes,' she said. 'We were almost like
strangers, which in a way we now were.'

Finally, they came to reshoot the scene that had sent Lee
Grant away in tears. Frankenheimer had decided not to
rehearse but got Sydney Pollack to run through the scene with
her. It was shot this time on the studio back lot and all that was
needed were close-ups of Shelley as they had all the necessary
coverage of Lancaster from the New York location.

The cameras turned and they began to speak the lines as
written. Each was blaming the other for the breakdown of their
love affair and, as the argument intensified, neither was acting
any longer. They lost themselves so completely in what was a
real-life emotive argument for them both that they forgot about
the written script and began using language that was so
colourful even the crew were embarrassed.

Frankenheimer yelled, 'Cut' and the camera stopped turning

but the actors were almost at each other's throats. Sydney Pollack got in between them and they stopped yelling. Shelley later wrote in her autobiography, 'I didn't know what Burt and I had been screaming about – was it the scene in the picture, or were we blaming each other for what had gone wrong in our lives in the last decades? Me – two broken marriages. Him – it was rumoured – an alcoholic wife.'

By the next day Lancaster had calmed down and so had Shelley. They apologized to each other and Frankenheimer set the scene up again. They covered it with two cameras, to get a close-up of Shelley and a two-shot, to be edited in with Burt's New York close-ups, the long shots and over-the-shoulder shots with Lee Grant. Everyone breathed a sigh of relief when they did the scene as written and with each in control. After that, Burt and Shelley learned to become friends again but they never resumed their affair.

Lancaster was hugely impressed with the work Sydney Pollack did with the young actors in the film as well as his work with Shelley Winters. He encouraged Pollack to take up directing and he personally called Universal Studios to see if they had a training programme. They were not currently training directors but they agreed, on Lancaster's personal recommendation, to allow Pollack to observe work on their sets for a six-month period after which they might, and eventually did, consider trying him as a director on one of their TV shows.

When *The Young Savages* was released in 1961, *The Times* said, 'The direction is fast and forceful and, if Mr Lancaster wears that habitual expression which makes him first cousin to a bloodhound confused as to the trail, that is not through any lack of pace in the action or, indeed, to any weakness in Mr Lancaster's own performance. There are a number of shots that drive home truth,' but the reviewer was not sure if the film was a 'fearless special document' or 'a gratuitous exercise in violence'.

Variety thought it was 'inventively, arrestingly directed by John Frankenheimer with the aid of cameraman Lionel Lindon.

Together they have manipulated the lens to catch the wild fury of gang pavement warfare; twisting, tilting, pulling way back, zeroing . . . But there is nothing Frankenheimer can do to make the yarn itself stand tall as screen fiction.' *Variety* noted also that the film was 'a non-musical east-side variation on *West Side Story*'. No doubt the overwhelming success of the Technicolor, 70mm-wide-screen, Leonard Bernstein musical overshadowed the modest straight drama shot in black and white and audiences did not rush to see *The Young Savages*. It was yet another nail in the coffin of the Hecht-Hill-Lancaster partnership.

14

Locked In

In 1909, convicted murderer Robert Stroud was sentenced to solitary confinement for life. He began studying and raising birds in his cell and became an expert on birds and their diseases, even writing several books on the subject. His life was published in a bestselling biogaphy by Thomas E Gaddis and, in 1959 Hecht-Hill-Lancaster purchased the screen rights to *Birdman of Alcatraz*.

By 1959 it seemed that Lancaster might be able to present a case for releasing the 69-year-old Stroud. He began to immerse himself in research.

Everything you see in the film is true. I read everything that was written about this case and I spent a lot of time with Stroud's lawyer. But I couldn't get to see Stroud because he just didn't want to see me. I read every letter he wrote and even though I never got to meet him, I felt like I knew him intimately, and I felt I had some idea what it was like to spend forty years in solitary confinement. At one time I thought I'd found his wife but it was a case of mistaken identity.

Making this film was like preparing an actual case. I felt like a detective or a lawyer. Ever since I made *Brute Force* I have had a strong, almost obsessive concern for the whole problem of penology. But the principal reason I wanted to do the film was because it was a good story. The fact that it dealt with the inadequacies of the penal system was certainly something that interested me, but the most compelling element was the emotional story of this man and what he went through. In the course of telling this story, we hoped to make people aware of the treatment of prisoners; not to say they shouldn't have been put in prison, but to show that there is room for improvement in the handling of convicted criminals.

The picture was due to begin early in 1960. Permission to film in an actual prison was refused by the director of the Federal Bureau of Prisons who had kept the Stroud story under wraps and did not want a public outcry over the case. So Alcatraz and Leavenworth had to be constructed at a cost of 150,000 dollars.

Lancaster brought Charles Crichton, who had made his name in Ealing comedies, over from Britain to direct. The picture got off to a bumpy start. Three weeks into shooting, after continuous arguments between the tempestuous star and his director, Lancaster fired Crichton and asked John Frankenheimer to take over.

'I told Burt I would only do the film if he let the director be the one who made the final decisions and not the star, even if he was the producer,' said Frankenheimer who had, in fact, previously been involved with a proposed TV production about Stroud that had been abandoned when the Bureau of Prisons told CBS TV that they would receive nothing in the way of co-operation.

Said Frankenheimer, 'In those days TV was done live, and I cannot to this day say what I was thinking of, intending to make the play because there is no way you can get birds to react the way we got them to behave in the film; it took months of training those birds. Well, we did not even train them because you can't really train birds like that. We had to let the birds get hungry before they would do what we wanted them to. Just to film the actions of one sparrow, we used about 27 different sparrows. Thank God we were shooting in black and white or we would have had to paint the birds to look like one sparrow!'

Portraying Stroud was a deeply emotional experience for Burt who, feeling he knew the man so well from all the research he had done, often wept real tears while preparing to shoot some scenes. 'I've never been so personally involved in a part before or since.'

Harold Hecht said, 'Burt became obsessed by Stroud. People are compelled to become what they are by the special circumstances of their lives. Look at Stroud and look at Burt. Burt became a good actor because he's locked in too.'

To achieve the ageing process, rather than wear wigs over his existing hair, Burt had his head completely shaved so that the wigs would fit naturally and appear more realistic.

His brother Jim, who worked on the film as an assistant director, suffered a fatal heart attack on the set. Such was Burt's attention and devotion to the part that he appeared not to grieve, having the body removed so that work could continue. The fact was, Lancaster had long managed to hide his innermost feelings from all but his closest friends and family, and he did his mourning in private.

Throughout filming, Frankenheimer kept telling the producers that the script was too long but they insisted it be shot as written. When it was complete, the first rough cut ran to almost four and a half hours. The producers then asked Frankenheimer to cut it but the director told them, 'You can't cut it. It's a film called *Birdman of Alcatraz* and there are a 120 pages of script before he even sees a bird, and that means a hundred and twenty minutes of screen time. You can't cut it. You have to rewrite it.'

It was a radical suggestion but Lancaster saw Frankenheimer's point and agreed. So Frankenheimer went to work on the script while Burt accepted a role in Stanley Kramer's *Judgment at Nuremberg*.

Abby Mann had written the story of the 1948 war crimes trials for *Playhouse 90* where it was a great success. Stanley Kramer asked him to rewrite it as a screenplay until he had a script that was twice as long as the original.

A superior cast was assembled to play the real-life characters: Spencer Tracy as the trial judge, Maximilian Schell as the defence attorney, Montgomery Clift and Judy Garland as victims of Nazi torture, Richard Widmark as the prosecution lawyer, Marlene Dietrich as the wife of one of the German generals, and Burt Lancaster as Ernst Janning, the principal defendant.

Some scenes involving Spencer Tracy were was shot in Germany but the Nuremberg courtroom set was constructed in exact detail in the Revue Studios in Hollywood where the rest of the cast did their scenes.

Lancaster had only a minimal amount of screen time and no artistic control but he clashed with Maximilian Schell on the set. Burt accused Schell of missing an important cue which Schell denied doing, saying that the proof would be in the daily rushes.

'This is a most unprofessional attitude,' complained Lancaster but, when the rushes were viewed, Schell was vindicated and Lancaster found himself the least popular actor on the set.

On 16 March 1961, Lancaster attended the Golden Globe Foreign Press awards ceremony to receive an award for *Elmer Gantry*. He told the gathering, 'Ladies and gentleman, if you want to see some real honest-to-goodness acting, you should come to our set of *Judgment at Nuremberg* and watch Spencer Tracy and Miss Judy Garland do some real emoting for you.'

Some Germans bitterly opposed the making of the film and historians said that the past was best forgotten. Kramer disagreed and said that the truth was important and that the Germans should make their own films about the Nazi past. Spencer Tracy publicly declared that he was playing his role truthfully and Maximilian Schell, born in Switzerland and brought up in Germany, stood firm in his support of the film.

Lancaster had finished his part in the film by the time the new screenplay of *Birdman of Alcatraz* was ready and that film went into production for a second time. If anything, making it this time round was even more difficult. Said Frankenheimer,

'When I was directing on television, I had complete control. But in movies there are too many people trying to interfere, especially the producer, who in this case was Burt. Also the writer was interfering and I just wasn't free. But I just kept working away at doing it my own way and did not listen to what anybody else had to say.'

Kirk Douglas, in his autobiography, wrote that John Frankenheimer told him that he and Lancaster got into a heated argument about how to shoot a particular scene. The director gave his instructions to the camera crew and then Burt asked, 'What are you doing?'

'The camera goes here,' Frankenheimer replied.

Lancaster picked Frankenheimer up, carried him across the room and put him down. '*That's* where the camera goes,' Lancaster told him.

While *Birdman of Alcatraz* was being edited, *Judgment at Nuremberg* was finished and made ready for release. It had a glittering première in West Berlin, the day before Eichmann was due to be sentenced in Israel. The studio put pressure on the stars to attend. Tracy, Garland, Schell, Clift and Widmark did but Lancaster, on hearing that 300 newsmen from 26 countries would be there, changed his mind, citing his attendance at previews for *Birdman of Alcatraz* as his excuse for having to remain in Los Angeles. He was certainly expected when the charter plane carrying the stars landed in Berlin.

Also missing was Marlene Dietrich who said at the last minute that she had an inescapable concert engagement.

Variety commented that 'Lancaster's role presents the actor with a taxing assignment in which he must overcome the discrepancy of his own virile identity with that of the character. This he manages to do with an earnest performance but he never quite attains a cold superior intensity.'

Alan Dent in the *Sunday Telegraph* wrote, 'Burt Lancaster, wearing an expression of undeviating grimness as the most remorseful of the doomed men, has a confessional outburst near the end which is easily the most striking thing this actor had ever done.'

The film grossed 5,500,000 dollars in America alone.

With work on *Birdman of Alcatraz* finished, Lancaster retired exhausted to his home. William, still walking with a limp despite several operations, had his own wing in the house, as did James. Joanna and Sighle had a suite each and so, with the children able to entertain their friends in their own secluded areas, Burt was free to relax. But not for long. In November 1961, Bel-Air was swept by brush fire; and among the 456 homes destroyed was Lancaster's.

Only a week earlier he had loaned 250,000 dollars worth of his finest paintings to the Los Angeles County Museum. As the flames reached his house, he evacuated the family to the safety of the Beverly Hills Hotel. James Bacon of Associated Press reported, 'It was an unusual fire – no refugees in Red Cross shelters. Most of those burned out checked into the Beverly Hills Hotel. It was probably the wealthiest group of refugees since the Bolsheviks drove the Czar and the Imperial household out of St Petersburg.'

Lancaster's house, worth half a million dollars, was burned to the ground. 'So many other people were affected by it that I couldn't feel particularly sorry for myself,' he said. 'It was just something that happened to all of us. The only things of real importance that I lost were pictures of the children when they were kids. The kids want me to rebuild it stone by stone, and I guess I will.'

This time he made it even bigger and better with a 30,000-dollar swimming pool complete with a waterfall, heating system and a tributary that ran into the living room. Burt did not swim much himself as he still had an irrational fear of the water. 'I never could explain it properly,' he said, 'but I do tend to get cold feet just looking at an expanse of water.'

It was 1962 before *Birdman of Alcatraz* opened. Stanley Kauffmann of *The New Republic* reluctantly said, 'The pleasant report about the film is that Burt Lancaster gives one of his few good performances.' Robert Beckley was more enthusiastic in the *New York Herald Tribune*; 'It couldn't have been an easy role, yet much of the suppressed power in the man and the film is due to Lancaster's performance.'

Time reported, 'Burt Lancaster plays with a firm restraint that never conceals a deep-felt conviction that Stroud should not be in stir at all.' *Variety* called it 'the finest prison pic ever made' and said, 'Lancaster gives a superbly natural, unaffected performance – one in which nobility and indestructibility can be seen cumulatively developing and shining from within through a weary exterior eroded by the deep scars of time and enforced privacy in a prison within a prison. Karl Malden is excellent as the warden. Four distinguished top supporting performances light up the picture. They are those of Telly Savalas as a fellow inmate and birdkeeper, Thelma Ritter as Stroud's mother, Neville Brand as an understanding guard, and Betty Field as the woman who married Stroud in prison.'

The film certainly caused a stir among the public as the whole subject of Stroud's long imprisonment was brought into question. Mr Bennet, the director of the Federal Bureau of Prisons, attempted to dissuade people from seeing it, saying on radio, 'I thought the glamorizing of a murderer like Stroud would not be in the public interest and would be detrimental to our national well-being, harmful to our impressionable youth and a handicap to law enforcement.'

Lancaster's public response was, 'Mr Bennet is not the censor of what the American people shall see, nor is he paid for this purpose. The public interest must not be confused with the hurt feelings of a group, nor does any such group represent the public. It is this "sacred cow" psychology which represents a real threat to the right of the public to freedom of expression. The President's Committee on National Goals has drawn attention to the need for controversy, not for unanimity of expressions.'

As the battle over the film raged on, Lancaster further said, 'This man has been behind bars for the last forty years and should, in my opinion, be freed. They say there is a new charge against him on grounds of homosexuality. Don't make me laugh. The first murder he did was for love of a woman. As for American prisons, they're clean and the inmates are properly fed and looked after? I think that such institutions are terrifying machines for destroying the human spirit. That's what I object to. But society evolves very slowly. I don't despair.'

Years later he reflected on the opposition to the film:

The prison authorities argued that we had not portrayed Stroud as he really was. In a way, that might be true, since I am me and not Stroud. But in a sense it wasn't true because we presented his story truthfully. It's nothing to do with whether Stroud was a good man or a bad man. It's to do with saying that society hasn't found out how to deal with criminals or how they should be treated. I don't claim to know all the answers, but we had to ask the questions, or to raise questions in people's minds. Society tends to want these people shut away out of sight but the ones who have to keep them that way aren't sure how to treat them either. We understand those things much more now than we did when we made *Birdman of Alcatraz*, and so when we made it, it was a true picture of what was happening.

In a rare TV appearance to promote the Stroud film, Burt was interviewed by Mike Wallace on 24 April 1962. Prior to the recording, Lancaster told Wallace he would not discuss his private life or the reported on-set battles on films such as *Judgment at Nuremberg*. Wallace decided to ignore Lancaster's directive and asked him about his inability to get along with other actors.

Lancaster replied, 'There's no reason to talk about it. My temper belongs to me.' He said it in a way that should have warned Wallace to back off but the TV host said that he was just being honest. 'I am suggesting you are not,' said Burt. 'I think this line of questioning is unreasonable.'

Wallace said that he had the advantage of asking his guests any questions he chose to put to them. Burt replied, 'I say you won't have the advantage long if we keep going on like this.' Wallace continued to goad Lancaster who finally got up and walked out. Wallace might have been thankful that Lancaster did not smash the set up on his way.

For whatever reason, the public were not interested enough to make *Birdman of Alcatraz* a box-office winner. 'The film wasn't a great success,' Lancaster reflected. 'But now people constantly talk to me about it. It proves something – but I don't know what.' He was nominated for another Oscar and had he won it would have added to the film's box-office results, but he lost to Gregory Peck for *To Kill a Mockingbird*. He did, however, receive the Best Actor prize at the Venice Film Festival.

With *Birdman of Alcatraz* came the end of the Hecht-Hill-Lancaster partnership. It had been deteriorating over the years. 'When a marriage is over, it's over, and there's no use staying together for the sake of the children,' he said. Ironically, that is exactly what he and Norma had done in their private lives.

15

Perfectly Mysterious Man

Stanley Kramer followed *Judgment at Nuremberg* with *A Child is Waiting* in early 1962 but this time he would only produce the film, planning to leave the directing to Jack Clayton. The screenplay by Abby Mann was from his own *Studio One* television play. Ingrid Bergman was cast as a teacher working at an institution for retarded children who becomes obsessed with the plight of one particular child.

It was only after Bergman had been cast that Kramer decided to give Burt Lancaster the role of the psychologist who heads the institution but when Ingrid heard this she pulled out, wanting nothing to do with the tempestuous star. So too did Jack Clayton, and Kramer replaced him with New York actor John Cassavetes who had directed two offbeat films to much acclaim.

Bergman's role was taken by Judy Garland for whom the part was difficult, not just because she lacked confidence in herself as an actress, but because it brought back memories of a visit to Peter Bent Brigham Hospital in 1949 when, at the end of her stay, an autistic little girl who had previously stayed silent, suddenly cried, 'Don't leave, Judy, don't leave.' Scenes in the film kept bringing the memory flooding back and her depression increased.

Lancaster liked Garland and, perhaps because she brought her own problems into the production, including an addiction to uppers and downers, he behaved himself and avoided any friction. He nevertheless helped her gently and, in her words, he was 'considerate and encouraging'.

Kramer managed to get Equity, the Actors' Union, to allow genuinely retarded children to feature in the film. Under Cassavetes's direction, the film had a raw quality, but both Lancaster and Kramer disagreed with some of the things he was doing. The problem was, Kramer had brought in an unconventional director to shoot what in the end was supposed to be a conventional film.

'Kramer had me replaced and the picture re-edited to suit himself,' complained Cassavetes. 'I didn't think his film was so bad, just a lot more sentimental than mine.'

Arthur Knight wrote in the *Saturday Review*, 'Miss Garland and Lancaster radiate a warmth so genuine that one is certain that the children are responding directly to them, not merely following some vaguely comprehended script.'

Variety said, 'Burt Lancaster delivers a firm, sincere, persuasive and unaffected performance as the professionally objective but understanding psychologist ... Judy Garland gives a sympathetic portrayal of an overly involved teacher who comes to see the error of her obsession with the plight of one child. That child, a deeply touching "borderline case", is played superbly by young Bruce Ritchey.'

Following this film, Lancaster joined a handful of other major stars to make gag guest appearances in Kirk Douglas's production, *The List of Adrian Messenger*, directed by John Huston. All the guest stars, including Tony Curtis, Frank Sinatra and Robert Mitchum, appeared in heavy disguise, and Lancaster was quite unrecognizable as a woman protesting against fox hunting. At the very end of the film, all their identities are revealed. It was not difficult to pick out which one was Robert Mitchum but Lancaster's identity was well and truly disguised by the dubbing of his voice. 'He was hilarious,' said Kirk Douglas about his old pal's unconventional performance.

When Italian producer Goffredo Lombardo went to Los

Angeles in 1962 hoping to interest Twentieth Century-Fox in backing *The Leopard* which Luchino Visconti was going to direct in Italy, he also wanted to see Burt Lancaster. He hoped to interest him in what Burt called, 'a *Ben Hur*-type movie', the script of which Burt thought was 'pretty lousy.'

It just so happened that Burt had a copy of Giuseppe Lampedusa's book *The Leopard* on his desk. Lombardi spotted the book and said, 'Have you read *The Leopard*?'

'Yes, I know it very well,' Burt replied.

'Would you be interested in playing the role of Prince Don Fabrizio?'

'I couldn't play that role. It needs an Italian to play him.'

'Yes, but Luchino is having trouble finding an Italian actor to fit Lampedusa's description of the prince: tall, blond, blue eyes, a man of German heritage as well as Italian. You would be perfect. I saw you in *Judgment at Nuremberg*. Think about it.'

Lancaster did but, as much as the idea intrigued him, the stumbling block was persuading Visconti to consider Lancaster in the part. When Lombardo returned to Italy, he told the director of his discussion with Lancaster. 'Aghh, terrible!' cried Visconti. 'He's a cowboy, a gangster. Awful, no, no, no!'

However, when Lombardo persuaded Visconti to see *Judgment at Nuremberg*, the director changed his mind and gave Lancaster the role without so much as a screen test. Burt recalled:

I got into Rome and met with Visconti for three hours, and he was surprised to know that I knew every nuance in the book, virtually page by page, and he was thrilled that I had been brought up in an area in New York where there were a lot of Sicilians and I knew about the Mafia, and he said, 'I confess to you that I didn't want you for this part. I wanted to get a famous Russian actor called Cherkasov who was in *Ivan the Terrible*. But when I went to Russia to see him, he was too old. Then I asked Laurence Olivier, but he was too busy to be able to begin when I wanted to begin.

Visconti later said, 'The prince himself was a very complex character – at time autocratic, rude, strong; at times romantic, good, understanding – sometimes even stupid and, above all, mysterious. Burt is all these things too. I sometimes think Burt is the most perfectly mysterious man I ever met in my life.'

Filming began in June 1962, in Sicily, with the unit of actors, crew and technicians from the Titantus film company based at Palermo. Those who could afford it hired villas along the coast. Burt and his family lived on his yacht and were considered aloof by the other actors who met each night at the villa of the younger leading man, French actor Alain Delon.

Lancaster prepared for his role by visiting the city's monuments and reading up on the island's history each evening. Scenes were to be filmed in the medieval village of Palma di Montechiaro but the Mafia demanded a levy and threatened the producer and director if they refused to pay up.

Shooting quickly transferred to Ciminna where the work began for an eleven-week period in the hot sun. As the pressure mounted on Visconti to get all he wanted in the time allowed by the budget set by Twentieth Century-Fox, the working day lengthened, beginning at four in the morning ending at ten at night.

The general populace of Palermo was alarmed that this rich American film star with the big yacht had arrived to portray what was essentially the spirit of their forefathers.

Visconti provided a mobile dressing room only for Alain Delon, of whom he was particularly fond. So Lancaster had to stand around in the sun, largely ignored by the mainly French and Italian cast and crew who considered him to be a big American star with a big American ego to match. They were suspicious of his enthusiasm for the work and the research he steeped himself in but he got on with it without complaint for either his discomfort or isolation.

He did not refrain from voicing his opinions and making suggestions to Visconti, and although the director ignored them, there was talk of growing friction between them. Nevertheless, Lancaster was fascinated by Visconti's method and style which

Burt the family man with daughters Susan and Joanna.

Lancaster often brought his children to the studios when he was working. Here he holds Susan up for the camera.

A rare informal shot of Burt relaxing with cowboy star Gene Autry.

The famous beach scene from *From Here to Eternity*, in which Lancaster and Deborah Kerr frolicked in the surf.

Lancaster's love of the circus resulted in his own hugely successful production, *Trapeze*. The film boosted the careers of his co-stars, Tony Curtis and Gina Lollobrigida.

'The Terrible-Tempered Twins' – Kirk Douglas and Burt Lancaster in
Gunfight at the OK Corral.

Fanatical about fitness: (*left*) assisted by Nick Cravat, Burt trained daily
to maintain his acrobatic prowess and (*right*) took a daily jog through
the Hollywood Hills.

Lancaster and Shirley Jones being directed by Richard Brooks in *Elmer Gantry*.

Burt scaring the devil out of the Long Beach Baptists in his Oscar-winning role as *Elmer Gantry*.

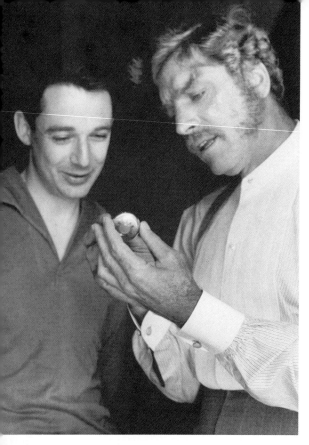

While making *The Leopard*, Burt was presented with a memento by Prince Gioacchino Lanza Tomasi, the adopted son of Guiseppe di Lampedusa.

Lancaster rehearses a comic scene from *The Hallelujah Trail* under the direction of John Sturges.

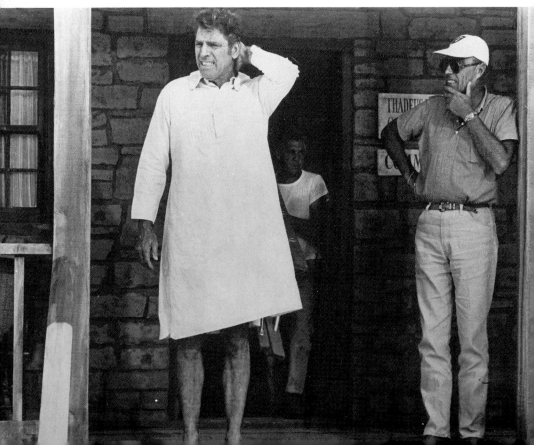

A bespectacled Burt Lancaster enjoying his night of tribute at London's
National Film Theatre in 1972.

Lancaster, a dedicated athiest, portrayed *Moses the Lawgiver* in Lew Grade's biblical TV epic.

Lancaster's last big-screen appearance was opposite Kevin Costner in *Field of Dreams*.

were unlike anything he had seen in Hollywood. 'Visconti is really a painter,' he said. 'He has the eye of an artist. He thinks that way. He will make the camera accommodate itself to what we are, to give a sense of real perspective, not a false one. It puts an enormous demand on the technicians but he gets marvellous results. A visual artist in the best sense of the word.'

As Visconti watched the early rushes, he began to realize that Lancaster was providing an extraordinary contribution and any tension between the two was soon dispelled as the director began consulting the actor. They became engaged in a remarkable collaboration. Lancaster's continual enthusiasm and professionalism began to win the Europeans over and they were soon calling him the 'anti star'.

He told me:

I knew I had to remember that I was a visitor to their country, and I have loved Italy and Sicily since the war, although I never got the chance to actually enjoy the country and its culture then. But when I went there to make *The Leopard* I wanted to discover the country more; not just see the sights, but learn about its culture. Visconti taught me a lot about Sicilian nobility. He was a difficult man to work with. He tended to push me around at first and I don't like being pushed around by anyone. He would storm off and sulk and we were all left stewing but after a while I got to know him, and he got to know me and we were able to sit and talk about the scenes, sometimes for an hour or more. But it was worth the time we spent talking because we got it right, and I don't take away any of the credit from Visconti because he was the master and I relied on him.

One day, Visconti and Lancaster spent three hours discussing the approach to a scene – much of that time devoted to Visconti trying to get his ideas over to Lancaster. 'They were far superior to anything I had in mind,' Lancaster conceded (although one wonders if Visconti felt the time was well spent in having to persuade Lancaster). Visconti was, said Lancaster, 'a perfectionist. He did not tell you how to play a scene because he trusted you as an actor. When he saw that you knew what you were doing he let you do it your way.'

Lancaster got on particularly well with Claudia Cardinale whom he found exquisitely beautiful. But he was not free to play around since he had Norma in Italy with him. Said Cardinale, 'We shared a love for Visconti, and I liked him as a very professional man and as a human being. To become the Prince of Lampedusa like he did was really good work. Burt did really marvellous work.'

Burt joined the Mondello Yacht Club where he always displayed impeccable manners towards the Sicilian members, and before long they were offering him warm hospitality and undying friendship.

In August he took time off from shooting to attend the Venice Film Festival where he was awarded the Best Actor prize for *Birdman of Alcatraz*. One reporter was brave enough to ask him about the moustache he had grown for the Visconti film. He replied good-naturedly, 'Have no fear. Five minutes after the last shot I'll shave it off. My wife and children never stop mocking my huge moustache. It seems, according to them, to make me look ridiculous.'

After the film was in the can, the matter of dubbing arose. Italian films are always shot silent and the complete sound track added on afterwards. This meant that the film could easily be dubbed into an Italian version and an English version. Since Burt's Italian was not quite good enough, he was dubbed by an Italian actor under Visconti's supervision.

In an agreement with Twentieth Century-Fox, Burt would direct American actors back in Hollywood in the voice-over sessions for the English-language version. He was willing to spend as many weeks at the Fox studios as it would take to get the English version as good as the Italian.

The Leopard, in its Italian form, won the Golden Palm at the Cannes Film festival in 1963 and was shown around Europe to critical and commercial acclaim.

Visconti was outraged when he saw the English version. Fox had transferred the rich Technicolor print onto the more garish De Luxe Color stock. It had also shortened the 185-minute film by 40 minutes.

Worse still, the dubbing of American voices cheapened the whole film. Visconti protested but Fox refused to waste further money and time by scrapping what it had produced under Lancaster's supervision. To be fair to Lancaster, he could not be held responsible for the shortening of the film or for the awful colour prints. His responsibility had been for the dubbing and no one has ever managed to successfully dub English-speaking voices over actors who were originally speaking in Italian or French. Nor could Lancaster really be expected to get American voice-over artistes to duplicate the nuances and subtleties of the original dialogue.

Yet the American critics looked very favourably upon the version they saw. And upon Lancaster. *Variety* noted, 'In the final reels, it is again Lancaster who gives the picture some of its deeply moving moments as he moves, a sad, lonely ageing figure no longer his own.'

Time said, 'Within definite limits [Burt Lancaster] is superb. True his Salina never quite becomes the figure of "leonine aspect, whose fingers could twist a ducal coin as if it were a mere paper". But as the scenes accumulate, the character complies impressive volume and solidity, and by the film's end, the Sicilian Prince stands in the mind as a man men shall not look upon again: one of culture's noblemen and a very imperfect gentle knight.'

The film was not a box-office success in America and perhaps Fox were not surprised, which would explain their reluctance to spend any more money on improving the English-language version.

When *The Leopard* was scheduled for a December 1963 release in Britain, Visconti publicly disowned the English version in *The Times*. 'I am a prisoner,' he wrote. 'It is not my fault. It is judged that American audiences are simple minded and will not understand, but the American version is a terrible disaster and the film is not what I intended it to be.'

He also wrote to the British Film Institute and asked them to show the Italian-language version with English subtitles but they were somehow unable to do so. Visconti, in a desperate bid to save his beloved film, threatened to sue Twentieth Century-Fox. Seymour Poe, executive vice-chairman of Fox, stated, 'If there is any suing to be done, we may be forced to initiate actions against Visconti. The print we are releasing throughout Britain and the US was prepared under the full and complete supervision of Burt Lancaster, the man delegated by Visconti for this responsibility. At all times Mr Lancaster had one hundred per cent artistic control and freedom.'

Burt Lancaster had been made the fall guy. The British press were allowed to see only the dubbed version, although Dilys Powell of the *Sunday Times* had seen the European version and wrote, 'Burt Lancaster as the prince is magnificent: each movement, each gesture has a noble authority, as if it were the product of authority. The high impatience with the fluttering of his wife, the touch of arrogance towards the family priest, the ironic contempt for new rich, the rage against a friend who cannot understand the impossibility of social survival without compromise, the sudden awareness of mortality: in everything, his qualities persist.'

Peter Baker in *Films and Filming* thought Lancaster gave 'a splendid performance', and that he succeeded in getting 'behind the character as though he knows and loves every subtlety of Lampedusa's writing.'

David Robinson, in *Sight and Sound*, said, 'Burt Lancaster has quite confounded all expectation by embodying the noble Prince of Salina, whose liberalism is half policy and half the indolence of an exhausted race.'

The British film critics, perhaps aware of Visconti's troubles and sympathetic to his concerns, overlooked the dubbing and tried to see the film for what it was. The *New Statesman*'s John Coleman wrote, 'Burt Lancaster's performance is, in many ways, very fine. He has the physical magnificence necessary to accommodate some of the Leopard's wilder moments, as when he plucks from the ground and embraces the vulgar new man whose daughter is to marry his beloved nephew. Unexpectedly, he also has the delicacy of the Leopard.'

Despite the reviews, the film was not a success in Britain and Burt was devastated that the film he regarded as one of his very best was such a controversial failure.

16

Great Buddies

Lancaster rarely saw any of his own films unless he had produced them. But in the case of *The Leopard*, he made an exception. He saw it in a public cinema to gauge the true response of those who pay to watch movies. He heard the man sitting behind him say to his wife, 'When's Lancaster going to screw Cardinale?'

Lancaster resigned himself to the fact that, 'once the public decide what you are, you might as well give up trying to be anything else. One of the most unusual and valuable experiences in my life was working on *The Leopard* but a lot of my fans couldn't understand why I'd made it. Strangely they all said the same thing – "Burt, I thought you were going to screw the girl, but you never did. What went wrong?" I guess I'm the guy who always screwed the girl – even if it was only after the movie had finished.'

If, when he remarked on his casual affairs, he had been thinking of women like Ava Gardner who, as she put it, had been swept off her feet by him, then he might have been delighted at the prospect of working with her again in 1963, in Kirk Douglas's production of *Seven Days in May*, a political thriller.

By 1963, Ava was a disenchanted and difficult actress and few producers wanted to take a risk on her. She lived in Spain for the most part but had returned to America to make Kirk

Douglas's film after the humiliating experience of losing many of her lines and scenes in the epic *55 Days at Peking*, Nicholas Ray, the director, having become so tired of her constant tardiness and temperamental behaviour that he cut down her part and had her character killed off so they could get on with the costly production.

While the battles between Luchino Visconti and Twentieth Century-Fox raged during 1963, Douglas got on with his film in which he also starred, alongside Lancaster and Gardner. They made an interesting trio since Kirk had also once been involved with Gardner. She was still, at the age of 41, absolutely stunning but now she drank heavily. Burt had the role of General James Scott, chairman of the US Joint Chiefs of Staff, who plans a right-wing military coup. Kirk Douglas was the general's aide who exposes the plot. Ava Gardner played Lancaster's mistress from whom Douglas obtains incriminating evidence.

Kirk, as producer, asked John Frankenheimer to direct. According to Douglas, Frankenheimer said he that he never wanted to work with Lancaster again and told his story of their battles on the set of *Birdman of Alcatraz*.

Douglas was shocked to hear the way Burt treated Frankenheimer and said, 'John, how could you take such a humiliating experience?'

'That's why I don't want to work with him again.'

'John, I promise you will not have any problems with Burt during the shooting.'

Frankenheimer agreed to do the film but he wanted it billed as 'A John Frankenheimer Film'. Douglas thought the whole idea of the film director as 'auteur' was ridiculous (as he once told me at length) but he agreed to the condition.

President John Kennedy gave the film his blessing and agreed to move to Hyannisport so that John Frankenheimer could film a riot scene in front of the president's residence. But the Pentagon was not happy about the project.

It is peculiar how so many people can work on one film and come away with so many different concepts of who did what to whom. Kirk Douglas wrote that Frankenheimer had problems with Lancaster, and also with Ava Gardner.

She was friendly with Lancaster still and on the set of *Seven Days in May*, he encouraged her with her work. But he kept out of her way after hours when she made a habit of getting drunk before summoning the director to bitch at him.

One night, after a long day's filming, Douglas and Frankenheimer were having a relaxing drink in Kirk's dressing room when the assistant director came in to tell Frankenheimer that Ava Gardner wanted to see him. Frankenheimer told Douglas, 'Every night, Ava downs a few drinks and then chews my ass out about everything. She's even accused you and me of having a homosexual relationship.'

Kirk said, 'I've known Ava for years. She must be a little high. Don't go.'

'Well, she might not come to work tomorrow.'

Douglas assured him she would come to work tomorrow. He said that since this was his production, he would take the responsibility. But Frankenheimer, according to Douglas, did go.

The director, however, told me of a different sequence of events. 'My problems were not with Lancaster but with Douglas. Before we began I told him that he would be playing a secondary role to Burt but he didn't like it all the same. I think Kirk was jealous of Burt. He wanted to be Burt. In the end I had to sit Douglas down and say, "Look, if you don't like it, get the hell out." '

According to Lancaster, it was during the making of that film 'that our friendship was really put to the test'. He said that Douglas tried to direct him in every scene. 'I really didn't mind because by then I had developed a profound respect for Kirk because single-handedly he ended the disgraceful Hollywood Blacklist by using Dalton Trumbo's name openly as the writer of *Spartacus*.'

Frankenheimer has said, 'Kirk wanted to be Burt Lancaster – he's wanted to be Burt Lancaster all his life.'

Douglas later wrote that John Frankenheimer in interviews

'played the role of the great auteur' and spoke as though Kirk were just an 'actor working under his tutelage, grateful for his guidance. He twisted the whole thing around.' Whatever the truth of the matter, Frankenheimer worked with Lancaster again but not with Douglas. Only a few months after the film was finished, in November, President Kennedy was ass-assinated.

When *Seven Days in May* was released in 1964, *Time* said, 'The movie is least successful when it tries to sound significant.' Judith Crist liked it and wrote in the *New York Herald Tribune*, 'Burt Lancaster combines a finely controlled fanaticism with innate conviction.'

Variety called it a 'strikingly dramatic, realistic and provocatively topical film . . . General James M Scott [is] played with authority by Burt Lancaster . . . The performances are excellent down the line, under the taut and penetrating directorial guidance of John Frankenheimer. Kirk Douglas is masterfully cool and matter of fact . . . Edmond O'Brien is standout as a southern senator with an addiction to bourbon and an unfailing loyalty to the president.'

Kirk Douglas, perhaps sensing his working association with Lancaster was over, joked, 'I've finally got away from Burt. My luck has changed for the better. I've got nice-looking girls in my films now.'

In early autumn 1963, Lancaster was in France making *The Train*, a Second World War adventure in which he played a French railway engineer trying to rescue a trainload of valuable paintings from the Germans who want the works of art to be taken to Berlin. Paul Scofield co-starred as the German colonel chasing Lancaster's runaway train which meets its end in a spectacular wreck.

Arthur Penn was directing – but not for long. After two weeks of filming, he disagreed with Lancaster who was producing as well as starring (although the film's credited producer was Jules Bricken) and Lancaster fired Penn. Associate producer Bernard Farrell took over the direction temporarily while Burt tried to find a replacement.

The press, of course, wanted to know what had happened between Lancaster and Penn. In good spirits, Burt surprisingly obliged the reporters who gathered in Paris, saying, 'I know what you've heard about me; that I am always difficult and grab all the broads. It's not true. I'm difficult only some of the time and grab only some of the broads.' It became a standing joke for Burt.

He went on: 'You have to make up your mind in this business whether you are going to make every operation a success or not. I don't have trouble with directors because I want to dictate to them. I think the director should have control of his province. But when you are the producer as well as the star and you see things are not working out right, you just have got to do something about it. Of course, a thing like that can bruise a director's ego. Sometimes they sound off a bit about it. But you must expect that.'

Of his marriage, he said, 'The truth is when I am not working I am just an ordinary family man. My wife and I may have had our disagreements but nothing like divorce has ever been whispered. When I'm at home, I go to the office every day, like anybody else. I find most of my spare time is taken up in driving the kids and their friends around.'

He was doing a very good job at covering up the truth about his marital history but he was never a man to make public his personal problems. He thought it was better to lie than to refuse to say anything at all because he knew that a 'no comment' gave reporters the freedom to speculate as much as they wanted.

When asked why he continued to work and do his own stunts, he replied, 'Because I just don't want to do anything else. I have all the money I shall ever need. The pleasure is not in making the money, but in doing what you want.'

Lancaster called Frankenheimer and asked him to join him in Paris to make the film. According to Kirk Douglas, Frankenheimer had not even finished editing *Seven Days in May* but simply dropped everything to fly to France.

On the flight to Orly Airport, Frankenheimer read the script and thought it was appalling. 'The damned train didn't leave the station until page 140,' he noted. So he rewrote the script to shorten the story, as he had done on *Birdman of Alcatraz*.

To film the spectacular train crash, he put five cameras around the railway track. A sixth camera was buried beside the rails and operated by remote control. The train was only supposed to travel at seven miles an hour but the French engineer had the engine going at something approaching 20 miles an hour. Frankenheimer relayed urgent instructions as he and the assistant directors hauled the camera crews out of the way. The five exposed cameras were destroyed in the wreck and only the buried camera produced the results of the crash.

The production limped on through into 1964. Heavy rain in Normandy brought work to a grinding halt and, taking advantage of the delay, Burt went to Washington for a single day in March 1964 to join a civil rights march. Filming resumed in the spring.

Frankenheimer enjoyed the experience of working with Lancaster on this occasion, and said, 'He was in his element, falling from trains, sliding down ladders, climbing walls, yet all the time living his part.' Burt was then 51 and, although he had occasional trouble with a knee that had been operated on a number of times since the days he kept knocking it in the circus, he remained incredibly fit and active.

'If Burt and I had that film to do over again,' Frankenheimer later said, 'we would both do it differently. Once Burt became involved he began to live the film so intently, he said to me, "My God, if only we had started this together, I would have played it with a French accent." '

It was too late because, although the French actors spoke English, their accents were thought to jar against Lancaster's own accent and United Artists decided to have their dialogue dubbed by American actors. It flawed the whole film.

The film's leading lady, French star Jeanne Moreau, who played an innkeeper who hides Lancaster from the Germans, was not impressed with him. 'Before he can pick up an ashtray, he discusses his motivation for an hour or two. You want to say, "Just pick up the ashtray and shut up!" ' She didn't, of course, and she stayed aloof from Lancaster while making sure she got on with the job she was paid to do.

When the film was released in 1964, it met with good business but mixed reviews. 'Lancaster lacks the grace that derives from true sophistication and his heedless acrobatics have a derailing effect,' said *Films in Review*. *Time* thought that 'not for a moment does [Lancaster] seem to be a French patriot.'

Bosley Crowther wrote in the *New York Times* that he found the film 'intensely engrossing', while *Variety* found that 'after a slow start, *The Train* picks up to become a colourful, actionful big-scale adventure opus . . . it is the railroad bustle, the trains themselves and some bangup special effects of bombing attacks and accidents that give the pic its main points.'

Lancaster and Frankenheimer agreed they would make more films in the future. Kirk Douglas, feeling not a little left out, wrote, 'It's ironic. I arrange this rapprochement between Frankenheimer and Burt, and then the two of them go off, great buddies.'

17

Western Sunset

By the mid-sixties, Lancaster's Bel-Air home had been restored following the 1961 brush fires. To the outside world all was well in the Lancaster marital home. Burt had agreed to stay with Norma while the children were still young but they were now growing up. In 1964, Sighle, the youngest, was 10, Joanna was 13, Susan was 15 and William was 16. Norma's son from her first marriage, James Stephen, was a grown man.

William had one more operation on his leg when he was 16 and considered to have reached his full height. He limped no more after that.

Burt was 51 and no doubt feeling time was passing by as he hung on to his marriage as agreed. In 1964 he was making plans to get away for a few months, the time it would take to make *The Hallelujah Trail*. The sixties was the era of the blockbuster film, lavish epics made for a big wide screen with stereophonic sound, shot in 70mm Panavision or Technirama or any of the other giant screen processes that were about then. The biggest of them all was Cinerama.

Technical discoveries had improved the you-are-there experience. When Cinerama was first revealed to the world in 1952, it caused a sensation. Lowell Thomas, speaking to the audience from a normal-sized screen, announced, 'Ladies and gentlemen, this is Cinerama,' and the curtains pulled right back across a deeply curved, extra-wide, ultra-high screen, plunging the audience into a rollercoaster ride. The depth of the curve and size of the screen gave the viewer the feeling of actually moving, and long preceded all the simulated reality rides now prevalent in the computerized funfairs of today. But the process in 1952 was flawed by the fact that, to achieve such a high, wide image the Cinerama camera had to have three lenses to produce it on three films, running side by side. These were shown on three separate projectors in the theatre to create a big picture but with two visible wobbly joins.

For the first ten years all the Cinerama films were travelogues and documentaries. By the time Cinerama came to make its first dramatic picture in collaboration with MGM, *How the West Was Won*, the improvements to the system were still negligible. The joins were a little less shaky and the thrill of seeing a drama unfolding on a giant curved screen was certainly breathtaking but the Cinerama company knew it had to find a way of making films with a single-lens camera to be shown on a single projector.

In conjunction with Panavision, it came up with a system, using 70mm-film, similiar to the type used for super-productions like *Ben Hur* and *The Alamo*, but which produced an image that had a slight squeeze at the edges of the picture frame, allowing the picture to be spread across the curved Cinerama screen without distorting the projected image. This also meant that the films could then be put on general release on 35mm anamorphic prints.

Cinerama's first films in this new technique were made in conjunction with United Artists, beginning with Stanley Kramer's *It's a Mad, Mad, Mad, Mad World*, followed by George Stevens's *The Greatest Story Ever Told*, and then John Sturges's *The Hallelujah Trail*.

Sturges had enjoyed exceptional success with box-office hits like *The Magnificent Seven* and *The Great Escape* since his first encounter with Burt Lancaster at the OK Corral. He was never a director to be intimidated by any star and he recognized that Burt Lancaster could be worth all the megrims. So when he asked John Gay to adapt Bill Gulick's comic novel of the old west into a screenplay, he immediately thought of Lancaster for the leading role of Colonel Thadeus Gearhart, the cavalry commander who gets the job of escorting a wagon train loaded with 600 barrels of Philadelphia-brewed whiskey and 700 cases of imported champagne to Denver to keep the thirsty miners from going dry over a long hard winter. Gearheart's problem is how to stop the wagon train from falling into the hands of, not only the Indians, but also the Temperance women. The Denver miners, seeing the potential hazards of either the Indians or the women getting their hands on their booze, go off to meet the wagon train mid-way in the hope of fending off the raiding parties.

The book was actually based on a true story but injected with some fictional humour. Sturges took it further by spoofing traditional western scenes. For instance, a circle of wagons was defended by drunken Indians against the US Cavalry, who ride around the outside whooping it up.

Above all, the film had to be funny and big. This was a Cinerama epic comedy and the idea was to keep an audience entertained for 152 minutes. 'We never intended it to be another *Paleface* or any of the other comedy westerns that had been made,' Sturges told me. 'It was a sort of reverse of what we did with *The Great Escape* which had been a drama with suspense and action but which also had a lot of comedy as a backdrop to the realistic events. *The Hallelujah Trail* had comedy, all played absolutely deadpan, played against realistic events as a backdrop. And the problem was, a lot of people didn't know how to take it.'

Lancaster did. He told me:

I liked the screenplay. I knew when I read it it would be fun. It was this huge-canvas western but very funny, and the best thing of all, we had to play it absolutely straight; none of that knockabout stuff or pies in the face. We were spoofing the western, and I liked that idea. The funniest thing of all about it was that the events in the film were absolutely true. There was that whole battle between the wagon train, the Indians, the cavalry, the miners and those women, and not one person got killed. John had the imagination to set the battle in a sandstorm so we could show all the different factions shooting all over the place and riding here and there without ever seeing the enemy.

Filming was due to begin in the summer of 1964 in Gallup, New Mexico, called 'The Indian Capital of the West'. Lee Remick had agreed to take the role of Cora Massingale, the Temperance leader who tries to hijack the wagon train, on the understanding she could be in New York by the autumn for her children's school term.

The cast, including Jim Hutton, Pamela Tiffin, Donald Pleasence, Martin Landau and Brian Keith, plus an army of supporting players, extras and film crew with heavy Panavision equipment, arrived in Gallup, where, Sturges had been told, it was hot and dry. From the beginning the location was struck by thunderstorms, rain and flash floods, holding up the filming. The unusual weather was, allegedly, due to the local medicine men who had been praying for rain following weeks of drought and did not know how to shut it off before the arrival of the film unit.

The long schedule became longer as Sturges had to delay filming until the rain eventually eased. Lee Remick's children did not object since they were consequently late back to school.

But there was a tragic side to the making of the film. The film featured many dangerous stunts which had to look thrilling and funny on screen. Some of these were classic western stunts such as the wagon that heads towards a cliff and plunges over seconds after the horses become detached and and the two men inside leap off in the nick of time. The wagon was rigged so the horses could be let loose by the stunt men who then had to time their jump perfectly before the wagon plunged over the edge.

Bill Williams, one of the stunt men, had been appearing in westerns for years, doubling for numerous film stars, including Kirk Douglas in *The Indian Fighter*. But Douglas thought he was not a particularly good stunt man. 'Anybody can do a stunt and get hurt; a stunt man is supposed to do it and not get hurt,' he said. 'Bill got hurt several times.'

But the money for doing stunt work had always been good and stunt men have been known to accept good pay for dangerous work they were not necessarily experienced at. Bill Williams's speciality was horse riding but he was willing to do the precarious wagon fall for John Sturges.

Williams's wife was photographing the scene and she was watching through the camera lens as the wagon reached the cliff edge. The horses went one way, one of the men jumped, but Williams left it too late and plunged to his death.

Filming was finally wound up early in 1965, after the last interior scenes had been shot in Hollywood. When it was released the same year it met with a mixed critical response. *Variety* noted its positive values: 'Producer-director John Sturges has pulled every plug in spoofing practically every western situation known to the scripter, and the whole is beautifully packaged. Screenplay, from Bill Gulick's novel, approaches the situations straight ... Performances, like situations, are played straight, and therein lies their beauty. Lancaster does a bangup job as the harassed cavalry colonel plagued with having to offer safe conduct to the whiskey train and to the temperance ladies.'

The film did well in its special Cinerama showings in 1965 and it is on the giant curved screen that the film plays best. 'It was shot for Cinerama,' said Sturges, 'and I made every effort to take advantage of the fact. It's purely a trick of film making since they got rid of that cumbersome three-lensed contraption, so you have to know what you want to capture on film. It has a lot to do with tempo and pace, and when you see the film on TV now, which it often is in America where it's really become popular, it just doesn't have the same feel to it.'

Certainly the film did not do particularly well when it went out on general release, by which time word had got around that some audiences were baffled by the style of comedy. 'It was a joke that few got,' said Lancaster. 'Yet today when it shows on TV it gets good ratings, because people have come to accept the mixture of gentle spoofing and large-scale action. They understand the jokes better. Why they did not in 1965, I have no idea.'

By the time *The Hallelujah Trail* was finished, Lancaster was seriously considering a film that would present him with a very personal and private challenge. The film was *The Swimmer*, the bizarre tale of a man who goes across country through private swimming pools. He was fascinated by the screenplay, by Eleanor Perry, which presented the marathon swim as a metaphor for the character's failed life. The problem was, Burt still suffered from hydrophobia. It was time to overcome it so he accepted the film, due to start production in 1966.

After the gruelling schedule for the Sturges film, Lancaster took it easy. Since making *Elmer Gantry* Lancaster had wanted to work once more with Richard Brooks. The opportunity presented itself when Columbia commissioned Brooks to write a screenplay based on Frank O'Rourke's novel *A Mule for the Marquesa*. While Brooks was working on his script, from which he would also direct, he began to gather his cast.

The Professionals, as it was retitled, was basically a western, although it was set in the early 1900s in Mexico. A millionaire hires four men to go deep into Mexico to save his wife whom, he says, has been kidnapped by a Mexican cut-throat called Jesus Raza.

Claudia Cardinale had already been cast as the wife, Ralph Bellamy as the husband and Jack Palance as Raza, when Brooks approached Lancaster about appearing. Lancaster recalled:

The script wasn't ready when Dick came to see me on the idea, so I read the book before we met. Naturally I thought he wanted me to play the leader of these guys, and when I said so, he replied, 'Oh no, Burt, that won't work. That's no good at all.'

I looked at him – stared at him – mental chess, see? – and said, 'Just how do you figure that, Dick?'

He knew the game I was playing and he said, 'You're

just so boring when you give orders with your stiff upper lip and all that shit. Just boring. No, Burt, the guy you play is a dynamiter. He's a clown; he's funny.'

'Dynamiter?' I said. 'I read the book, Dick. There's no dynamiter in the book.'

'I know,' he said, 'but there will be when I get the screenplay finished.'

I said, 'What's this dynamiter like?'

He said, 'He's like you, Burt. He's funny, and good at his job, and a hell of a pro.'

He'd sold me. I said, 'Okay then, I'll do it as long as we start by October. By the way, just who is gonna play the leader?'

He said, 'Columbia want Lee Marvin. He's under contract to them. I'll meet with him and see if I think he'll work out.'

Richard Brooks knew he was playing mental chess, not only with Lancaster, but with Lee Marvin too. Fortunately, Brooks is a master at the game. He quickly sized Marvin up. 'Lee watches you – all the time, because he wants to know why you really want him. He'd just done *Cat Ballou* and before then he'd always been second and third banana, and all of a sudden he was being sought for greater things. And he wanted to know if you really cared about him or did not.'

Lee Marvin remembered Brooks selling him the film:

Brooks was giving me all this shit about what a great part he had for me, and what a great film it would be, and what a great kick-off it would be for me as a leading man after *Cat Ballou*, and I'm thinking: let's see how much he wants me, and not just some new boy on the block who's either gonna make it big or fall flat on his ass.

So I looked at him kinda offhandedly – you know, take this how you like it – and said, 'I hear you're quite a tough guy. Is that right?'

He said, 'No, I'm not tough. Look, Lee, if you want to

be in the film say so. If not, tell me to go away.'

So I said, 'No, no, just hold on there. I'd like to do this picture. But what do I play? One of Lancaster's stooges?'

He said, 'No, you give all the orders. You're the guy in charge.'

Now, whoaaa! He's telling me I give all the orders! I said, 'I like the sound of that. Do I give Burt Lancaster orders?'

He said, 'Yes, Lee, you give Lancaster orders.'

I said, 'In that case I'm in.' I mean, how can anyone pass up the opportunity to give Burt Lancaster orders?

In October 1965, Brooks began directing the film in Nevada's Valley of Fire State Park. As well as Lancaster and Marvin, Brooks also had Robert Ryan and Woody Strode to complete the professionals who go after Jack Palance to save Claudia Cardinale. In a way the film was not unlike *The Magnificent Seven* except there are only four in the band, but this film had the surprise twist of the professionals discovering that Cardinale was not kidnapped at all, but had run away from her husband to be with Palance.

Because the film was shot not too far from Hollywood, the stars were able to commute. Lancaster made Claudia Cardinale welcome at his home. 'I was a bit lost there,' she said. 'It was my first time there, and he was very sweet to invite me to his home to see his family.' In doing so, Burt broke one of his own strict rules about never entertaining actors he was working with.

Lancaster continued to keep in shape by running three miles daily before breakfast, then spent four hours in the gym. Away from the set, Burt saw little of Lee Marvin who was too busy to socialize anyway with so much to keep him entertained in Las Vegas where he was housed for the duration in a hotel. One night Marvin got arrested for firing arrows at the famous animated cowboy which beamed night and day just across the street from his hotel. Marvin said he had been 'provocated', and the police let him go.

On the film set, Marvin, who was renowned for raising hell and occasionally getting drunk, behaved himself to start with. Then, three weeks later while they were filming a scene in the desert under an uncomfortably hot sun one Friday morning, Marvin began missing his marks and his lines. (He once told me, 'The art to being a professional is to hit the lines and say the marks!') Brooks realized he was drunk. It was only eleven o'clock.

Lancaster, Ryan and Strode patiently redid take after take to accommodate Marvin until Brooks said, 'Okay, hold everything,' and took Lee aside for a private discussion.

'What the hell's the matter, Lee?' Brooks asked. 'You're missing everything today.'

'Oh bullshit!' cried Marvin. 'Jesus, just because I'm not the big star. Are we all supposed to be Burt Lancaster?'

Lancaster and the others, hearing these remarks, stayed cool. They all liked Lee despite his hellraising. 'What is this? Is it because Lancaster's the star? Is that what it is?'

All Brooks said in response was, 'You're drunk.'

Marvin persevered with the argument. 'That doesn't change a damn thing. It's the truth, isn't it?'

Brooks finally lost his reserve and said, 'No. It isn't the truth at all. You're being disrespectful to all the people around, not just to Burt because you think he's the star, but to everybody else. And it won't work that way.'

'Yeah, but that's the way it is, baby, isn't it?'

Brooks hustled Marvin back to work and they continued with the scene, but it just wasn't working.

Lancaster recalled:

I like Lee; he's a fine actor and we had some fine times making *The Professionals*. But when he got drunk and hadn't sobered up by the time he came on the set, he was a total screw-up, that's for sure. It only happened once; he was so drunk he couldn't stand straight or say his lines. Dick was getting so mad with him and gave him a dressing down. It was all most unprofessional for any actor; at least when I yell at a director it's to do with the film. But Lee had a chip on his shoulder, I think, about not getting treated like a star. But that wasn't true because he got treated the same way we all were.

Well, Dick had Lee removed from the set and taken back to his hotel to dry out over the weekend. We had to shoot around him for the rest of the day while he was dragged kicking and fighting into the car and driven away.

At the end of the day Woody Strode and his wife looked in on Lee, and when Lee started shouting about how he didn't want to stay there, Strode and his wife sat on him.

Monday morning Lee was back on the set and, although he was sober, he was not repentant. So Dick showed him a can of film and said, 'This is the negative from Friday morning. If this film ever gets seen, it'll be the end of your career. Now, if you ever do this again, I'll rewrite the script so your character gets killed off and then Burt will be the leader.' Then he took out the negative, unrolled it in the sunlight, and Lee was a good boy after that.

There was one time we were in the middle of filming and we'd taken a break. It was so damned hot, and we were standing on this rock in the desert, and Lee looked at me and said, 'Burt, you were in the army, right?' I said, 'Sure, I was a private.'

He said to Bob Ryan, 'What were you, Bob?' He said, 'I was in the marines, Private First Class.'

'Dick, you were in the marines too, Private First Class?'

'Yeah!'

And Lee had been in the Marines, Private First Class.

He looked at each of us and said, 'All these millions of dollars riding on the backs of us privates. I wonder what all those fucking generals are doing now?' That was Lee. He could really piss you off, but you have to love him.

When the film was released in 1966, Judith Crist, in the *New York Herald Tribune*, thought it 'a sleek, slam-bang adventure suspense film. Burt Lancaster has never been more athletically suave.' Pauline Kael wrote in the *New Yorker*, that it had 'the expertise of an old whore with practised hands and no thoughts of love.' Arthur Knight stated in the *Saturday Review* 'rock solid professionalism pervades every shot, every line and every performance.' *Variety* thought it 'a well made actioner . . . Marvin underplays very well . . . Robert Ryan is in the relative background, as is Woody Strode. Lancaster is the most dynamic of the crew as a light-hearted but two-fisted fighter.'

The Professionals was one of the biggest hits of 1966 and is today highly regarded not just as a fine example of an action film but for the sumptuous Panavision/Technicolor photography by Conrad Hall, who was nominated for an Oscar for his work. Richard Brooks had two Oscar nominations, one for his direction, the other for his screenplay.

Of the film, Lancaster said, '*The Professionals* sets out to be an entertaining, ribald kind of western. Let us not overlook the fact that our business is a business industry and we have to make films that make money. There are still a bulk of people who like to go to a pure escapist film, and these films are bread and butter. *The Professionals* is a good film – highly entertaining. People were stimulated and excited by it. People can't live in the darkness of life all the time, saying, "Oh my God, it isn't true." We have to be able to laugh, you know, and have a little fun.'

In Phil Hardy's definitive book on the western, titled simply *The Western*, he listed the most successful western movies up to 1983, and when he adjusted the list to take inflation into account, he placed *The Professionals* at number 21. One point above was *Vera Cruz*, and one below was *Gunfight at the OK Corral*.

With *The Professionals* following *The Hallelujah Trail*, and then with his next release, *The Scalphunters*, turning out to be another western, it appeared that Burt, who had been threatening to retire, intended to ride out of screen history into the western sunset. In fact, before he made *The Scalphunters*, he worked on *The Swimmer*, but this was a film that the distributors, Columbia, did not know what to do with.

18

From Swimming Pools to the Ocean

When Burt first read the script for *The Swimmer* he knew it was going to be something very offbeat. It was hardly the kind of film that would make money but he wanted to do it because it was so different.

The film unfolds a bizarre story of a man swimming through other people's swimming pools on his way home, who appears to be perfectly sane at first but who is actually out of his mind. Towards the end of the film, throughout which he is only ever in his swimming trunks, he visits the home of his former mistress, then arrives home where the audience is expecting him to be greeted by his wife and daughters. But his home is seen to be deserted and the film finishes with many questions unanswered.

Burt said, 'I liked the concept of the film. You find yourself asking, where has this man been? Was he in prison perhaps? Has he had a mental breakdown? Was he forced to leave his home to start with, or did he go of his own accord? Did his wife and girls leave him, or are they dead? Each pool he swims across, each person he meets, tells us something about the mores of American society and culture. It's all allegorical. It was an exciting concept.'

Exciting enough to make Lancaster fight to overcome his

hydrophobia and spend three months improving his swimming. When the film was made in 1966, he was in superb physical shape. The muscles were still hard and the face looked much younger than his 53 years.

The film's director was Frank Perry, husband of Eleanor Perry who wrote the screenplay. He assembled a good, strong cast that included Janet Landford, Janice Rule, Kim Hunter, Diana Muldaur, Joan Rivers and John Garfield Junior. He filmed this symbolic tale in Fairfield County in Connecticut where local home owners were paid 500 dollars each for the use of their swimming pools.

To protect the privacy and property of the locals, sanitary and catering facilities were set up for the cast and crew to keep them from messing up gardens and homes.

'I was gasping one evening for a vodka martini,' said Burt, 'and had nothing in my caravan, so I put on a robe and knocked on the back door of some lady, and asked, "Are you the lady of the house? I'm Burt Lancaster. I wondered, may I have a vodka martini please?" She seemed to love the idea of making me a drink. When you're a star, you can take all kinds of liberties.'

Being so many miles away from home, Burt turned out not to be homesick or lonely. Norma was back home in Hollywood. Lancaster had kept his promise: he had stayed with Norma for the sake of his children. He clearly had no love for his wife by this time and, not wishing to see any more of his life pass by before he found someone to love, he had met and fallen for Jackie Bone, the company hairdresser. But he made sure she was kept out of public sight when they were together and he maintained a strict control over the usual media interest in a Burt Lancaster film.

Frank and Eleanor Perry knew about the new love in Burt's life but they did not have to be forced to pledge their silence over the private matter. They were concerned only with getting the film made and for Burt to give his best efforts.

After the film ended on location, Jackie Bone retired to her own home while Burt returned to his. After the film was edited, some concern was raised at Columbia by the producer Sam Spiegel over the scene between Lancaster and his former mistress in the film, played by Barbara Loden. Spiegel was unhappy with her performance and demanded that it be reshot using a different actress. Frank and Eleanor Perry protested and, refusing to have anything to do with it, left it in the hands of Spiegel.

With Spiegel wondering how best to deal with the problem, Lancaster suggested that Sydney Pollack be given the scene to refilm. Spiegel agreed, and so the scene was shot again, this time in California, with Janice Rule in Loden's part.

Then Columbia hesitated, wondering what they were going to do with such an unusual film. Meanwhile, Lancaster went off to Durango in Mexico to make *The Scalphunters* for Sydney Pollack. Leaving Norma at home, he took Jackie Bone to keep him company through the long location shoot in 1967.

Durango had become a favourite location for makers of westerns. Burt had been their several years before with John Huston to make *The Unforgiven* and, since then, John Wayne had really put the town on the map with a succession of westerns. Durango was wild and uncompromising, allowing only a certain amount of luxury for visiting film companies and offering some authentic western dangers. The major cause of death for men between the ages of 25 and 40 was gunshot wounds and the local hospital had a 24-hour scorpion treatment unit to cope with the 2,000 scorpion stings a year, which resulted in 128 deaths.

In the film, Lancaster played a fur trapper who teams up with an escaped slave, played by Ossie Davis, to track down a band of scalphunters led by Telly Savalas who has taken furs from the Indians who had taken them from Lancaster in the first place. To infiltrate the band, he and Davis enlist as fellow scalphunters. Burt liked the civil rights angle and wanted Sydney Pollack to highlight them even more than the screenplay permitted. But Pollack, who was however always grateful to Burt for getting him started as a director following their meeting on *The Young Savages*, refused to give in just to pander to Lancaster's social conscience.

There was another link with *The Young Savages*. Shelley Winters was playing Telly Savalas's cigar-smoking mistress. All past bitterness forgotten, Lancaster and Winters joked around and laughed. Remembering the 3,000 dollars in cash he had brought to her along with the roses when she was in Cedars Hospital after she broke off their affair, he said, 'What about those 3,000 dollars I loaned you?'

She replied, 'What 3,000 dollars?'

'And just who was that guy in your apartment that night?'

'Nobody,' she told him. It wasn't until she published her autobiography that Lancaster learnt that her guest had been Marlon Brando.

Lancaster loved Durango and explored the whole area to discover its Mexican culture. In the evenings he took Spanish lessons and attended the Gian-Carlo Festival of Opera that was playing at the opera house in Durango.

Lancaster rented a house, as did Sydney Pollack, and Jackie Bone stayed with him during the long, hot months of summer. When it was over, they went again back to their respective homes in Hollywood, meeting secretly and privately while Burt still tried to maintain a public image of being happily married.

The Scalphunters was released in 1968 to moderately good business, but it hardly broke records. *Variety* thought 'the whole ensemble works to a remarkable degree. Lancaster and Davis work particularly well together, ditto Savalas and inters. There are talky periods of slow pace, but they are terminated before undue damage has been done.'

Columbia finally released *The Swimmer* in 1968, after *The Scalphunters*. Even if there was no audience for it, the critics found it a fresh, intriguing film. 'A grim, disturbing, and sometimes funny view of a very special segment of upper-middle-class American life,' was how Vincent Canby described it in the *New York Times*. *Variety* thought it 'a minor triumph in collaborative film making. Performances, direction and writing hit the target. Lancaster emerges with a strong achievement, that of a pitiable middle-aged Joe College.' Judith Crist of the *New Yorker* called Lancaster's performance 'perhaps the best of his career'.

Sadly, few but the film critics ever saw it, although it has become something of a cult classic now.

Even before the dust on the set of *The Scalphunters* had been kicked up, Lancaster and Pollack had agreed to work together again to make *Castle Keep*.

The long hot summer of 1967 was about to be followed by the long winter of discontent in Yugoslavia where the offbeat war film was made. Pollack must have felt like reneging on the agreement after all the arguments he had had with Lancaster in Durango but he had signed a contract with Columbia, and so had Burt. They were tied to the project and, while Burt probably did not give it a second thought since he was used to directors complaining about him, Pollack must have wished he had never got himself involved.

Set in the Second World War, Lancaster played a one-eyed American army major who entrenches his men in a tenth-century castle in the Ardennes forest in Belgium. The resident count reveals that he is unable to father a dynasty and asks Lancaster to provide the young countess with a child. In the event, Lancaster decides he and his men must remain in the castle to defend it against the Nazis. In the final battle, everyone is killed except for the young countess and a black private.

For the film, the old Petrovaridan fortress was converted partly into the castle of the film's title, and partly into a hotel for the cast and crew. On arriving, Lancaster and Pollack once more took up battle positions, disagreeing on the interpretation of the story.

The verbal assault from both parties was so ferocious that the young actress Astrid Heeren, who was cast in the role of the count's young wife, hailed a taxi and fled to the airport. When Lancaster and Pollack were told of her departure, they raced to the airport where Astrid was about to board her plane home and talked her into staying, explaining that this was how they best communicated with each other and she should not be alarmed. They promised they would both refrain from shouting at each other again – at least in her presence.

Lancaster's idea of the film's theme was that it 'concerns the fact that every one of us has our own castle; we can be pushed so far, but when it comes to the crunch we make our stand. In the final analysis every man will retreat only so far, and no further. That's what this movie's all about.'

Later Lancaster actually said of Pollack, 'He was the man who worked me hardest and the man I best communicated with.' Lancaster ran every morning, paced by actor Bruce Dern, who had once been an Olympic runner and who was well known for either running with the stars, or getting them to run when they did not want to. Lancaster did not need any encouragement.

When filming began, there was no a sign of the snow that Pollack wanted. His Castle Keep was supposed to be covered in snow. A giant snow-making machine was flown in to throw out 60 tons of artificial snow. But it was not enough. In the hope that the winter would bring real snow, Pollack concentrated on interior scenes.

The first eye patch Lancaster wore for the film was made with tiny holes so he could see through it but he discarded it. 'I felt it was better to go for realism, so I insisted on the real thing,' he said, 'and now I find I'm getting everything out of perspective.'

At last the snow came. Despite the three-foot drifts, Lancaster donned his tracksuit each day and went for his run. He told journalist William Hall on the set of the film that he was even considering retiring. 'Two years more, then I want to quit acting altogether. Some actors go on for ever, into the grave. I don't want to be like that. I've been in the business most of my life, and I'll stay in it – but as a producer. I like being a producer. Reading scripts, testing the artists, talking to the writers and directors. I do more work that way than when I'm acting. When I get away to do a movie, it's like a paid holiday.'

He said that he knew he could still improve as an actor. 'We've all got to keep trying to reach new horizons. The trouble is, the right scripts don't seem to be there any more. And some of the people behind the scenes believe audiences want to see me as they saw Gary Cooper, in a high hat and boots. Maybe they're right. But these days the super-hero is on the way out. You don't have to be handsome to be a hero any more. The good-looking guys like Gable and Cooper, the stories aren't geared their way any longer.'

So far Lancaster had successfully managed to keep his affair with Jackie Bone under wraps but one evening an incident occurred that was reported in newspapers all the way back to California. He had taken Jackie to a restaurant and had managed to get into an argument with her. To settle the argument, she picked up a bottle and hit him over the head with it. He was taken to hospital with concussion and scratches but fortunately she did not succeed in breaking his skull open. Nevertheless, filming had to be cancelled for a few days while he recovered. If Norma had not known about her husband's infidelity, she did now.

Perhaps the fact that Lancaster and Pollack could not agree on what the film was really all about is what, in the end, made it a failure when it opened in 1969. It featured huge battles and pretentious dialogue with some black comedy thrown in for good measure. The critics seemed unable to agree on what it was about either. *Variety* said, 'the film carries fast and savage action once the actual battle sequences are reached, but it's strictly a conversational war in footage leading up to these moments. Lancaster enacts with one of his fast-talking roles with a glib, almost tongue-in-cheek approach, and gets good mileage out of it.'

Film Quarterly's Paul Warshow thought the film 'an artificial, forced allegory which could never decide whether it was operating from a realistic base or from one of abstract poetic myth. On either level the film is awful . . . and the shift back and forth between the two levels was excruciating.'

William Wolf in *Cue* thought 'the artistry to bring it off successfully simply isn't there', and Vincent Canby in the *New York Times*, said that it was 'never as impressive as the sum of its very expensive parts'.

At the end of filming in early 1968, Lancaster returned to

Hollywood to face the music from Norma and to rejoin John Frankenheimer and Deborah Kerr to make *The Gypsy Moths*. Lancaster, Gene Hackman and Scott Wilson were three sky divers who arrive in a small Kansas town to barnstorm it, staying at the home of Wilson's aunt, played by Deborah Kerr. She is unhappily married to a professor and inevitably she and Rettig, played by Lancaster, have an adulterous affair. Rettig wants her to leave with him but she refuses to go, so the next day he simply allows himself to fall to his death.

To capture the breathtaking scenes of the divers, cameraman Carl Boenisch jumped with the stunt men to film their acrobatics on the way down, capturing shots of the three divers that look like a ballet of death performed by human moths.

Deborah Kerr, when accepting the film, stipulated that she would not do the nude scenes required by the script. 'I think it's totally unnecessary and unreal that these two people would strip stark naked in the living room,' she told John Frankenheimer. 'In reality they simply wouldn't do it.'

Frankenheimer was not going to argue the point, nor did he really expect Deborah Kerr to reveal all. He explained that they would be using a stand-in.

Deborah Kerr watched the nude scene being filmed in which Lancaster cavorted with an uncredited actress with less inhibitions than Miss Kerr, and later said, 'I really didn't think Frankenheimer would do it. To do it there in the living room, on the couch – to have this stark naked backside staring at you was, quite frankly, just laughable.'

She asked Burt, 'Do you think they're really going to show this?'

'I shouldn't think so,' he answered. But when it came to sex, Burt had a much more permissive attitude towards the subject, whether it was on the screen or in real life. His answer was more polite than honest, since he was not about to give a reply that might indicate he thought she was being somewhat starchy.

Some time later he said, 'I never had any objection to stripping in a film if I felt there was good reason for it. But to strip to play a love scene doesn't make any sense at all unless it is pertinent to the film. I have nothing against pornographic films – looking at the beautiful body of a man or woman is a beautiful thing – it depends on what manner they attempt to titillate me. I tend to be permissive because it's in my nature to say to anybody, "Go ahead and do what you want as long as you don't harm me." '

As Burt obviously knew, and as Frankenheimer had always intended, the film showed plenty of bare flesh but none of it belonging to Miss Kerr.

Frankenheimer had now made five films with Lancaster and on every one of them there had been some arguments. But, he told me, he had nothing but respect for Burt:

You know, he has this reputation for fighting with everyone. And he does. But it's only because he cares deeply about the work. And it's never because he wants to have the focus on himself. He is very generous to other actors and he works harder than almost anyone else. And he knows a lot about cutting and the problems of filming. I don't know that I'd say he was the best director ever – he probably wouldn't either – but because he does know about producing, I find it easy to work with him. He is one of the most hard-working individuals I have ever met.

Gordon Gow of *Films and Filming* thought *The Gypsy Moths* 'conveys the essence of the novel . . . particularly in the enigmatic nature of Lancaster's interpretation of the Rettig character, whose philosophy is: To face death is hard, but to face life is harder . . . It seems ages since Deborah Kerr has been given a role so worthy of her talent. It requires great skill in the playing, especially since Frankenheimer surrounds it expertly with realistic notations of the small-town mentality, against which she fortifies herself in her own pathetic way. She is permitted a neat little speech which sums up her formative years and the things that went awry. She tells Rettig her tale with a concise and heightened terminology, in a few minutes so impeccably controlled by Frankenheimer, so beautifully spoken by Kerr and so perceptively listened to by Lancaster that the dimension of the medium is expanded to contain the speech – virtually a thing of the theatre.'

Variety said, 'At best, aside from exciting sky-diving episodes, [the] picture is a lack-lustre affair insofar as the character relationships are concerned. The stars do not appear to be particularly happy with their roles. Lancaster seldom speaking, Kerr not particularly well cast. Lancaster delivers well enough considering what the script requires of him, and Kerr is mostly grim. Hackman and Wilson are forceful, both giving excellent accounts of themselves.'

Life's Richard Shickel was 'uncomfortably reminded of the romance these two enacted in *From Here to Eternity* – and of the passage of time since. As he has grown older, Mr Lancaster has developed a capacity, unique in established stars, to "give away" scenes that his status in the movie pecking order entitles him to dominate. He did it in *Castle Keep* and he does it again in *The Gypsy Moths* and he deserves full credit for its shrewd selflessness.'

Wrote Vincent Canby in the *New York Times*, 'It's a weekend of dimly articulated emotional crises for everyone, including Miss Kerr, an unhappy, highly unlikely Kansas housewife who has a brief affair with Lancaster, principally, you feel, because she remembers meeting him in *From Here to Eternity*.'

The film flopped in America. In Britain, MGM, taking no chances with it, put it out as a second feature with the James Garner thriller *Marlowe*.

In September 1968, Lancaster was stopped along Pacific Coast Highway at Malibu for exceeding the speed limit. When asked to sign the police officer's ticket which calls for an appearance in court, he refused and was told he would spend the night in jail if he did not come to his senses and sign.

He chose to go to jail. Burt later claimed he wanted to be educated and, although he could have easily bailed himself out of jail, he did not. Only in the morning did he hand over the 65-dollar bail money and go home.

In November 1968, he took part in a four-hour television marathon to support Hubert Humphrey's bid for the presidency against Richard Nixon. Paul Newman, Joanne Woodward, Edward G Robinson, Sonny and Cher and Kirk Douglas were also there, giving their comments and expressing their support.

In June 1969, Burt attended the funeral of Judy Garland in Manhattan. She had died of a drugs overdose, a fact which did not surprise Burt. 'I liked Judy – very much. But I could see she was on a self-destructive path,' he told me.

Then, in July, the Lancaster marriage finally came to an end. Norma sued for divorce on the grounds of mental cruelty and was granted custody by the Santa Monica court of Susan, Joanna and Sighle, and more than two million dollars' alimony. Norma remained curiously loyal to Burt, presumably for the sake of the children, and never made a public statement about the marriage, the divorce or the reasons for it.

But, as it had been agreed between Burt and Norma that they would stay together while the children were still young, the time had come for them to agree it was best to end the marriage that they both knew had been a sham for many years. The children were much older and, by the time of the divorce, William Lancaster had been married for three years to Kippe Kovacs, daughter of the late comedian Ernie Kovacs. The fact that Burt was known to be involved with Jackie Bone was something Norma could no longer ignore. It was time to end the charade which had become too embarrassing to keep up for both of them.

Burt moved in with Jackie Bone, publicly saying only, 'We have no plans to marry. There's no point in matrimony unless a couple plan to have children. And at my age raising another family is not exactly uppermost in my thoughts. The relationship between Jackie and me is great. There is no ownership between us. We aren't possessive.'

For a time Burt considered moving out to some mid-western retreat. 'You can't live by swimming pools alone,' he said. 'Think of the starving children. It has been a constant source of guilt to me that I have become so luckily rich. But I haven't yet found a method of salving my conscience, though I give a lot away to good causes. The trouble with money, when you have it in bags, is that you don't count it. Yet I remember my father, who earned 48 dollars a week in the post office, considered that he was making a fortune.'

Instead of moving to the Midwest, he acquired two apartments: one in the Century Towers in Century City where Gig Young, George Raft and David Janssen lived, and the other in Rome. There he furnished the place with paintings – mainly by unknown artists whose works he chose simply because he found them aesthetically pleasing rather than for any financial gain – and elegant furniture.

For much of the time, in between filming in America, Burt and Jackie lived in Rome; in many ways he felt more at home there than he did in Los Angeles. Or perhaps he liked to think he did. Italy has always treated its film stars like royalty and actors like Clint Eastwood, Lee Van Cleef and Burt Lancaster – Americans stars of the Italian screen – were welcomed as their own.

Jackie, however, was not known and she had some trouble with the Italian police when she found herself driving through a strictly pedestrian area of Rome. The police stopped her and, she alleged, while searching through her papers, stole 90 dollars from her passport folder. She was arrested and jailed overnight but released the next morning when Burt Lancaster turned up, persuading the police to drop the charges or face a formal accusation from Jackie – Burt Lancaster's girlfriend – for the theft of 90 dollars.

He did not spend all his free time in Rome. He still had his business affairs to take care of in Los Angeles but he needed somewhere where he and Jackie could be left alone at weekends. He bought a small house – small in comparison to the Bel-Air house – at Malibu Beach. The ocean outside no longer held any fears for Burt Lancaster since his triumph over hydrophobia in *The Swimmer*. He did not necessarily swim in the sea, but at least he could face it.

19

Smoking Ears

If it had not become clear to Burt Lancaster, it had certainly dawned on most film producers that Burt Lancaster's name above the title of a film no longer assured it of success. Even *The Professionals* had, like *The Magnificent Seven*, been a film where the success was due more to the combined efforts of a talented ensemble cast rather than to any one name, not to mention the obvious commercial appeal of the story. And, since *The Professionals* in 1966, Burt had not been able to boast of a box-office success.

After his divorce in 1969 he seemed to take stock of his life. He had said, in 1968, that he would retire in two years and, if his rejection of Franklin Schaffner's offer to play in *Patton* was part of his exercise in running down his career, then somewhere along the line he had an about-turn when he accepted Ross Hunter's offer to join another ensemble cast for *Airport*.

Based on Arthur Hailey's bestselling novel about an attempted bombing on board a passenger airliner, the film was a blatant and unapologetic stab at bringing in the masses. The star-studded cast included Dean Martin, Helen Hayes, Barbara Hale, George Kennedy, Van Heflin, Jean Seberg, Barry Nelson, Dana Wynter, Lloyd Nolan and Maureeen Stapleton.

Filming began in Minneapolis-St Paul in the autumn of 1969 and Universal ploughed 10,000,000 dollars into it.

Producer Ross Hunter hired a Boeing 707 at 18,000 dollars

a day and made the actual plane land in a snowstorm. It was so cold that film froze in the cameras and the faces of the cast and crew swelled despite wearing protective masks as they shivered in temperatures that reached 43 below zero.

Interiors were filmed in the luxury and warmth of Universal Studios where a mock-up of the plane assured that none of the cast ever had to actually take off. The critics seemed to stick their noses in the air at the film. Judith Crist called it 'the best film of 1944'. Alexander Walker of the London *Evening Standard* said, 'For sheer contentment there is nothing to beat the sight of constant catastrophe happening to others.'

Variety recognized it was 'glossy, slick . . . handsome,' but felt that 'the ultimate dramatic situation . . . does not create suspense because the audience knows how it's going to end.'

So far the film had earned in the region of 45,000,000 dollars, so it was not surprising that Universal were eager to create a series of sequels, although they gradually deteriorated in quality and credulity. The first film was the best, earning six Oscar nominations, including Best Picture. It won one only, for Helen Hayes as Best Supporting Actress.

If Lancaster, not to mention Dean Martin, had found the film was perhaps a little too blatant in its crass commercialism, they did not complain on their way to the bank to deposit handsome cheques. 'It's the biggest piece of junk ever made,' said Burt.

Dean Martin was equally unkind about a film that paid him more than generously since he had agreed to do it for a percentage of the profits and these earned him 7,000,000 dollars a year after the film's release. Since then he has undoubtedly earned far more. Lancaster must have been on to a similar deal.

Said Ross Hunter, 'Lancaster and Martin both accepted their roles even before a script was written, banking on the success of the book and my promises to develop their roles importantly within the framework of a superior production. They were also reassured by the fact that a man like George Seaton would be both author of the screenplay and director of the film.'

Forgetting all about his decision to retire, Burt went to Spain

in 1970 to make another western, *Valdez is Coming*, directed
by Edwin Sherin. He played an ageing Mexican-American
lawman, who becomes the victim of racial prejudice in a small
border town. He kills a suspected murderer in self-defence and
then attempts to help the victim's Indian wife, played by Susan
Clark. The man he killed turns out to be innocent and finally
Lancaster must face the band of real killers.

When he was 57, he said, 'I'm too old to get the girl any
more. Filmgoers these days aren't about to accept me winning
the girl in movies, although I've been doing it pretty well for
more than 25 years. For me romance is out. Soon I'll be
pushing 60, so I can't go chasing some young woman. I can still
play leading men, but guys with more character than sex
appeal.'

He did note, however, that this film allowed him, 'a brief
fling with Susan Clark'. There would not be many more
on-screen flings for him. He felt his age and he was so miserable
making *Valdez is Coming* that he said, once more, he would
retire.

> If it was a cold day, I'd try to get into my trailer and
> there'd be eight guys in there lying on my bed, warming
> themselves, drinking everything in the icebox, reading my
> books, playing cards. I'd walk in and they'd all look at me
> like, 'What the hell do you want?' On warm days, when I
> might be looking for company between scenes, they'd be
> off playing ball, chatting up the girls, and nobody would
> come near me. I sometimes got a picture of what it will be
> like when I'm dead and lying in my coffin. All these friends
> are going to lean over, spit down on me and say, 'You
> bum! Couldn't you have waited another year until I get my
> Cadillac paid off? Even this you couldn't time right.'

The film was released in 1971 to generally poor reviews.
Time said, 'The film offers little besides its star. Continual
editorials about racism give it contrived relevance. Edwin
Sherin's directing may best be described as functional; the

members of the cast do not bump into each other. Call it a Burt Lancaster picture: that says it all.'

Perhaps more determined than ever not to be put out to pasture, Lancaster went straight into another western, *Lawman*, directed by British film maker Michael Winner who spent a year preparing the 3,000,000-dollar production. Burt found himself back in Durango again with the scorpions still stinging 2,000 people a year but managing to avoid being stung himself. He arrived in his personalized jet and was met by an accountant who handed over his 30,000-dollar advance. On top of that he would get a percentage.

On the set Winner treated him with deference, calling him Mr Lancaster – 'partly because I respect him,' Winner explained in an interview with *Empire* magazine, 'and partly because he's one of the few actors around who's ever paid for dinner while I've been around.'

Lancaster did not mind being called 'Mr Lancaster' and said, 'If people have a preconceived idea about you, they resent it if you turn out to be different. Nowadays they want me to be Mr Lancaster, so I am Mr Lancaster. In the early days when they called me that, I'd always say, "Call me Burt." I don't do that any more. Now I'm a little older and a little more cranky, I'm beginning to feel like Mr Lancaster.'

While Winner rented the house in Durango usually reserved for John Wayne – the only house with a swimming pool – Burt, Robert Ryan and Lee J Cobb had to settle for second best.

Winner soon learned what Lancaster's temper could be like if he chose to argue with the director, saying to William Hall, 'I can tell you that smoke came out of his ears.'

In one scene, Lancaster had to shoot his horse, using a Colt .45. A later shot for the same sequence was set up and this time Lancaster used a Winchester .73 rifle. Winner said, 'Excuse me, sir, you actually shot the horse with a Colt .45.'

Lancaster went into a frenzy, shouting, 'I shot it with a Winchester!' He stormed over to Winner and towered over the director. 'What do you know about directing?' shouted Burt. 'You're a moron.'

'The crew were loving it,' Winner later said when describing the incident. Lancaster kept up a stream of abusive language, finally grabbing Winner, picking him up and walking over to a nearby cliff where he hung the poor, struggling, terrified director over the edge.

'What did I fucking shoot the horse with?' he yelled.

Winner replied, 'You shot him with a Winchester, no doubt about it. I was completely wrong.'

Lancaster released Winner and strode back to his place. The script girl complained, 'But this will never cut together.'

'Keep quiet,' Winner told her. 'I'm not going to die over this.'

Winner cleverly distracted any attention from the Winchester by cutting to a stock shot of a vulture.

This episode, although it does Lancaster no favours, certainly does not paint a picture of Burt hating his director. It was, it seems, just Burt's way of bringing an argument to a quick end. He liked and respected Winner, despite his way of showing it, and said of his director, 'He's sharp, bold, without respect for convention. This could be one hell of a western.' Unfortunately it wasn't.

When the film was finished and Lancaster sat down with Winner to watch it, Winner told Burt, 'You will notice in this scene, if you look very closely, you will see at one point the wrong gun.'

Lancaster replied, 'Oh, that is very careless of you, Michael. How did that happen?'

'Lancaster, as usual, is a highly convincing marshal, tough and taciturn,' said *Variety*. 'Ryan is also excellent as the faded, weak marshal with only memories. But it's [Lee J] Cobb who quietly steals the film as the local boss who, however, unlike in many such films, is no ruthless villain.'

In April 1971, Lancaster appeared singing on the American Academy Awards show and was a surprise hit. It helped him make up his mind about his next career move – to do a stage musical. He accepted the part of Peter Stuyvesant, the Dutch governor of New York during the 1600s, in *Knickerbocker Glory*, by Maxwell Anderson and Kurt Weill.

The production was a real boost to Lancaster's flagging morale after so many disasters with films. Not only did Burt have to sing, but he had to play the entire role on one leg, with the other doubled up in a 'straitjacket'. He called the part, 'the most challenging of my career'.

Although he had a reasonable voice – he had sung on the soundtrack of *Elmer Gantry* with some conviction – he needed some formal singing lessons. He asked Frank Sinatra, still a good friend since the days of *From Here to Eternity*, if he could suggest someone and Sinatra offered his services. Said Lancaster, 'I have the finest, most expensive voice teacher in the world. Frank offered to do it purely out of friendship. We've been going at it three or four times a week.'

The show opened on 11 May 1971 and played for seven weeks in San Francisco's Curren Theatre, before transferring to the Dorothy Chandler Pavilion in LA. 'I'm no great singer, not that that's any handicap nowadays,' he said. 'I've never sung in public before but, with my vaudeville background, the idea of a musical has always intrigued me. Besides, very few pictures come along now that an actor really wants to make. Most scripts add up to just another film to walk through. I think my last one, *Lawman*, is a good movie, but it's still another western. There were some Las Vegas people who wanted me to do *The Music Man*. The money was very tempting, but then *Knickerbocker Glory* came along, and it's such a rich, juicy part. So here I am doing this for one-tenth that I could make in Las Vegas.'

Because he had to perform, dance and do everything else on one leg, the show presented its own unique problems for him. 'Physically and psychologically, it's a brute of a part. But if there's anything I do well, it's move. And if I'm not really driving in the part, I get cold. That strap becomes a sack of cement. I simply have to defeat it. Then it isn't there any more. The trick is to get out there and throw caution away.'

Dan Sullivan, in his review of *Knickerbocker Glory* in the *Los Angeles Times*, wrote, 'Oddly enough, his singing isn't at all bad. It's the acting side of the role that gives him trouble. To begin with, he is no more comfortable in period dress on the stage than he is on the screen. Secondly, he has to hop around on a silver peg leg that gives him too much to think about. Finally, he is simply not at home in sly, twinkling, mock-ferocious comedy. Lines that should come out with deft irony sound like heavy camp, as if the actor were doing a parody guest shot. It's an uphill fight all the way, and the applause at the end is more for effort than achievement.'

During the show's Los Angeles run, Lancaster and Jackie attended a late night party following the performance on 5 August. At three in the morning they left the party and Burt was driving home when the police pulled him over and charged him with drunk driving. At the police station he made no attempt this time to guarantee a night behind bars as he had previously and he was released into Jackie's custody.

When he appeared in a Los Angeles municipal court, he testified that he had drunk only one beer and one martini. The jury believed him and he was acquitted – it was virtually unknown in Hollywood circles for Burt Lancaster to get drunk.

Despite the threat he made to retire when making *Valdez is Coming*, he kept on seeking work. When asked why, he said:

I can't afford to quit. Not because I haven't enough money, but because, over the years, I've acquired too many people whose livelihoods depend on my labours. I try to use people whose work I like from one film to another. I'm very fond of them and I know they love me – as long as I keep acting. If I say, one day, I don't want to do another film for six months or a year, to take it easy, they get furious. One by one they come to me and ask, 'What the hell's the matter with you, you no-good bum? Listen, I've just broken ground for a swimming pool in my back yard. How can you think of quitting at a time like this?'

And God forbid that I should plead poor health as a reason not to work. They couldn't be less sympathetic. 'What's wrong – your back? Tape it up and get on with the job,' they say callously. 'My kids have four more years of college.' So I feel obligated – because they've been loyal to me over the years – to go to work, sick or tired. It's a good thing I enjoy acting.

He may have been speaking with his tongue in his cheek, but there was a certain ring of truth to these remarks. There was a generous side to Lancaster that few people saw. He did try to make sure people he liked got regular work. He once asked Kirk Douglas to put Nick Cravat, who was not exactly sought after in Hollywood, into one of his films.

Kirk invited Cravat over to his office and said, 'Nick, I'd love you to be in my next picture. There's a good part for you.'

Cravat replied, 'Go fuck yourself! Don't give me any crumbs! I don't want your fucking picture.'

When Kirk told Burt what had happened, Lancaster shrugged and said, 'Well, that's Nick.'

Another actor whom Lancaster liked to work with was Ed Lauter, who eventually went on to become one of Hollywood's favourite supporting players in scores of films and TV shows. But, in 1971, Ed Lauter was an ex-soldier struggling to make it as an actor. He told me:

After I'd been in the services, a pal said to me, 'Burt Lancaster is in town [in New York] at the Plaza; why don't you call him up. You never know, he might have a job for you in a movie. What have you got to lose?' He was kind of baiting me on, so the next day I got home and I called him up at the Plaza Hotel, and I'll never forget it.

The receptionist comes on, I say, 'This is Ed Lauter, I'd like to speak to Burt Lancaster.' The next thing I know is I'm hearing Burt Lancaster say, 'Hello.'

I said, 'Mr Lancaster, you don't know me and I know how you respect your privacy, and I hate to intrude on you, but I'm just starting out in the business as an actor. I wonder if you can give me some advice.'

He said, 'I really don't know what to tell yah. There's

really no formula for making it in this biz-ness. However, if you wanna make it in the movies, stick with the theatre.'

Fade out – fade in. About three years later I'm doing *The Great White Hope* on Broadway, and he's in the audience. He came back stage and I related the story about the phone call. He went, 'Ha Ha! Ha! Ha! Good advice! You're doing the right thing.' He didn't even remember it, but I got to know him very well.'

Whenever there was a part for Lauter in one of Lancaster's films, Burt saw he got it.

To round off 1972, Lancaster did another western, *Ulzana's Raid*, reuniting him with Robert Aldrich. Burt thought the screenplay, by Alan Sharp, sensational. He said, 'I'm not kidding, but during my whole career I have only read two first screenplays that I really liked. One was Guy Trosper's for *Birdman* and the other was written for *Ulzana's Raid*. It's about the treatment of the Indians, the total inability of any race which controls another to understand the culture and lifestyle of the subject nation.'

Lancaster played a hardened, veteran cavalry guide who helps a fresh, graduate officer, played by Bruce Davison, to track a band of Apaches. But it was not the run-of-the-mill cowboys 'n' Injuns story. Rather, it said more about the White Man's hatred for the Red Man. It was something of an allegory about Vietnam, and in the process it proved to be a violent picture:

We were trying to draw a parallel to a condition like Vietnam, where Americans don't know the people, don't understand them, and don't care to. This is what happened when the White Man went west. Another point we make is that the White Man had many of the same bloody instincts as the Indian, only they were kept in check by the thin veneer of civilization. But the Indians did kill savagely and brutally – they were probably driven to it by the way they were treated, by the way they were debilitated, by the fact that they were taken from their lands and confined to reservations where their spirits began to die. Ulzana tries to rekindle them.

I loved doing the picture. I thought the script was very well written. Alan Sharp is very talented, and the whole approach to the Indian problem, the whole background, I found highly interesting.

Unfortunately, Universal seemed scared by what Aldrich had presented them with. They had probably expected a conventional western with lashings of violence. So they made two different versions of the film with some cunning editing: one for the American and British markets and the other for the rest of the world.

Vincent Canby in the *New York Times* thought that 'Aldrich's west is a timeless place where noble motives lead to disastrous actions. Loyalties are hopelessly confused and the only possible satisfaction in life is behaving well for the immediate moment. This Burt Lancaster does with ease, along with the rest of the predominantly male cast.'

Variety found it a 'sort of pretentious US Army-vs-Indians period potboiler that invites derision from its own dialogue and situations. Whatever the film's aspirations, the effect is simply another exploitation western which crassly exploits the potentials in physical abuse, and in which plot suspense is not what is going to happen, but how bestial it can be.'

The film did not do well at the box office and Burt Lancaster was bitterly disappointed.

20

The Light of Experience

In 1972, Burt Lancaster ushered at a fund-raising function held in Los Angeles for Senator George McGovern. Lancaster supported McGovern's outspoken opposition to the Vietnam War. He also made a rare television appearance, in *Sesame Street*.

He broke his own rule about never appearing in TV commercials by narrating a number of commercials made on behalf of consumer groups, one of which concerned the dangers of certain pain-relieving drugs, and another exposed the potentially dangerous flaws in Chevrolet cars.

After the failure of *Ulzana's Raid*, he could have been forgiven for sitting back and thinking it really was time to retire. But he accepted an offer from Michael Winner who paid him 750,000 dollars plus a percentage to star in *Scorpio*. 'You can count the number of stars who rate that kind of money on one hand,' said Winner, 'and still have a couple of fingers to spare. I have a respect for a man who knows his own market value.'

Filmed in London and Vienna in the summer of 1972, *Scorpio* featured Lancaster as a CIA agent whose young mentor, played by Alain Delon, is hired to kill him.

While in London, Lancaster rented a house in Mayfair. Very few journalists were granted an audience and those who were were diverted to a nearby hotel where he answered sensible questions and lost patience with those reporters who sought only trivia.

When one female reporter asked him about his diet, he replied, 'Madam, I burp in exactly the same way as you do.'

I was not a journalist at that time but worked for a film company in the publicity office. By pulling a few strings I was allowed to meet Lancaster and he generously and patiently answered the many burning questions I had. Some years later I had the chance to interview him formally, but, for now, he seemed pleasantly flattered that I showed so much interest in his career.

He also arranged for me to come and see him give a John Player Lecture at the National Film Theatre where he enjoyed answering questions put to him by Joan Bakewell and the audience, all of whom knew as much about his films as he did, if not more.

He told the audience a little about the film he was about to start for Winner. 'I'm going to make a straightforward whodunnit, but with some slight comment on police corruption. But basically it'll be a light film – something for me to get back in stride with. When you reach my sort of age, and have done so much, acting-wise, you begin to look around and wonder what to do next. I feel it's about time I made a move towards directing again. I'm always trying to tell my directors what to do, so I really ought to go away and do it myself.'

He said, 'I'll be 59 in November. I'm getting on. I don't run up the stairs any more.' He still managed to run each morning around Hyde Park. 'It's one way of getting my heart started in the morning.' But from time to time he still suffered pain in his knees.

A mobile dressing room was provided for him on the London location and every day Winner had lunch from the exclusive London restaurant Wiltons delivered to Burt's caravan by Rolls-Royce and served by a waiter. Lancaster felt that at his age he could afford to bask in this luxury and elegance, eating fresh salmon and drinking chilled white wine.

In the evenings he indulged himself in London culture, usually going to the opera to see *Elektra*, *Otello* and *La Traviata*, and to the ballet to see Rudolf Nureyev and Margot Fonteyn. He told Roderick Mann that he would love to direct opera. 'That's my great passion. I love it. I'd like to see opera singers trained as actors. As it is, they never seem to know how to behave on stage. When I went to see *Otello* the other night, it was on the verge of being ludicrous. I'd like to change all that.'

Jackie Bone was with him throughout filming but he never spoke publicly about her. As for the film, he was blunt and to the point. 'It's an entertainment, a glamorous one, because of the European backgrounds. It's a CIA story, nothing incisive, just a lot of action. It's one of those things you do as part of your living but you try to avoid doing them as much as you can. There's an awfully good cast but it's pure entertainment of no real lasting significance.'

The film was concluded in Vienna where Lancaster still managed to run about through the Viennese construction site for the climactic chase scene. Afterwards he took a holiday in Salzburg to see more opera, and then to Munich to watch the Olympic Games.

He was not surprised when *Scorpio*, released in 1973, was not a hit with the critics. *Variety*: 'Despite its anachronistic emulation of mid-1960s cynical spy mellers, *Scorpio* might have been an acceptable action programmer if its narrative were clearer, its dialogue less "cultured" and its visuals more straightforward.'

Robin Bean in *Sight and Sound* thought that 'technically, for anyone interested in the art of film-making, it is a must since the technique is pretty near flawless – the construction and the editing are a delight, as is the harsh realistic lighting of Robert Paynter.'

Jay Cocks in *Time*, wrote, 'Lancaster, always good at playing brashness, was never an actor to show much warmth. His role in *Scorpio*, a double agent on the run from both East and West, gives him a chance to project the kind of dead-eyed savagery he has nearly patented his own. He has the proper cunning and just the right kind of careful menace and restrained violence.'

He spent months after finishing *Scorpio* considering an offer he had from David Miller to star in a controversial thriller called *Executive Action*. Dalton Trumbo wrote the screenplay which was based on a book by Mark Lane and a considerable amount of research into the murder of President Kennedy. In effect, it supported the theory that JFK was the victim of a conspiracy by right-wingers who opposed his stance on civil rights and his decision to withdraw troops from Vietnam.

It was almost twenty years before Oliver Stone could make his staggering contribution to the conspiracy theory with *JFK*. Whereas Stone was able to work in an environment that allowed him the freedom to name names and tell the story of the assassination as told by New Orleans District Attorney Jim Garrison, David Miller's film had to maintain an air of fiction about it. Therefore, Lancaster's role of an ex-CIA spy who works with a financier played by Robert Ryan and a senator played by Will Geer, was purely fictitious. Miller did, however, intercut his movie with actual footage of the assassination, a device many found offensive in 1973.

Lancaster had been a supporter of JFK's and, after deciding to take the role, he discarded his usual six-figure fee and accepted the Equity minimum, as did all the other actors.

He told me:

I did a lot of private research before accepting the role and I was convinced that what the book was saying was basically right: that President Kennedy was the victim of a conspiracy. In fact, I am convinced of it. In all probability Lee Harvey Oswald was a fall guy, which he said he was. I decided to make the film because it is based on the facts, otherwise I wouldn't have gone near it. I wanted to do it as a warning against the dangers of powerful men playing God and deciding who should live and who should die, especially when it has such long-lasting effects upon the world. There's no question that there was a conspiracy. Otherwise, why did so many witnesses die? And who is to say we shouldn't have made it? It was the perfect time to make it because of the Watergate break-in. I had hopes that the film would make people in high places ask questions they should have been asking in 1963. But it didn't. Everyone ran scared from it. I hope some day someone will ask.

Ed Lauter, who had asked Lancaster for his advice on getting on as an actor, had a supporting role and kept Lancaster entertained for hours in between takes by reciting dialogue from many of Lancaster's films, while Burt proved his memory had not faded with the years by naming and dating each film.

A sad footnote to the filming of *Executive Action* was that Robert Ryan was terminally ill while making it. He made one more film, but he died before *Executive Action* was released.

Executive Action hit the cinemas in 1974 and in some areas of the United States it was well received but in some Southern areas it was hardly shown. Some TV stations even refused to show trailers for the film because, they said, the ads were 'overly violent and violated the standard of taste'.

It was obvious that, as Burt said, they were running scared. He publicly stated, 'I have made many films much more violent than this one and the commercials for them, none of which was ever censored or refused, were more violent than these.'

He said that he felt it was 'possibly the most important film I've ever been involved with'.

Pauline Kael, in the *New Yorker*, said, 'It's a dodo bird of a movie, the winner of the *Tora! Tora! Tora!* prize – in miniature – for 1973, with matchlessly dull performances from a cast that includes Burt Lancaster (looking very depressed). It could hardly be called a thriller, and it's so worshipful of Kennedy (while treating him insensitively) as to seem to have no politics.'

Variety called it 'an emotional after-shock to the event . . . dramatized with low-key terror.'

Because he was still involved in producing films, Lancaster maintained an office in the Century Towers block. He went to the office every day when there was no location work to whisk him away. Although not as extravagant as the Hecht-

Lancaster offices, Burt still liked to decorate his room with antiques, leather sofas and books. Each day he read scripts and met writers. He was always casually dressed, some might say untidy. He was most comfortable in tracksuit trousers and jogging shoes.

From his office he set into motion plans to direct a movie himself. The story he chose to film was *The Midnight Man*, about a paroled ex-cop who takes a security job on a university campus and stumbles into a series of murders.

Lancaster played the lead role and surrounded himself with actors he could rely on, including Susan Clark and Ed Lauter. Nick Cravat also featured in a small role, as did William Lancaster. It was filmed for very little money in South Carolina and working in collaboration in the director's seat was Roland Kibbee. They had also written the screenplay together, basing it on a book called *The Midnight Lady and the Mourning Man* by David Anthony.

'It was a concession to me because I wanted to make some money,' Kibbee admitted. 'It certainly wasn't the kind of project Burt would have picked out for himself. He is one of the most intellectual actors I've ever known. He has no taste for pulp fiction, and his reading is on a very high level. I had to talk him into reading [the book].'

Although he had not directed another film since *The Kentuckian* in 1955, Lancaster said, 'I've been sort of directing ever since but this one's official. I'm cutting my ancient eye teeth on it.'

In making the concession to Kibbee, the film allowed Kibbee to direct for the first time, aided by Lancaster who liked the idea of being able to make decisions as a director but without having the complete responsibility resting on his still considerably broad shoulders. It proved to be a smooth collaborative effort without any of the fireworks some might have expected and with Burt sharing the director's credit.

Said Kibbee, 'It seems contradictory, but he actually detests violence and I have never heard of him hitting anyone. He has always been forceful, sure-footed and strong in his opinions, although a certain mellowness has come with the years, but he is difficult in regard to the standards he sets in his works. He has always felt that it was his job as a star to be involved with production, and scripts have always been his primary concern. He is thoroughly honest, his candour can be brutal, but he is critically and constructively valuable at production conferences. He is, to put it as simply as possible, an unusual man. He fits no moulds.'

When released in 1974, *The Midnight Man* was liked by the critics, if not the public. Said Richard Schickel of *Time*, 'Burt Lancaster is turning into an attractive hard-working actor as superstardom fades.'

Vincent Canby in the *New York Times* wrote,'Mr Lancaster is an intelligent actor. He thinks about his characterizations. He makes choices. He moves through *The Midnight Man* with studied humility, saying, "yes, sir" and "no, sir" more often than is always necessary, listening attentively when spoken to. The mannerisms don't suggest a middle-aged parolee, uncertain of his future, as often as they suggest a reformed alcoholic trying desperately to succeed as a liveried chauffeur.'

He was still being offered scripts and film roles but the films either did not interest him or the parts were simply cameos that required only his presence and not much in the way of acting. But he had finally come to the conclusion that he was not going to just give up and leave.

'This business is essentially one of mediocrity,' he said at the time. 'I thought for a while of giving up acting. It may have been a momentary dissatisfaction, which I am working out, but I think we all come to a point where we take a measuring stick and place it against the past. Then the mood passes and I just get on with acting. I've decided that the best way to carry on is just to step out there in front of a çamera, read a line, and hope I can get away with it. We change from time to time in the light of experience. I suppose that's called understanding.'

21

When in Rome

In 1974 Lancaster made a decision that was a surprise to all who knew him. He had previously fought off all offers from TV producers but in 1974, he gave in to Lew Grade and agreed to star in *Moses – The Lawgiver*.

Perhaps even more surprising was that he should agree to do a Biblical subject. By way of explanation, he told me:

> I am an atheist in that I do not believe in a Christian God and I don't believe in heaven or hell. I don't mind if God exists, but I don't concern myself so long as I have my own set of values to live by.
>
> That's why I did not want to make *Ben Hur*, although I think Chuck Heston did a wonderful job in the role. It's only in the last half-hour of *Ben Hur* that the film becomes over-religious for my liking. But the first three hours show that Heston is a formidable actor, and I'm glad I could oblige him with the part.
>
> So when a huge script for *Moses* arrived on my desk, you can imagine what I first thought. First, I asked myself, didn't Charlton Heston already do this? Then I asked myself, do I even want to do a religious TV film? But then I began reading it, and I began to see that Anthony Burgess saw God as a pretty tough customer with whom Moses was always in conflict. It reminded me of me and Hal

Wallis. Well, that really caught my attention; I thought about me fighting God. That really appealed to me.

Before going to Italy where the film had its base at the RAI Studios, he announced, 'My Moses will be very different from the version put on the screen by Cecil B De Mille. None of that larger than life stuff. My Moses will be a real man. Not a hero, not a leader, but a man who is aware of his own and other people's failings.'

Six million dollars were poured into the enterprise, a huge amount for a TV production. Lancaster said, 'This is not just another TV series. It has dignity and quality.'

To help him prepare for the role, he spent hours reading the Bible, and came up with some unconvincing arguments. 'It might seem strange that a thoroughly Anglo-Saxon man like myself should be chosen to play the greatest of Jewish prophets. But nowhere is it established that Moses was a Jew. He was found in the bulrushes of the Nile. He could have been an Egyptian. He's not spoken of by Jews as part of their lives after bringing them to the Promised Land.'

Lancaster is right in saying that Moses was not a Jew. But he is erroneous in the way he reaches that conclusion. At that time in Biblical history, the nation of Israel was split into twelve tribes. The Jews were of the tribe of Judah. Moses was of the tribe of Levi.

Grade, his producer Vincenzo Labella and director Gianfranco de Bosio, secured an impressive international cast that included Anthony Quayle, Ingrid Thulin, Irene Papas, Aharon Ipale and even Burt's son William, to play the younger Moses.

'Billy happens to be a very talented actor,' said Burt, 'even though I don't think he has any desire to be one. He got involved in *Moses* by accident. The producer liked him and thought he'd make a great young Moses. I told Bill, "If you think you're going to be a star and get fame and fortune, forget it! You've got to love the business and accept the fact that maybe you'll never be terribly important. Then, and only then, you've got a chance to be someone, and then you'll love it too." '

Most of the shooting was done on location in Israel, right in the middle of the Yom Kippur War. One morning the cast and unit awoke by the shores of the Dead Sea to hear tanks rolling down the street in front of their hotel. Unable to film, the unit returned to Rome where Labella and de Bosio debated whether to head for Spain or Morocco to continue filming. An armistice was then agreed in Israel and, when it became certain it would hold, the unit returned.

There were times when Lancaster lost his temper at the inefficiency of the joint Israeli-Italian film crew. He was heard screaming obscenities on top of a dune in the Sinai. He also lost his temper with the ever-present paparazzi. He got so mad when one photographer refused to leave that he finally lost control and hit him.

There were arguments on the set too, between Lancaster and his director. 'We argued over the voice of God,' Lancaster explained. 'I wanted to use my voice. That is to say, the voice of Moses which is the concept of God. They wanted something else. We tried my voice and it was fine. It would have been wrong in this story of men to insert a booming, God-like voice.'

Whenever William Lancaster came on to the set to do a scene, Burt never stayed around to watch. 'I don't want to overshadow Bill. I walked off the set every time he began a scene, and I wouldn't even stay to watch him secretly.'

The parting of the Red Sea was filmed at Sharm el Sheikh. The Golden Calf sequence was shot at Amram's Pillars in the Negev Desert. Hundreds of extras, mainly real Bedouin complete with camels, were gathered and, for 32 weeks, Lancaster and the large cast endured the desert heat. The only respite was when the principals returned to Rome to shoot in the studio.

Lancaster said, 'I'm glad I did it, but I'd never do anything like it again. You have to shoot so fast for television, and for the kind of series we were making you needed many more weeks. Yet having said that, it was a long, tiring shoot, and I was exhausted when it was over.'

After filming, Lancaster went to London to help in the editing process of getting the film down to six two-hour episodes which were premièred on Italian television to much acclaim. The film was supposed to go on the air in America during Easter week of 1975 but instead it was seen by Americans between 21 June and 2 August 1975. Before it reached its final episode, viewers had lost interest and the initial high viewing figures dropped drastically. Nobody seemed to care about Moses as an ordinary man after all.

The series was then abridged into an appalling feature film running to 140 minutes and released in America in 1976. Lancaster was furious. 'The English butchered a perfectly respectable TV movie for release in theatres so they could have a "turnover". It was dreadful.' Curiously, Britain got to see the film version before the TV series. *Variety* said of the feature-length theatrical version, '*Moses* is another attempt at compressing a big slice of Biblical drama, and the inevitable result is superficial story telling. The film was impressively photographed in Israel and has Burt Lancaster in a restrained portrayal. [The film] strikes a reasonable balance between spectacle and narrative. But the net effect is one of flat earnestness, a tale more of tribute than of dimensional human saga. Lancaster delivers his usual polished professionalism.'

Except for the trip to London to help cut the series, Lancaster decided to remain in Rome to work again for Luchino Visconti in *Conversation Piece*. Here he played an ageing American art historian who lets an apartment to a beautiful Italian woman, Silvana Mangano, her rich fiancé and her teenage daughter. On to the scene comes the woman's lover, Helmut Berger, and from there it is all very talky and tangled as Lancaster gets involved in their lives. Visconti asked Claudia Cardinale to appear briefly in a flashback sequence and so enthusiastic was she to work again with the director and with her old friend Lancaster that she rearranged her busy schedule to do the cameo.

Visconti was his typically 'intransigent' self. Recalled Burt, 'I remember being with Luchino Visconti on *Conversation Piece* when he stopped all shooting because he saw three TV antennae in the distance. I was getting 50,000 dollars a week overtime and said maybe he should take some of my money back. He didn't approve of that. "I stop shooting so my producers and crew learn I'm serious when I say no antennae. At times like this you must be intransigent." '

The film opened at the New York Film Festival in September 1975. Pauline Kael, in the *New Yorker*, asked, 'Whose idea can it have been to cast Burt Lancaster as a gentle intellectual? He is as extroverted as an actor can be. His performance made me realize that I've watched him for almost 30 years and I don't know the first thing about him. Whatever goes on inside that man, he doesn't use it as an actor; he doesn't draw from himself. So how can he play a character whose life is all inner? Lancaster simply negates himself in the role, as if by not using any physical energy and by moving slowly with a long face and a demure expression, he would become a thinker . . . he keeps waiting for the professor to make a pass at Konrad (Helmut Berger). I was profoundly grateful to Visconti that he didn't – the audience might split its sides if Burt Lancaster were to be shown coming out – but part of what makes the film giggly is that it's set up as if he should.'

Time said, 'Visconti forsakes the wit of the opening for a kind of tongue-tied general valedictory. He is interested not so much in exposing his character, as in having the professor embrace all of them, opening his arms to their indulgences and sanctioning their moral impotence.'

Variety said, 'Visconti has kept this talky but rarely verbose pic in the two apartments with only an outside studio view of Rome. The assorted accents are justified and even the peppering of blue lingo Americanisms fit these jetsetters. Lancaster is highly effective as the professor.'

Nigel Andrews of the London *Financial Times* wrote, 'Lancaster alone lends the film some of the dignity and resonance it may once have had in Visconti's head. Rueful, aristocratic, stoically polite, his performance is a perfect companion piece to the role he played ten years ago for Visconti, as Don Fabrizio in *The Leopard*. But the odds are stacked against him and even Lancaster can do nothing with dialogue that alternates between stilted would-be profundities and sudden eruptions of banality.'

Vincent Candy, of the *New York Times*, thought that Lancaster's performance was 'a formidably intelligent piece of work.'

It was not, however, a commercial work and, despite Lancaster's cavalier attitude towards making films for the sake of making money, he still needed to find something to please the masses as well as the critics. He thought the film to do that would be Bernardo Bertolucci's epic *1900*.

Bertolucci was still riding on the success of *Last Tango in Paris* and, on the strength of that, he persuaded Twentieth Century-Fox, Paramount and United Artists to give him 6,000,000 dollars for what was supposed to be a three-hour movie. Burt's third Italian film in a row covered some fifty years of life and social conflict in the Emilia region of Italy.

'Bertolucci came to me and we talked and talked,' Lancaster recalled. 'He was raising the money and there was no way to talk about what my salary might be. So finally I said, "Look, I'll do it for you for nothing." And I did. I wasn't doing anything at the time and it was only two weeks' work. So I went to Palma – right near where Bertolucci was born – and treated the whole thing like it was a vacation. I found the ageing character I played a very rich, exciting part.' He described the character he played as a 'ruthless aristocrat, a man who hates his son but loves his grandson. Eventually, I become old and senile.'

Bertolucci had acquired two young up and coming stars, one from America, the other from France: Robert De Niro and Gérard Depardieu. The script that Lancaster saw was only for the first half of the movie. It ran to 180 pages alone. Donald Sutherland was among the other stars who appeared in the second half of the movie.

Lancaster did not particularly enjoy making the film which was shot in 1975. 'Bertolucci was brilliant but extremely difficult to work with because every morning we came on the set, every single thing in the shooting schedule had been changed, and we had to waste three or four hours so the changes could be made. These were conditions I simply wasn't used to.'

Maria Schneider, who had starred in *Last Tango in Paris*, got into a serious row with Bertolucci over his seemingly preferential treatment of Dominique Sanda and she walked off the set. Bertolucci fired her and replaced her with Stefenia Sandrelli.

Paramount became alarmed when they realized that *1900* appeared to be a communist film. Bertolucci explained, '*1900* is the century of a great Utopia which will become a reality. It's the century of the end of the bosses and the death of the social and moral role of the bosses.'

The censor was kept busy eliminating scenes and shots from the film. 'One of the scenes that was lifted in Italy because of the censors was where I attempt sexual intimacy with a little girl. In anger, and impotence and shame, I hang myself,' said Burt.

Part of a scene in which De Niro and Depardieu were either side of a woman in bed was trimmed. The opening of the scene, which the censor cut, showed the woman fondling both men's genitals. Bertolucci decided that such an act could not be faked, so he filmed the real thing. 'It doesn't matter that Bertolucci was naughty,' Lancaster insisted in the director's defence. 'He went ahead and made a marvellous movie, his creation.'

The American studios were not completely in agreement, especially when the film's budget rose to 9,000,000 dollars. And to have a film running for five-and-a-half hours really threw Fox, Paramount and United Artists into turmoil. American distributors have never treated innovational and imaginative Italian directors well. Visconti had his beloved *The Leopard* ruined. United Artists cut Sergio Leone's *The Good, the Bad and the Ugly*. Paramount butchered Leone's *Once Upon a Time in the West*, and Warner Brothers slaughtered his *Once Upon a Time in America*. The five-and-a-half-hour version of *1900* was screened at the Venice Film Festival and hailed as a masterpiece. But the American studios wanted it shortened.

Lancaster, living much of the time in Rome since 1974, had acquired an enormous respect for many European directors. 'These men – Fellini, Visconti, Bertolucci, Antonioni – are extraordinary human beings. We have a whole thing in our system where people direct only for the sake of saying they are directors. Where is their background for directing – their education, intellectuality, imagination? You think of Ingmar Bergman. These are informed, erudite, knowledgeable, creative people. But because ours is a business of mediocrity, nine out of ten directors are only average craftsmen but not imaginative. They are also part of a system where how much money the picture makes is the criterion for goodness.'

Despite his admiration for these men – and despite his pontifications – Lancaster's Italian films had not added much to his own prestige and in 1976 he decided it was time to go back to Los Angeles.

There Robert Altman made him a tempting offer – a week's work as Ned Buntline, the dime-novelist in *Buffalo Bill and the Indians*. The film was based on Arthur Kopit's failed Broadway play called *Indians*. Altman had taken many liberties with it when transferring it to the screen. Paul Newman had been assigned to play Buffalo Bill Cody.

Buntline wrote about Buffalo Bill in his book *King of the Border Men* in 1869 and created the famous Buffalo Bill Wild West Show in 1883. The film features Buntline as a man disenchanted with the legend he created. It was not really a traditional western at all and Burt liked Buntline's philosophy: that America is all about show business.

Of Altman's improvisation method of filming, Newman said, 'Altman is less restrictive than any director I've ever worked with. He demands and depends a great deal on actors outside the confinements and construction of the script.'

Lancaster was not happy working this way. 'I like to work to a script,' he told me. 'I've spent months – years – working on some of the scripts for movies I've produced or starred in, but Altman encouraged us, not so much to improvise, but to create our own concepts. He didn't want to hear what your concept was, or argue about it, and that makes work very difficult for me if I can't argue with my director.'

The film reached American screens in the summer of 1976. It

was not received well by the critics and the public did not want to go to see it. Nigel Andrews, in the *Financial Times*, said, 'Only Burt Lancaster's elegantly rueful performance as Ned Buntline manages to give some contours in a flatly conceived role.' Michael Billington in the *Illustrated London News*, wrote, 'Whereas Kopit's play offered a hallucinatory mosaic, Altman's script has the one-dimensional clarity of a cartoon.'

Newsweek's Jack Kroll, however, thought it an 'ambitious, impudent, brainy, sorrowfully funny movie'.

Meanwhile, the controversy over the length of *1900* raged on. The three Hollywood companies insisted Bertolucci cut his film. He refused and sued them all. They counter-sued. In October 1976, Lancaster attended a special two-hour showing of scenes from the film at the Palace of Fine Arts Theater as part of the San Francisco International Film festival where he said about the controversy:

> I think Bertolucci out-manoeuvred them. Paramount, Fox and UA all gambled on Bertolucci because of his *Last Tango* success and gave him 5,000,000 dollars for a three-hour film of *1900*. And all he did was bamboozle them because he knew he wasn't going to give them a three-hour film. The script I saw, which was only the first half, concerned only me and the old peasant, Sterling Hayden. It was 180 pages long. Our two sons, Robert De Niro and Gérard Depardieu, were still little boys when it ended, so I knew there was going to be another whole movie there. As Carol Reed might have said, 'It was all very naughty.' As yet, I haven't seen the movie in any of its versions but I would be very surprised if it wasn't a marvellous film. The guy is tremendous.

Bertolucci finally compromised and agreed to a four-hour version shown in two parts by Paramount in America and Fox in England. The American critics couldn't make up their minds what to say about this serialized, cut version. *Newsweek* called it 'a "yes, but . . ." masterpiece'.

The *New Yorker* said, 'Bertolucci tried to write a nineteenth-century novel on film: the result is appalling, yet it has the grandeur of a classic visionary folly.'

Time found it 'exasperatingly uneven, but its most powerful moments can't be matched by any movie since *Godfather II.*'

The American and British cinema-going public were not prepared to watch a film in two parts, and the film was seen little outside Europe.

22

Autumn Years

Throughout the years, Lancaster had made certain that his children were not exposed too much to his business and only William showed an interest in films at this time, although Joanna would later become a film producer. In 1976, William saw his first screenplay reach the screen, *The Bad News Bears*, a comedy about a team of kids coached in baseball by Walter Matthau. No doubt William was inspired by all the baseball his father had taught him in their own private baseball park.

Burt maintained close links with his family, whether they were still living with Norma or had set up on their own. 'When they were young I felt it was reasonable to help them and advise them and I thought as they grew older I'd finish with that. But no. They're still babies to me. I still worry about them. I have to remind myself that I have no right to go on exercising authority. "Oh, look, dad", they say when I start on something, and then it sinks in.'

By 1976, he badly needed something to earn him some money, so he accepted a part from Lew Grade to appear in the star-studded disaster movie *The Cassandra Crossing*. Said Burt, 'There are times when I do a film like *The Cassandra Crossing* simply because I need the money. I kid you not. It's a matter of lifestyle. I have only one dress suit to my name, and a few jackets and pants but it still costs me 300,000 dollars a year just to live. I must continue to work.'

The Cassandra Crossing came at the tail end of a cycle of disaster movies. This one featured a train full of plague victims which cannot be admitted to any country, so it is diverted towards the Cassandra Bridge where it will meet its inevitable fate. On board the train were Richard Harris, Sophia Loren (whose husband Carlo Ponti was producing for Lew Grade's ITC company), Ava Gardner and Martin Sheen, among others.

Lancaster played an intelligence officer who, with Ingrid Thulin, must decide on the train's destruction from their secret headquarters. While much of the film was shot on location in Poland, Lancaster and Thulin worked in the studio.

> I worked on it for two weeks and got a lot of money for it. It was a terrible script so George Pan Cosmatos [the director] and I worked together on the script, and I think actors like Harris and Loren were saying, 'Who does Burt Lancaster think he is rewriting the script?' George just yelled at them, 'Lancaster and I worked our asses off writing these lines for you. If you don't like them, you can have the original lines back and then see how you like that.'
>
> Making the film was fun really. Ingrid and I worked for ten days; she's a marvellous person and a wonderful actress, although the film didn't actually show anyone's talent to great effect. I remember my best line in that whole movie was 'Listen, why don't you just take the dog for a walk?' And I'm on the phone saying, 'Hello? Yes. Yes. The train is approaching.'

Of Lew Grade, Lancaster said, 'Wonderful man, great businessman. But he does have this occasional wish to interfere. The film's about a plague. It ends with me ordering a train blown up. So he rings up and says, can't you say something like "My wife and two children were on that train." He always wants these happy endings.'

Released in 1977, the film met with howls of derision from the critics. Even *Variety*'s reviewer had trouble keeping a straight face, finding it 'a tired, hokey and sometimes unintentionally funny disaster film. Mismatched leading players all play directly to the camera for themselves only, without betraying a hint of belief in their script.'

As a respected elder statesman of the movie business, Burt Lancaster was invited to lecture students on film acting and producing, politics and world affairs; and politics and religion. He thoroughly enjoyed having the chance to speak his mind about all those topics.

In early 1977, he went to the Virgin islands to make *The Island of Dr Moreau*, based on an H G Wells story which had been filmed in 1933 as *The Island of Lost Souls*. Charles Laughton had played the part Burt now had. Dr Moreau experiments with genetics, producing half-human, half-animal creatures.

'Our version was different to the Laughton film,' Lancaster said. 'Laughton was a mad scientist, but I play him as a dedicated scientist who feels what he is doing is a nobler thing – then he goes mad. But who's to say that what Moreau does in the story is unlike anything that goes on in our own governmental laboratories? That's what fascinated me about the story.'

Directed by Don Taylor, the film also starred Michael York, Nigel Davenport, Richard Basehart and Barbara Carrera. Burt managed to find a small role for Nick Cravat to play.

Don Taylor and the film's producers, John Temple-Smith and Skip Steloff, faced the full weight of Lancaster's temper when they tried to change the script. Said Lancaster:

The film's opening scene had Michael York washed up onto the island half drowned. He runs through the jungle and sees strange things – a cloven hoof, just shadows of a face like an animal. He thinks he's mad. He falls in an animal trap. They were worried that the opening scene was too slow. They wanted a *Jaws*-type opening. They wanted another man to be in the boat with Michael – almost dead. As Michael goes into the jungle, an animal hand would pull the man into the bush and then you'd see this bloody stump – the man being eaten.

I blew my top. My contract protects me from any producer changing the whole concept of the script. It was important that the movie reveal slowly the boy's mind. But they just wanted a bloody opening sequence.

To create the so-called 'humanimals', make-up experts John Chambers and Dan Striepke, who worked on *The Planet of the Apes*, created some excellent make-up. No expense was spared with 6,000,000 dollars to spend, and the results were favourable.

Variety called it 'a handsome, well acted and involving piece of cinematic story telling,' but *Sight and Sound* thought it was 'cursed with lush colour photography instead of black and white atmospherics, and Lancaster's stolid mania instead of Laughton's maniac zeal.'

In 1977, Burt had an operation on his troublesome knee. More bothersome was his lack of box-office clout. His list of failures had resulted in a loss of credibility at the box office. There seemed a chance to redeem himself when Robert Aldrich came to him with *Twilight's Last Gleaming*.

This American-West German co-production made in 1977 featured Lancaster as a US Air Force officer who seizes a nuclear missile site to force public disclosure of secret Vietnam war policies. 'I thought the film had some important things to say,' said Lancaster, 'but Bob Aldrich didn't quite succeed in bringing them out.'

This further collaborative effort between Lancaster and Aldrich was not much marked by arguments. 'Bob is a sweetheart,' Burt said, 'and I love him.'

Richard Widmark played a general who mobilizes his operation to forcibly recapture the missile base and Charles Durning played the president of the United States.

Variety called the film an 'intricate, intriguing and intelligent drama', and highlighted the performance of Charles Durning which it thought 'outstanding'. But, in 1977 when the film was released, few people seemed to want to see a film that starred Burt Lancaster any more.

Scripts sent to him were usually mediocre at best but when he read a Vietnam War tale, *Go Tell the Spartans*, he was immediately enthusiastic. 'It was,' he said, 'the best project offered me in Hollywood for years.'

Certainly director Ted Post wanted him but the independent producers, Allan F Bodoh and Mitchell Cannold, could not afford him nor could they hope to raise much money on his name. Studios were also backing off because it was the first film to suggest that the American soldiers in that war were not invincible. So, desperate to make the film, Lancaster put 150,000 dollars of his own money into the budget.

'It was a difficult idea to sell to the American people, that we can be beaten. The studios wouldn't put money into it and it was a struggle just to get it made. But what we finally achieved was excellent, I thought, and I am very proud of it.'

Lancaster played the commander of an advisory group at Penang who orders a raw detachment of American and Vietnamese mercenaries into the jungle to occupy an outpost abandoned by the French a decade earlier. But when the Vietcong move in on the outpost, rather than stay and fight a battle the Americans cannot win, Lancaster orders their evacuation.

When it was made, in 1978, it was the first film since John Wayne's *The Green Berets* ten years earlier to be set in the Vietnam War. Wayne's film, which was a box-office success despite what the critics said, portrayed the American soldiers as heroes. *Go Tell the Spartans* was the first film not to show them as heroes, preceding films like *Platoon* and *Full Metal Jacket*. But it was not a success.

In 1978, despite his poor ratings at the box office, Burt was an icon in Hollywood and that year he donated his five-feet by seven-feet canvas painting *The Kentuckian* by Thomas Hart Benton to the Los Angeles County Museum. It had been painted in 1955 but had been kept stored in a warehouse since then. Lancaster was happy to attend the ceremony at which the museum's director said, 'It's rare to have the patron, donor and subject on hand at a presentation.'

In 1979 Lancaster was again an actor in search of a commercial winner. This time he thought he had found it in *Zulu Dawn* a 'prequel' to the hugely successful 1964 epic *Zulu*. But first, before arriving in South Africa to make *Zulu Dawn*, he took Jackie on holiday to Australia and Bali.

Despite a heavyweight cast that included Peter O'Toole, Simon Ward, John Mills, Nigel Davenport and Denholm Elliott, Burt was top-billed. As desperate as he was to make a successful film, he still maintained his personal values when it came to choosing scripts. He had previously turned down *The Wild Geese* because he did not think it told the truth about South Africa. Of *Zulu Dawn* he said, 'This is an honest film, full of action and courage. It is very realistic with an almost documentary approach that follows the course of history accurately. It makes a real change from some of the films being made today. I've turned down a lot of garbage lately.'

But the makers of the film had made a big mistake. Cy Enfield, who directed the original *Zulu*, had worked hard on the screenplay for this prequel for years, although it was Douglas Hickox who finally directed it. Its action begins before the brilliantly recreated attack on Rorke's Drift in *Zulu*. But the climax of *Zulu Dawn* was the battle that is featured fleetingly in the opening of the first film; a battle in which 1,300 British soldiers were slaughtered. So all who had seen the first film knew the outcome of the second, and audiences were not persuaded to see the build-up to that finale.

'The action sequences are superbly handled,' said *Variety*, 'as are the scenes in which the men and material are assembled and manoeuvred. For sheer scope . . . *Zulu Dawn* is positively De Millesque in scale.'

Lancaster was still a highly respected man in Hollywood and in 1979 he was asked to run for president of the Screen Actors Guild. He considered the offer but discovered he was ineligible because the rules stipulated that no one who employed actors could be the president. Lancaster had a small company,

Norlan, which he had kept running since the breakdown of Hecht-Hill-Lancaster, even though he had not made a film through Norlan. Nevertheless, he was a potential employer of actors and, although he could have closed the company down and thereby become eligible to run, he decided to hang on to it, 'just in case'.

An offer for a western came along and he decided to take one, possibly last, stab at the genre. The film was *Cattle Annie and Little Britches*, made in 1979 in which he played ageing desperado Bill Doolin whose gang is pursued by lawman Rod Steiger. Two teenage girls, played by Diane Lane and Amanda Plummer, go west in search of adventure and meet up with Lancaster. They join his gang but, finally tired of the girls, he allows Steiger to catch up.

Variety slated it: '[It] is as cutesy and unmemorable as its title. [The] whole film washes over the viewer, with no images or moments sticking in the mind.' Although Derek Elley wrote in *Films and Filming*, 'the playing of Lancaster and Steiger is beautifully shaded, Lancaster especially good as the ageing outlaw with life in him yet, gently philosophizing over the impertinence of his profession and the needs which drove him to assume it.'

The film was hardly shown either in America or Britain. In 1979, Lancaster announced, 'I'm at an age where I'm phasing out my work. There are very few pictures that interest me. It's too much personal involvement. I want to take it easy. I've had several offers to do things at considerable money, but they just don't interest me.'

He did not hesitate to disagree with those who complained that it was not like the good old days in Hollywood. 'It's a better situation in pictures today. We look back with nostalgia at the films of the past but all of them were not that good. We think of that as the Golden Era – but I think this is the Golden Era. Better movies are being made today.'

Towards the end of 1979 he began feeling unwell, which surprised him as he had always been so fit and healthy. In January 1980, when he was 66, he was admitted to Cedars-

Sinai Hospital suffering from abdominal pain, and rushed into surgery for what the hospital would only describe at the time as 'intricate abdominal surgery'. Rumours spread that he had cancer but a spokesperson for the hospital assured the gathering reporters that Lancaster's ill health was 'not cancer-related'.

He was on the operating table for eleven hours, during which surgeons removed his gall bladder because of gall stones. But complications set in during what should have been a much shorter, routine operation. His stitches would not hold and he was constantly losing blood. Pints of blood had to be pumped back into him as surgeons battled to save his life. Jackie Bone later admitted, 'He could have died right there and then on the operating table.'

For a while he was on the critical list but once the danger had passed, he recovered quickly. Among the get-well messages he received was a letter from Michael York. Lancaster wrote back to him: 'I was on the table for eleven hours. When I came to I thought they'd turned me into a Moreaurian Monster, what with endless tubes and things sticking out from all parts of my body. Believe me, Michael, I treated you much more kindly when I had you on *my* table in St Croix.'

Despite the light approach displayed more for the benefit of others, the whole experience had actually shaken him to the core. When he left hospital people were shocked to see that he now had a pot belly and a shock of white hair. He walked with some difficulty because of the arthritis in his knees.

'My romantic leading days are over,' he announced. 'I can look at nineteen-year old girls but I'm not allowed to get too close.'

He suddenly became perfect casting for Louis Malle's *Atlantic City*, the story of a white-haired, ex-gangster who can remember when 'the Atlantic Ocean was really something'; he runs errands for his landlady and becomes fascinated by his young female neighbour. Robert Mitchum had been offered the part but turned it down as being too much of a blow to his ego.

Malle offered the role to Lancaster and he grabbed it eagerly.

'It's good to reach out and try something different,' he said. Louis Malle said:

> It was an act of heroism for Burt to allow himself to be seen so starkly as an old-timer. It is all the more remarkable because he has the reputation of being very difficult and temperamental and a long history of making trouble with his directors. Yet from the start, he was enthusiastic about this project.
>
> When I first saw Burt, I thought, My God! What great irony if a man, whose image is so much the opposite, should play this silly old man who is a voyeur, watching a girl undress in the opposite apartment. I did not want to make him completely ridiculous. I wanted to show something moving about him. But because he is Burt Lancaster, an actor who carried around a heroic image all his life, there is that extra sense of humiliation.
>
> I am told he saw a copy of the film and reacted very well. I would hate to have had an unhappy Burt Lancaster. He can really get mean.

He was not unhappy at all. Susan Sarandon, the neighbour he takes to spying on, said, 'Burt Lancaster was thoroughly professional and accessible – although he did not hang out.'

The critics loved the film when they saw it in 1981. Pauline Kael said, 'In shallow action roles, he played bloody but unbowed. When he was working with Visconti or Bertolucci, he wasn't afraid to be bloody and bowed. And that's how he is here, but more so, because this time he isn't playing a strong man brought down by age and social chance; he's a man who was never anything much – he was always a little too soft inside.'

Richard Schickel wrote in *Time*;

> The highest pleasure *Atlantic City* has to offer is a little essay on fastidiousness by Burt Lancaster. That is not a quality one automatically associates with a star who was

once the most macho of leading men. But in the past decade, he has become a resourceful and wide-ranging character actor. Here he is playing Lou, a small-time crook who seems to feel neatness just might count in the battle to keep his withered dreams intact. You can practically smell the blue rinse in his hair; the pressing of a tie, the caressing of a whisky glass, the sniffing of a wine cork, incantatory gestures. They are supposed to ward off the new tawdriness of the gambling casinos, which is replacing the old salt-water-taffy funk of the boardwalk town. While the wrecking balls swing all around him, Lou complains that even the ocean isn't what it used to be.'

Variety said, 'The film is well limned by Burt Lancaster, Susan Sarandon, Kate Reid, Robert Joy and Hollis McLaren. Atlantic City is also a character as director Louis Malle adroitly uses decrepit old and new façades.'

Towards the end of 1980, after finishing *Atlantic City*, Lancaster returned to Rome to make *La Pelle* (*The Skin*) for Liliana Cavini. Set in Naples in 1943, it was a Second World War drama in which he played General Mark Clark. Claudia Cardinale was also in it, as was Marcello Mastroianni, but it was never seen outside Europe. It was, however, well received at the Cannes Film Festival in 1981.

Burt remained in Rome to appear as Pope Gregory X in *Marco Polo*, a huge but undistinguished television saga which was only well received in Italy. He spent his time wisely in between scenes of *Marco Polo*, improving his Roman apartment. He bought a new dining room table which he discovered being made:

This was the perfect look, a strong design of black-enamelled wood, with inlays of brass, and brass legs. It accommodates six or eight, which is my ideal number for a dinner party. I like to cook and entertain when I'm in Italy. I've mastered the skill of preparing pasta, which so many Americans ruin by overcooking, and all my sauces are authentic, whether I'm serving spaghetti *carbonara* or *matriciana*. I grow my own herbs – basil, rosemary and oregano – just as the Italians do, and I plant flowers in between, which is an Italian custom. There's a huge market in Rome, the size of two Twentieth Century-Fox sound stages, that's filled with flowers. I buy them there at half the price I would have to pay at a fancy flower shop.

It seems that in Rome Burt broke all his own rules; he entertained at home and he talked happily about trivial things. He continued to redesign the interior, bringing over Jim Vance from Carmel in California to design his library. Roman artisans worked on the rest of the apartment. His bedroom pillows were covered with Italian silk in soft muted colours, designed by Enrico Sabbatini who created the costumes for *Marco Polo*. A hand-sewn picture of a classical view of Rome by Italian artist Maria Teresa Capoanno hung over his bed. He placed Turkish rugs, which he had bought years before in Istanbul, over the bedroom floor.

The place was devoid of movie memorabilia – except for a single giant photograph of Claudia Cardinale and himself dancing in a scene from *The Leopard*. He had a huge soft spot for Cardinale; he loved Italian people and things.

He was back in America by August 1981, for what he expected to be a very special event. For years Kirk Douglas and he had talked about doing a play together and, eventually, they found *The Boys of Autumn*. In it Lancaster played Hucklebrry Finn and Douglas played Tom Sawyer – meeting for the first time after many years since their adventures.

'We begin by meeting on a hill looking over the Mississippi,' Douglas told me, 'and at first I don't recognize him. We're in our sixties now, so we sit down and talk about our lives. It turns out we've both done things we're unhappy about. He confesses to the mercy killing of his wife, I confess to molesting children. It was damned hard work. After rehearsing in San Francisco one day for twelve hours, I said, "Burt, aren't we too rich for this?" '

Lancaster said at the time, 'Neither of us is used to such hard work. But working together in a play like this we've learned a lot about each other. The show was a hit, and we could have gone on doing it as a sort of personal appearance in a number of theatres. But both of us knew it wasn't good enough, and it was damned hard work. I was relieved when we agreed that it was too exhausting. I much prefer film.'

The friendship between the two actors had been rekindled and all memories of *Seven Days in May* forgotten. Kirk was full of admiration for Burt as an actor. He said, 'When you compare Burt Lancaster with John Wayne, you find that Wayne was a great star and always played John Wayne. Anything less than that he did not regard as manly. But Burt is just the opposite. He's a great star and a great actor. He is living proof that you can be sensitive and macho at the same time.'

In Hollywood, in 1982, Lancaster won the Best Actor award from the Los Angeles Film Critics Association for *Atlantic City* and, on accepting it, said, 'Maybe the award will help, for apart from myself, Kirk Douglas and my immediate family, I don't think anyone else has seen the picture.'

He was also nominated for an Oscar. The film received other nominations, for Best Picture, Best Screenplay (John Guare), Best Actress (Susan Sarandon) and Best Director. When Oscars time came around in 1982, the film failed to win any but Lancaster, losing to Henry Fonda for *On Golden Pond*, said, 'I'm glad he got it. First of all, it was a wonderful performance. Secondly, after forty years . . .'

23

A Hero in Scotland

David Puttnam had come to the fore in British films when he made the Oscar-winning *Chariots of Fire*. In 1982 he was about to produce *Local Hero* in Scotland from a screenplay by Bill Forsyth who had won an Academy Award for *Gregory's Girl*. Forsyth was also going to direct this story of an American oil executive who goes to Scotland to buy an entire village where his company intends to construct a new oil refinery. The local Scots, far from being outraged and immovable, cannot wait to sign away their town in exchange for vast amounts of money.

For the part of a Houston-based oil magnate who is more concerned with his psychiatrist and astronomy than in what is going on in Scotland, Forsyth thought immediately of Lancaster, even as he was writing the script. Said Forsyth, 'In my head I began to hear him saying the dialogue. Then I think I started writing it specially for him. I knew we needed a big name, although I don't usually work with stars. Happer has to be a man of power and influence, and there aren't too many 65-year-old American unknowns around who can put that over. However, I'd never met Burt Lancaster and had some qualms about approaching him because of the effect his acceptance might have had on the budget. If he were to accept then we would be committed to him. At the same time, we knew his name would help in terms of cable and television rights. We spent some time in Los Angeles looking for people who might play the part if he turned it down.'

Lancaster received the script at his office where his daughter
Joanna worked for him. When he had read it, he said, 'Hey
Joanna, you gotta read this. I've gotta make this movie.'

He later said, 'Good scripts are rare and this was the best I'd
received since *Atlantic City*. It was light and satirical, with no
villains, just eccentrics. It was like those lovely old Ealing
movies. I don't particularly care if I don't act any more unless I
find a piece of work that really excites me. You've no idea the
rubbish that's sent to me. Tits and sand. That's what we used to
call sex and violence in Hollywood. I had never heard of
Forsyth before I received the script.'

'Of course,' said Forsyth, 'it was amazing when he read it
and was interested in doing it.' Unfortunately, clinching the
deal was not quite so easy.

Lancaster's agent called David Puttnam and told him how
much Lancaster would cost. It was more than Puttnam could
ever afford. He recalled, 'I spent four or five weeks shuttling
back and forth across the Atlantic to try and arrange it. Bill was
equally stubborn. He'd written it for Lancaster and wouldn't
budge.' When Burt got to hear of the problem he told the agent,
'If these guys can't afford it, let it ride. I want to do it.'

Filming for Lancaster began in Houston in the early spring of
1982. It took only a day and a half, during which associate
producer Ian Smith nervously said, 'Mr Lancaster, it would be
just wonderful if you could give some interviews.'

'But I never give interviews.'

Smith pleaded and handed a list of names to Burt. 'I've
prepared a list of those we'd like you to talk to.'

'You mean these people will come and write nice things
about the picture? It's to be for the good of the picture?'

Smith nodded.

'Okay,' said Lancaster, 'I'll do it.' He dropped the list in the
nearest wastepaper basket.

On the Houston location, Bill Forsyth spoke to the Texan
cops through whom Lancaster has to push his way to get to his
limousine. 'We had real cops,' Forsyth explained, 'who were a

bit timid of Lancaster. He was supposed to barge through them and part them, and they backed off. I said to them to allow Burt to push through and went back to the camera from where I saw him talking to them, and I thought, He's going to be okay. He's helping out.'

And he was, relaying the message to the cops in frank American terms so they would not misunderstand. When he saw that Forsyth had noticed, he said to the director, 'I hope you don't mind me talking to the other performers but I thought I could help.'

Forsyth told him he could do whatever he liked.

With Jackie to keep him company, Burt flew to London and then on to Fort William in Scotland to meet the rest of the cast. Peter Riegert was playing the executive whose job is to buy the village. Jenny Seagrove had the role of a marine biologist, and Denis Lawson played the village pub owner and chief negotiator for the village folk.

Burt recalled, 'When I arrived in Scotland I was told, though not by Bill – he is an extremely modest, rather shy man, very strong when he wants but very quiet – that he wrote the part with me in mind.'

About the part and of Forsyth's writing, he told me:

It wasn't really easy for me because Forsyth writes about these characters who are all sort of mad, but not really mad. Forsyth is a very perceptive person about human nature, and the frailties of human beings. From his point of view, everybody is a little strange. But he treats them all very gently with a very sweet, light kind of humour. He doesn't put them down; he indulges them and looks upon their weaknesses with affectionate humour.

You have to be careful playing a character like this who is just a little mad. When he isn't getting one over his business rivals, he's shoring up his psyche with 'abuse therapy'. His office is a private planetarium with a telescope NASA would kill for. Forsyth is a superb writer on the frailties of human nature. The temptation is go overboard with it but you have to be careful that you don't 'farcialize' it. You have to let the total effect of what is happening evoke an attitude of charm and mirth in the audience. At first I was not sure what I was doing, but I came to feel pretty comfortable about it after I'd seen some of the rushes.

Burt filmed for two weeks at Morar beach, 37 miles from Fort William. He and Jackie stayed with David Puttnam and Bill Forsyth in the exclusive Inverlochy Castle.

A late snowfall hampered the first few days of filming, followed by rain, but then the weather brightened. On Saturday nights Burt visited the Glenfinnan pub to listen to bagpipes and drink with the locals. Other nights were spent in nearby pubs, often just standing round with members of the unit and signing autographs for astonished drinkers. He even played snooker with Alex Higgins. 'I just beat that guy Alex Higgins at the snooker table,' he proudly announced. 'He looks like he survives on booze and nerves – but he sure can put those balls in the pockets.'

One night he took Jackie to eat at the Holly Tree Restaurant, a converted railway station at Kentallen. It turned out around forty of the film's unit were also eating there. He agreed to talk to the owner's wife's mother on the phone to prove Burt Lancaster really was eating there and before he left he secretly paid the bill for the crew.

News came that he won Best Actor from New York Film Critics Circle for *Atlantic City* and, although he didn't win the Oscar, he was nominated by the British Academy of Film and Television Arts for the Best Actor award. He agreed to attend the BAFTA ceremony in London where he was duly awarded the Best Actor award.

Back in Scotland he had trouble remembering the long speech on the beach. He knew he was getting a little too old and was frustrated by the limitations old age was imposing on him.

He towered over Peter Riegert so it was suggested that

Riegert should stand on a board to raise him. Burt noticed he was shifting a good deal and asked, 'Are you comfortable on that thing?'

'No.'

'Then don't stand on it.'

'But I agreed.'

'Don't agree. That's their problem, not yours. Don't let them hassle you.'

Burt found he had a particular rapport with Fulton Mackay, who had appeared in a TV play, *Going Gently*, which was about terminal cancer patients and in which Burt had tried to interest American TV networks two years earlier. The networks turned him down, even though he and Art Carney were prepared to do it for nothing.

Burt did the interviews he had been asked for but, because he had thrown away his list of names, he kept asking the publicist, 'Was he on the list? Okay then.'

He still jogged for two hours each day but said he preferred to stay at home to read or make love.

The whole cast and crew loved him, as summed up by Denis Lawson who told me:

He was wonderful to have on the picture. We did all our stuff with him on the beach in Scotland, and they could only afford him for three weeks, so he did his half week in Houston and then he did two and a half weeks with us in Scotland. And he was very enthusiastic about the film. I think as a film it was unique. We all had a wonderful time doing it and Lancaster felt exactly the same way.

When he finished shooting, they gave him a party and they presented him with a kilt and socks and the full bit. He just took off his trousers in the middle of this reception and put the kilt on. There was a great sense of loss the day after he left because it's wonderful to work with somebody like that, especially under those circumstances because his involvement seemed as heavy as anybody else's. It wasn't just a job for him. I'm fascinated to watch people like him who have spent their lives in front of movie cameras. Yes, I kind of learned bits from him, I think.

There were 120 people at the party they threw for him. 'He was a prince,' said Ian Smith.

Lancaster did not fly straight home but went to Turnberry, Gleneagles and St Andrews to play golf for a fortnight.

In October 1982, he narrated a 30-minute TV programme which attacked right-wing groups for their 'political intolerance reminiscent of witch-hunts, slavery and McCarthyism'. It was really a lengthy commercial produced for 200,000 dollars by Norman Lear and his organization 'People for the American Way'.

Millions of Americans tuned it to watch it and listen to Lancaster explain, 'You'll see that we, as a nation, are besieged today by a powerful wealthy movement with one dangerous goal.' The movement he and the backers were attacking was the Moral Majority, although it was never mentioned by name in the programme. However, Cal Thomas, a spokesman for the Moral Majority, accused the programme of being 'a total piece of blatant propaganda'.

Then Burt went to work on *The Osterman Weekend*, a violent picture in which Rutger Hauer is convinced by a CIA agent, played by John Hurt, that his three closest friends are Soviet agents. Lancaster appeared much further down in the cast list than usual, playing the CIA chief who wants to be the president.

This was Sam Peckinpah's first film in six years; as Burt had a minor role, he did it quickly and for no other reason than the money. For Peckinpah, it was intended to be his comeback to the big time since his disappointing trucker's film *Convoy* in 1977. But Twentieth Century-Fox did not like *The Osterman Weekend*, which they had paid for, and took it away from him to re-edit. *Variety* described it as 'a competent, professional but thoroughly impersonal meller', and noted that 'Burt Lancaster socks over his bookend cameo as the scheming CIA kingpin'.

But Lancaster was not much interested in what was said

about that film; he was waiting eagerly for the response to *Local Hero*. And the reaction in London in 1983 was excellent, both critically and commercially. When it opened in the US, however, the reviews were virtually all raves but the American cinemagoers were not so interested in what the *Hollywood Reporter* called 'a quaint, sardonic and laudably unpretentious film'.

Vincent Canby wrote in the *New York Times*, 'Though he is not on screen as long as one would like, Mr Lancaster is splendidly unpredictable as the oil tycoon. In Mr Lancaster's perfectly controlled nuttiness lies the secret of Mr Forsyth's comic method, which is as stylish and original as that of any new director to come along in years.'

Pauline Kael said, 'The humour is dry, yet the picture is romantic in spirit, and Burt Lancaster has something to do with that. He is convincing as a sturdy, physically powerful man, and even more convincing as a man of authority whose only intimacy is with the stars above . . . he belongs there, on top of a tower under the stars, and I doubt if there are many actors who could convey so much by just standing there.'

In 1983 he hosted the Italian TV series *The Life of Verdi* in which Ronald Pickup played the composer. Also that year he attended a special tribute to Kirk Douglas who was being awarded with the Albert Einstein Award from Israel's Institute of Technology. It was a rare public appearance for Burt in which he displayed the warmth and affection he felt for Kirk when he greeted Douglas with a kiss on the lips.

He told the gathered audience, which included Robert Mitchum, Gregory Peck and Ernest Borgnine, 'I've worked with him many times over the span of years, and I think I know him pretty well. Let me start by telling you something about him. To begin with, he is the most difficult and exasperating man that I know – except for myself. He fights with his wife, he fights with his children, he fights with the maid, he fights with the cook. God knows, he has fought with me.'

When it was time for Kirk to give his speech,he said, 'I'm glad that years ago I did not desert Burt Lancaster – stood by him in spite of a hacking cough, fought it out with him at the OK Corral. As I listened to my life story, I thought what a wonderful movie it would make – and there is only one person to play it – Burt Lancaster!'

In May, Burt and Jackie took a holiday on Kapalua Bay on the Hawaiian island of Maui. He was enjoying a much needed rest before taking on a difficult and demanding role in the homosexual drama *The Kiss of the Spider Woman*. It was to be directed by Hector Babenco in Paris and Brazil and co-star Raul Julia. But when Lancaster returned to Los Angeles he was informed that the film had been delayed until October.

Since *Local Hero* there was now a fresh interest in Lancaster from producers and directors. He had other projects he was looking forward to: *Maria's Lovers* with Nastassia Kinski and John Savage, to be directed by Andrei Konchalovsky, a much acclaimed Soviet director; *AD*, an epic mini-series in which he was to play the Roman Emperor Tiberius; and *Firestarter*, which William Lancaster had adapted from Stephen King's tale of a girl with pyrokinetic powers, to be directed by John Carpenter.

In June, after his holiday, he checked in to Cedars for what was supposedly his annual check-up, but he had in fact been experiencing chest pains. Rumours quickly spread that he had suffered a heart attack. Tess Griffin, speaking on behalf of the hospital, told the press, 'It is correct that Mr Lancaster is here. Our records show that he came in for his annual exhaustive physical check-up. Tests will include checks on his heart but this was not an emergency admission and he has not suffered a heart attack.'

Doctors told him that his coronary arteries were blocked. Despite all his attempts to remain fit, he had never been able to deal with the one thing that in the end was most likely the cause of his illness – smoking. He still chain-smoked, excusing his habit by saying, 'I know, I live in a land full of health nuts and I still smoke. But I run every day to offset the effect.'

But smoking could not be offset by running and he was now, at the age of 69, paying the price. His only chance was to have a quadruple by-pass operation to relieve blockages in the coronary arteries. Although it was never confirmed by the hospital, it seemed that Burt had, indeed, suffered a mild heart attack, and he was kept in for a couple of weeks for constant observation.

Despite the warning from his doctors, Lancaster was resisting the operation. He had not forgotten the time he had spent eleven hours under the knife for the removal of his gall bladder when his life had hung in the balance, and he seemed convinced he would die this time. As it was, his heart muscles needed time to recover from the heart attack and so he was allowed home in July where he went through a daily routine of careful exercise to strengthen his heart muscles.

Then he returned to Cedars and underwent a five-and-a-half-hour operation. Because of his exercise routine, he was surprisingly well the next day and managed to read the newspaper. 'They told me the only other one who did that was George Burns,' he said.

He spent three days in intensive care and was then moved to a private room. The following day he was up and walking, and only ten days after the operation, he left. His recovery was remarkable and he was eager to get back to work. He was due to start on *Firestarter* in a month's time. But that film was scrapped after Carpenter's *The Thing* flopped. It was eventually produced by Dino de Laurentiis who replaced Carpenter with Mark L Lester and Burt with Martin Sheen.

There were further blows – he was replaced by Robert Mitchum in *Maria's Lovers*, and by James Mason in *AD*.

Perhaps to ease producers' anxieties, Burt announced, 'I feel great. I've been leading the life of a saint; no smoking, no drinking, no sex – I cheat a little.' He and Jackie were still together and still not married. 'She hasn't yelled for it yet,' he said.

She never would. Their relationship suddenly ended.

Ironically, at this the most depressing and difficult time of his entire career, one of the films that meant the most to him which had been so cruelly treated on its initial release, was restored and reissued in September 1983 – *The Leopard*. The critics rediscovered it in its complete, though dubbed, version. Alexander Walker of London's *Evening Standard* said, 'Lancaster can, in a word, *impose* himself. It takes some doing to dominate the most lavish and sensual setpieces of social ostentation ever seen on the screen.'

Lancaster was delighted with the film's critical reception, saying, 'When *The Leopard* first came out it got good reviews, but the critics laughed at me. I was a bum. Twenty years later they're saying, "It's his *chef d'oeuvre*, his great acting piece." I don't know what happened to these people, but suddenly I've become a hell of a performer.'

24

A Tough Guy

Lancaster was well enough to go to Spain in 1984 to start work on *Le Marchand des Quatre Saisons*, written and directed by Chilean director, Miguel Littin. But financial problems hit at the last minute and the film was cancelled. After a couple of weeks in the Spanish sun, he flew back to LA to play an old crook who is reunited with his daughter, played by Margot Kidder, in *Little Treasure*. He dies, leaving money from a bank robbery buried in a ghost town somewhere in New Mexico. The film's distributors tried to compare it to *The Treasure of the Sierra Madre* when it was released in 1985 but most agreed that, after Burt's scenes, the film had little going for it.

If he had expected the re-release of *The Leopard* to rejuvenate his career, he was wrong. He was looked upon as a veteran with past glories who should sit back on his laurels. But few stars had ever done that – Dietrich, Garbo and Cary Grant were among the rare ones who did retire – and Lancaster, despite the times when he said he would retire from acting, seemed intent on going on.

'You can't just give up and die,' he told me, 'not when you're on the operating table, nor when you're an actor. You just don't give up. There are character parts for old actors like me. Henry Fonda found the perfect one in *On Golden Pond*, and that's the kind of role I would like.'

So he kept searching for his own *On Golden Pond*. But by

the mid-eighties, much of Hollywood's output was for television. And while many of the TV-made feature-length movies were of a high standard, they could never hope to receive the same accolades and acclaim accorded to theatrically released movies. But that was where much of the work was for ageing actors and that is what Burt turned to.

In 1985, he starred in *Scandal Sheet*, playing the owner of a newspaper which specializes in publishing salacious gossip about show-business personalities. Pamela Reed played a successful freelance journalist who is hired by Lancaster, and unwittingly helps him to destroy a film star, played by Robert Urich. The plot sounded like *Sweet Smell of Success* but this time Pamela Reed, unlike Tony Curtis in the former film, is a likeable character who becomes tainted after Urich kills himself.

His old screen sparring partner Kirk Douglas had been finding the same problem as Burt; as much as Kirk did not want to admit to getting older, he was, even though he was still extremely trim and fit. He was younger than Burt by only three years but had managed to keep in magnificent shape. To find something suitable for himself and Lancaster was something they both kept an eye open for.

'We had wanted to work together once more for many years,' Lancaster told me, 'and we thought it would be great to do something on the stage, so we did *The Boys of Autumn*. But that was hard work so we decided we ought to try and find a film to do. It took a few years, but these two guys, James Orr and Jim Cruikshank, came to us with a script they'd written especially for us, called *Tough Guys*. It just seemed perfect for us.'

Orr and Cruikshank had seen Lancaster and Douglas do another song-and-dance routine at the 1985 Academy Awards Show and had decided that they personally wanted to see the two stars in another movie. So they came up with the story of two robbers who, released from prison after 30 years, decide to 'do it right this time'. So they plan to hold up a train.

Orr and Cruikshank, having got Burt's and Kirk's

commitment to it, took the idea to Disney. Kirk was eager to make the film through his Bryna company in collaboration with Disney's then new subsidiary, Touchstone Pictures. The Disney people gave it the go-ahead. The screenplay needed some revision so, while that was being done, Lancaster went to Mexico to appear in another large-scale television mini-series, *On Wings of Eagles*, based on real events in Iran in 1979 when two Americans were imprisoned in Tehran and rescued by a band of ex-army civilians. Lancaster played the colonel who hires Richard Crenna to lead the rescue mission. It was an easy role for Burt to play and required little effort from either his acting or his physical muscles. But then, at the age of 72, after a by-pass operation less than three years earlier, he was not expecting to go on being an action man.

In *On Wings of Eagles* he left all the running and fighting to the younger actors, but his solid performance as another military officer earned him good reviews.

Disney wanted work to begin on *Tough Guys* but there were various hold-ups; Douglas had to go to Washington to testify before Congress about abuse of the elderly and then Burt decided there was a picture in France he wanted to make with Alain Delon, which was then cancelled when the director died. But he was also required in Germany to appear in *Sins of the Fathers* as the manufacturer of chemicals whose son-in-law turns the enterprise into the means of mass extermination. Julie Christie played his daughter. The film was a German-Italian-French co-production mini-series for TV and did not appear on American or British screens for a further two years.

At this time a new lady came into Burt's life. She was 33-year-old Susan Schere whom he met at a party. She was born in Santa Barbara and had graduated from Marymount College. As usual, he remained cautiously silent about his private life, giving nothing away about his break-up from Jackie, or his new-found love, Susan. 'I have always been secretive about my life,' he told me. 'People think because you're an actor and can perform on stage or in front of the cameras that you are outgoing and extrovert. I'm only those things with people I know. I'm not easy with strangers, as most reporters and journalists are. It's hard for me to know what the public has a right to know about me, and what they haven't a right to know.'

At first, before becoming romantically involved with Susan, Burt had asked her to become his secretary. Within months they had fallen love. He then promoted her to production co-ordinator on his films. Meanwhile, his daughter Joanna had progressed to producing films, her first being *Ruthless People* made in 1985 (released in 1986).

His children, now all grown up, seemed to accept Susan and did not seem to mind the 38-year age gap. 'They love Susan just about as much as I do,' he said. 'They tell me that being with Susan makes me look and act at least ten years younger.'

While his private life was getting back into some semblance of happy order, Disney complained that they had invested almost a million dollars in *Tough Guys* with no results. It was looking as though the Lancaster-Douglas screen reunion might never happen. But eventually, in the spring of 1986, filming began.

Both Burt and Kirk had a great time making the film, even though it never was going to live up to the expectations of so many. 'It's a film that spoofs both our careers,' Lancaster told me. 'It probably said a lot about the way we feel today, Kirk and me. There we are, two swashbuckling rogues who don't like what they find in the modern world, especially the lack of chivalry. So they go back to their old ways, to do things the way they did them 30 years ago. Only now the world doesn't work that way. Nobody holds up trains any more. These two bandits are not what they used to be, and neither are Kirk and me.'

To Kirk the film had one mission. 'We were creating make-believe with no aim but to entertain,' he said. 'I think that's really a very worthwhile purpose, to allow millions of people all over the world to forget their problems for a couple of hours and lose themselves in the make-believe world we were creating on screen for them.'

Despite the title of the film, Kirk was quick to point out that the reference was not to the real Kirk Douglas and Burt Lancaster. 'After doing a scene, I didn't go around saying, "I'm a tough guy." I might say, "Oh, my back aches!" Burt and me, we're not so tough. He loves opera and I love poetry.'

The ever-lengthening career links between Lancaster and Douglas really did make it difficult for some people to distinguish one from the other, as Laurence Olivier experienced when they were all making *The Devil's Disciple*. Kirk had a favourite example of this sort of confusion: 'Burt and I were once sitting in a booth in Ruby's Restaurant in Palm Springs. A guy who's drunk walks in, sits down next to me and says, "Mr Mitchum, I want to tell you how great you were in *Trapeze*." '

Charlton Heston, one of Lancaster's and Douglas's generation of actors, has a similar story. 'A man approached Jeff Chandler and said, "Excuse me for intruding upon your privacy, but I just wanted you to know how much I admired you in *Ben Hur*." Chandler replied, "But that wasn't me in *Ben Hur*." The man said, "If you're not Burt Lancaster, then who the hell are you?" '

Tough Guys opened in September 1986. It had been made very quickly, and it showed. '*Tough Guys* is unalloyed hokum that proves a sad waste of talent on the parts of co-stars Burt Lancaster and Kirk Douglas,' said *Variety*. 'It's all silly, meaningless and vaguely depressing, since the awareness lingers throughout that both actors are capable of much, much more than is demanded of them here.'

They would not get another chance to resolve the situation. Towards the end of 1986, Kirk had a pacemaker installed. The need for it, due to an unusually slow heartbeat that caused him to faint, frustrated him. A few weeks after its installation, he returned to Cedars for a check-up and there, in the waiting room was Burt, waiting for his annual check-up. They did not discuss their reasons for being there, just smiled, and when they were both called at the same time, each went through different doors. Douglas did not fail to notice Burt's 'voluminous medical file'.

Lancaster went back to doing another TV movie but one which was something of a labour of love for him, playing the title role in *Barnum*, the flamboyant showman in nineteenth-century America.

In 1987, he returned to Italy to make *Control* for cable TV. He played a retired nuclear scientist who is summoned by Ingrid Thulin, as head of a nuclear fallout shelter manufacturer, to test the shelter. He chooses 15 people, including Ben Gazzara and Kate Nelligan, and convinces them that war has really broken out to make the test more authentic.

He remained in Italy to make a very brief appearance in a movie called *The Betrothed*, which was never shown in America or Britain.

Then he was in *The Jeweller's Shop* which was based on a story written by Karol Wojtyla who became Pope John Paul II. Set in Poland in 1939, it concerns two couples who marry in Cracow and buy their wedding rings from Burt Lancaster's jeweller's shop where he explains to them the significance of their actions and the rings which will bind them together even after death.

At the press conference to promote the film, Lancaster said how impressed he was with the story but the film failed to gain a wide showing and was hardly seen.

In 1988 he thought he had found his *On Golden Pond*. *Rocket Gibraltar* was made by Columbia and was for cinema release. Lancaster played a blacklisted writer who, in his old age, gathers his family around him at his home on Long Island. He announces he is soon to die and declares his great love for the sea. When the writer dies, he is given a Viking funeral by his children who cast him adrift in his burning boat.

But there were stirrings within the Columbia offices where David Puttnam was reigning briefly as its head. Among the upheavals was the removal from the picture of director Amos Poe who was then replaced by Daniel Petrie. When the film was finished, it was shelved.

As if having his hard work so casually dismissed was not enough, Lancaster next underwent the humiliation of having a film pulled out from under him because of his age and health. He should have been in *Old Gringo*, produced by Jane Fonda who had promised him the starring role. But the necessary insurance needed to cover him was refused. No insurance company was prepared to take a chance on him. Nevertheless, some kind of spoken promise was made that this would not prevent him from making the film, yet he was suddenly replaced by Gregory Peck.

Lancaster promptly sued the producers for his estimated loss of earnings which came to 1,500,000 dollars.

On the political front, Lancaster continued to show liberal sympathies on TV in support of ACLU, which had been criticized by presidential candidate George Bush. He also maintained his cultural links by reading Ogden Nash's verses in a performance of Saint-Saëns's *Carnival of Animals* with the California Chamber Virtuosi at the Smothers Theater at Pepperdine University in San Francisco in 1989.

Now offered only small roles, he accepted one in *Field of Dreams* with Kevin Costner. It was only a cameo but it gave him the chance to be in a movie that was widely seen. It was a mystical film about a farmer (Costner) who hears a voice telling him to transform his corn field into a baseball diamond. The voice sends him on an odyssey across America, through time, on a mission to make forgotten dreams come true. Along the way he meets Lancaster, a saintly but ghostly old codger with unfulfilled wishes, and James Earl Jones, as a reclusive writer.

'A wonderful film,' is how *Empire* magazine described it. *Variety* said, 'In spite of a script hobbled with cloying aphorisms and shameless sentimentality, *Field of Dreams* sustains a dreamy mood in which the idea of baseball is distilled to its purest essence: a game that stands for unsullied innocence in a cruel, imperfect world.' The film was a hit in America, less so in Britain. Lancaster was glad to be a part of it. It was his last appearance in a made-for-the-cinema movie.

He next received the kind of offer he had always turned down – to appear in a TV commercial. This was for Foster's Lager and, to the surprise of many, he accepted because, he said, 'Bill Forsyth was directing them and each commercial was like a short story. I wanted to work with Bill again and this seemed a good way of achieving that. And I'm sure if I get into trouble with my acting, Bill will help me out!'

He and Susan arrived in Britain in December 1989 and he made two 70-second commercials under Forsyth's direction, each costing in the region of half a million pounds. What Lancaster's share of that was, he didn't say.

In 1990 he starred in another TV film, yet another retelling of *The Phantom of the Opera*, in which he played the managing director of the Paris Opera House, Charles Dance playing the Phantom. One of the things Burt said he enjoyed most about making the film was having the chance to hear operatic excerpts sung by members of the Hungarian State Opera. He was still an opera buff but he rarely went in 1989 because, he said, 'the voices are not around'.

Lancaster's part was not from the Gaston Leroux novel but was the creation of Arthur Kopit who wrote the screenplay from his own stage play.

'Leroux's novel was schlocky even for its time; a real melodrama,' said Lancaster. 'The Phantom was a terrible man, a murderer who killed a lot of people. In Kopit's version, there is a link between my character and that of the Phantom that adds a new twist to the story.'

Under Tony Richardson's direction, the three-hour film suffered from a typically tight TV shooting schedule. It lacked any tension and looked like just another lavish TV film with little to distinguish it but Lancaster's presence. But nevertheless it attracted much attention when it was screened in Britain on the BBC in August 1990.

He had other projects, including another mini-series, this one with Sidney Poitier called *Separate But Equal*. Susan was working on the picture as production co-ordinator. Just before they were due in South Carolina to begin filming, Burt suddenly proposed to Susan, and she accepted.

Lancaster announced, 'I'm getting married because the time is right. This is what we want. We're doing the wedding privately – just the family.'

Not even Kirk Douglas was in on this one as not a single celebrity was included in what Burt was determined would not be a media circus. Including the bride and groom, only fourteen people gathered in the garden room at the Four Seasons Hotel in Beverly Hills in September 1990. Lancaster's daughters Susan, Joanna and Sighle served as witnesses. James was also there, as was William, as well as Susan's own 21-year-old son John and her mother. The only business associates included were Burt's business manager Jack Ostrow and his wife.

The ceremony was conducted by Judge Wopner, famous on American TV for his series *The People's Court*. Burt actually bought a new suit for this special event – a double-breasted black suit. Susan dressed very simply in a lightly striped suit and white pill-box hat with a small veil.

Burt looked trim, having lost a lot of weight in a very short time. He insisted his loss of weight was due to dieting but he looked sadly gaunt. And, as it turned out, he was not well, which may have precipitated his decision to marry, although he said that Susan convinced him they should get wed after hearing that Gene Kelly, then 77, had married his 31-year-old bride in July.

Two days after the wedding, Burt and Susan flew down to South Carolina to begin work on *Separate But Equal*. Their future plans included going to Washington DC when the film was finished, and then returning to Los Angeles to decide where to take their honeymoon. They did not get the chance. And the film was never finished.

On 1 December Burt went to visit a friend in a nursing home where he himself became unwell. He lost all feeling down his right side and his speech became slurred. He was rushed to hospital where tests confirmed that he had suffered a massive stroke. He underwent emergency treatment for four hours in a battle once again to save his life.

A hospital spokesman told reporters, 'I think he's going to be okay. He's a tough old bird.' Jack Ostrow said that Burt was 'in fine spirits'.

But, as his condition stabilized, it became clear that his right side remained paralysed and he was struggling to speak. Now Burt had become what he had always dreaded – he was, he decided, a burden to other people. But neither Susan, nor his children looked upon him that way.

When he was well enough to leave hospital, Susan took him back to their Los Angeles flat. Their Christmas was a muted one, brightened only by the fact that Burt had beaten death yet again. All he hoped for was to be able to regain his strength and the feeling in his right side, and walk out of his apartment block.

He never did. For four more years, he remained a prisoner in his apartment, unable to move freely, struggling to speak, knowing that his days as an actor had this time finally come to an end.

He saw few visitors; he could not bear anyone to see him in his condition. Kirk Douglas did visit, so did his children. Most other well-wishers he tried to discourage from coming; he did not want sympathy or to be thought of as a cripple. For his remaining years he was unable to come to terms with his disease.

Reporters inquired after him, TV interviewers sought to gain access to his home for an 'exclusive', but Susan, nursing him constantly, politely turned them all away. He did not want the world to see him then but to remember him as he had been.

Kirk Douglas hated to see his friend dissipating and paid a small public tribute to him at an American Film Institute gala evening thrown in Douglas's honour in 1992. He said that he knew Burt wanted to be there that night but was not well enough to make it. He said little more, keeping his private thoughts to himself.

Lancaster's condition slowly deteriorated until, on 21 October 1994, he died at home with Susan by his side. Until then, the world had heard hardly more than a word about him. It was the way he wanted it.

The last four years of his life were a sad end to such a vibrant personality. If he wanted so desperately not to be seen in those final years but to be remembered as he was, then fortunately he had already prepared a small list of films which, he told me in 1986, he would most like to be remembered for.

'There are not many,' he said, 'just a handful, that I liked myself in and would hope to be remembered for. *From Here to Eternity, Sweet Smell of Success, Elmer Gantry, The Leopard* and *Atlantic City*. They are the highlights of my life in movies. I figure if people will remember me for those – even if for no others – then I'll be a satisfied man when my time comes.'

Afterword

From an interview with Burt Lancaster in 1982

I won't write my autobiography. I've had a lot of offers, but I have nothing I want to say that I can't say either on film or to people like you, provided you write what I say and not what you wish I'd say. I won't write about my life because there are things that are strictly private and I have no desire to tell the whole truth about myself. I want to keep a little of it back.

I admit that when I was a kid I thought acting was real sissy stuff but I did it at school because I got extra marks for it which meant I could go to summer camp which was a really special thing for a kid living in East Harlem in those days. I was into athletics, and what I wanted to do was perform in a circus. So I ran away to join the circus. So I was in excellent physical condition when Lady Luck took over and made me an actor in movies.

It was all luck; being the right man in the right place at the right time. If I'd started as a bit part actor in films instead of going on Broadway I might never have become an important actor because when you start in bit parts, you can get stuck there, or you might come to the attention of the public very slowly. But being in a Broadway play, in a good part and being exciting in it was a showcase. I also got a break because I had the physical equipment for movies. How you look, how you move is so important, and I was physically exciting and so I did well at the beginning in movies.

And it was luck that I came in at the right time when drawing-room dramas were going out of style and I was part of a new fashion that was tough, less polished, gritty. I recognized that and exploited that side of myself, but I always wanted to reach new horizons – and always will.

I thought I would probably quit acting by the time I was sixty and just produce films. That's what I wanted to do at the very beginning – produce films with Harold Hecht and later James Hill too. We wanted a company that was different to the other actors who produced because lots of them did it just to turn a quick buck through tax concessions. We wanted a company that continued and we weren't concerned with turning a quick buck but in just being independent.

After the war, America went through an enormous catharsis and I knew that people needed more from movies than just pap or even good entertainment; they also wanted some of the realities of life, so we made films that reflected that, I think.

But everything changes. We became too big as a company and we never wanted to be that big. And we all got older. I'm at an age now where I can't play romantic leads but there are a few roles when the older man gets the young girl, like William Holden in *Breezy*. I may be older but I'm not immune to the charms of a younger woman, even a nineteen-year-old.

An actor can always improve. God knows, I can improve. I have no illusion about that. I am always trying to reach new horizons.

It's true that I'm a very emotional person – even a violent person. But there's a part of me that doesn't like what goes on inside of me, so I try to control it. I've not become more tolerant; I just try to stay calm. And I hope at the end I will have left something to be remembered by.

When I do go, I promise I won't make a fuss. I'll be like the old soldier who just drifts away quietly.

Bibliography

Bosworth, Patricia, *Montgomery Clift*, Bantam Books, 1978.

Braun, Eric, *Deborah Kerr*, W H Allen, 1977.

Crowther, Bruce, *Burt Lancaster – A Life In Films*, Robert Hale Ltd, 1991.

Douglas, Kirk, *The Ragman's Son*, Simon and Schuster, 1988.

Gardner, Ava, *Ava, My Story*, Transworld Publishers Ltd, 1990.

Gow, Gordon, in *Films and Filming*, interview with Burt Lancaster, January 1973.

Graham, Sheilah, *Confessions of a Hollywood Columnist*, William Morrow & Co (New York), 1969.

Hall, William, and Crawley, Tony, in *Game*, interview with Burt Lancaster, February 1975.

Hall, William, in *Photoplay*, interview with Burt Lancaster, August 1968.

Hardy, Phil, *The Western*, Aurum Press, 1983.

Hibbert, Tom, in *Empire*, interview with Michael Winner, November 1993.

Hill, James, *Rita Hayworth: A Memoir*, Simon and Schuster, 1983.

Hunter, Allan, *Burt Lancaster – The Man and His Movies*, Paul Harris Publishing, 1984.

Hunter, Allan, *Tony Curtis – The Man and His Movies*, Paul Harris Publishing, 1985.

Mann, Roderick, in the *Sunday Express*, interview with Burt Lancaster, 2 July 1972.

Morley, Sheridan, *The Other Side of the Moon*, Guild Publishing, 1985.

Munn, Michael, *Kirk Douglas – A Biography*, Robson Books Ltd, 1985.

Munn, Michael, *Tony Curtis – The Kid from the Bronx*, W H Allen, 1984.

Olivier, Laurence, *Confessions of an Actor*, Weidenfeld and Nicolson, 1982.

Shipman, David, *Judy Garland*, Fourth Estate, 1992.

Thompson, Douglas, in the *Radio Times*, 'Vocal Hero', 18-24 August 1990.

York, Michael, *Travelling Player*, Headline Book Publishing, 1991.

Walker, Alexander, *Audrey, Her True Story*, Weidenfeld and Nicolson, 1994.

Wallis, Hal B, and Higham, Charles, *Starmaker*, Macmillan, 1980.

Winters, Shelley, *Shelley, Also Known As Shirley*, Granada, 1981.

Zinnemann, Fred, *An Autobiography*, Bloomsbury Publishing, 1992.

Filmography

The Killers. 1946. Universal. Produced by Mark Hellinger. Directed by Robert Siodmak. Screenplay by Anthony Veiller, based on the short story by Ernest Hemingway. Photographed by Woody Bredell. Music by Miklos Rozsa. Cast: Burt Lancaster, Edmond O'Brien, Ava Gardner, Albert Dekker, Sam Levene, Charles McGraw, William Conrad. 105 minutes.

Desert Fury. 1947. Paramount. Produced by Hal Wallis. Screenplay by Robert Rossen. Photographed by Charles Lang in Technicolor. Music by Miklos Rozsa. Cast: Burt Lancaster, Lizabeth Scott, Wendell Corey, John Hodiak, Mary Astor. 96 minutes.

Brute Force. 1947. Universal. Produced by Mark Hellinger. Directed by Jules Dassin. Screenplay by Richard Brooks, based on the short story by Robert Patterson. Photographed by William Daniels. Music by Miklos Rozsa. Cast: Burt Lancaster, Hume Cronyn, Charles Bickford, Yvonne de Carlo, Ella Raines, Ann Blyth, Anita Colby, Sam Levene, Charles McGraw, Howard Duff, Jeff Corey. 98 minutes.

Variety Girl. 1947. Paramount. Produced by Daniel Dare. Directed by George Marshall. Screenplay by Edmund Hartmann, Frank Tashlin, Monte Brice and Robert Welch. Photographed by Lionel Lindon and Stuart Thompson. Cast: Mary Hatcher, Olga San Juan, De Forrest Kelley, William

Demarest and guests stars Bing Crosby, Burt Lancaster, Gary Cooper, Alan Ladd, Bob Hope, William Holden, Lizabeth Scott, Robert Preston, Veronica Lake, Sterling Hayden, Macdonald Carey. 93 minutes.

I Walk Alone. 1948. Paramount. Produced by Hal Wallis. Directed by Byron Haskin. Screenplay by Charles Schnee, based on the play *Beggers Are Coming To Town* by Theodore Reeves, adapted by Robert Smith and John Bright. Photographed by Leo Tover. Music by Victor Young. Cast: Burt Lancaster, Kirk Douglas, Lizabeth Scott, Wendell Corey, Marc Lawrence, Mike Mazurki. 98 minutes.

All My Sons. 1948. Universal. Produced by Chester Erskine. Directed by Irving Reis. Screenplay by Chester Erskine from the play by Arthur Miller. Photographed by Russell Metty. Music by Leith Stevens. Cast: Edward G Robinson, Burt Lancaster, Mady Christians, Louisa Horton, Howard Duff, Frank Conroy, Arlene Francis. 94 minutes.

Sorry, Wrong Number. 1948. Paramount. Produced by Hal Wallis. Directed by Anatole Litvak. Screenplay by Lucille Fletcher from her own radio play. Photographed by Sol Polito. Music by Franz Waxman. Cast: Barbara Stanwyck, Burt Lancaster, Wendell Corey, Ann Richards, Ed Begley, Leif Erickson, William Conrad. 89 minutes.
    Academy Award Nomination: Barbara Stanwyck.

Kiss the Blood Off My Hands, UK title: *Blood On My Hands*. 1948. Universal/Norma. Produced by Harold Hecht. Directed by Norman Foster. Screenplay by Leonardo Bercovici from the novel by Gerald Butler. Photographed by Russell Metty. Music by Miklos Rozsa. Cast: Burt Lancaster, Joan Fontaine, Robert Newton, Lewis Russell. 79 minutes.

Criss Cross. 1949. Universal. Produced by Michael Kraike. Directed by Robert Siodmak. Screenplay by Daniel Fuchs from the novel by Don Tracy. Photographed by Franz Planer. Music by Miklos Rozsa. Cast: Burt Lancaster, Yvonne de Carlo, Dan Duryea, Stephen McNally, Richard Long, (Anthony Curtis appeared way down the cast list). 87 minutes.

Rope of Sand. 1949. Paramount. Produced by Hal Wallis. Directed by William Dieterle. Screenplay by Walter Doniger. Photographed by Charles Lang. Music by Franz Waxman. Cast: Burt Lancaster, Paul Henreid, Claude Rains, Peter Lorre, Corrine Calvet, Sam Jaffe. 105 minutes.

The Flame and the Arrow. 1950. Warner Bros. Produced by Harold Hecht and Frank Ross. Directed by Jacques Tourneur. Screenplay by Waldo Salt. Photographed by Ernest Haller in Technicolor. Music by Max Steiner. Cast: Burt Lancaster, Virginia Mayo, Robert Douglas, Frank Allenby, Nick Cravat. 88 minutes.

Mister 880. 1950. Twentieth Century-Fox. Produced by Julian Blaustein. Directed by Edmund Goulding. Screenplay by Robert Riskin, from articles by St Clare McKelway. Photographed by Joseph La Shelle. Music by Sol Kaplan. Cast: Burt Lancaster, Edmund Gwenn, Dorothy McGuire, Millard Mitchell. 90 minutes.
   Academy Award Nomination: Edmund Gwenn (Best Supporting Actor).

Vengeance Valley. 1951. Metro-Goldwyn-Mayer. Produced by Nicholas Nayfack. Directed by Richard Thorpe. Screenplay by Irving Ravetch, from the novel by Luke Short. Photographed by George Folsey in Technicolor. Music by Rudloph G Kopp. Cast: Burt Lancaster, Robert Walker, Joanne Dru, Ray Collins, John Ireland, Carleton Carpenter, Hugh O'Brian. 83 minutes.

Jim Thorpe – All-American, UK title: *Man of Bronze*. 1951. Warner Bros. Produced by Everett Freeman. Directed by Michael Curtiz. Screenplay by Douglas Morrow and Everett

Freeman, based on the autobiography by Jim Thorpe and Russell J. Birdwell. Photographed by Ernest Haller. Music by Max Steiner. Cast: Burt Lancaster, Charles Bickford, Steve Cochran, Phyllis Thaxter, Dick Wesson. 107 minutes.

Ten Tall Men. 1951. Columbia/Norma. Produced by Harold Hecht. Directed by Willis Goldbeck. Screenplay by Roland Kibbee and Frank Davis. Photographed by William Snyder in Technicolor. Music by David Buttolph. Cast: Burt Lancaster, Gilbert Roland, Keiron Moore, John Dehner, Jody Lawrance, Mike Mazurki, George Tobias, Mari Blanchard. 97 minutes.

The Crimson Pirate. 1952. Warner Bros/Norma. Produced by Harold Hecht. Directed by Robert Siodmak (some scenes were directed by Burt Lancaster and Roland Kibbee). Screenplay Roland Kibbee. Photographed by Otte Heller in Technicolor. Music by William Alwyn. Cast: Burt Lancaster, Nick Cravat, Torin Thatcher, James Hayter, Noel Purcell, Eva Bartok. Christopher Lee, Dana Wynter, Frank Pettingill. 104 minutes.

Come Back Little Sheba. 1952. Paramount. Produced by Hal Wallis. Directed by Daniel Mann. Screenplay by Ketti Frings, based on the play by William Inge. Photographed by James Wong Howe. Music by Franz Waxman. Cast: Shirley Booth, Burt Lancaster, Terry Moore, Richard Jaekel, Philip Ober. 99 minutes.
   Academy Award: Shirley Booth. Academy Award Nomination: Terry Moore.

South Sea Woman. 1953. Warner Bros. Produced by Sam Bischoff. Directed by Arthur Lubin. Screenplay by Edwin Blum from the play by William M. Rankin. Photographed by Ted McCord. Music by David Buttolph. Cast: Burt Lancaster, Virginia Mayo, Chuck Connors, Arthur Shields, Veola Vonn, Paul Burke. 89 minutes.

From Here to Eternity. 1953. Columbia. Produced by Buddy Adler. Directed by Fred Zinnemann. Screenplay by Daniel Taradash from the novel by James Jones. Photographed by Burnett Guffey. Music by George Duning. Cast: Burt Lancaster, Deborah Kerr, Montgomery Clift, Frank Sinatra, Ernest Borgnine, Philip Ober, Mickey Shaughnessy, Jack Warden. 118 minutes.

Academy Awards: Best Picture, Daniel Taradash (Best Screenplay), Fred Zinnemann (Best Director), Burnett Guffey (Best Black and White Photography), Frank Sinatra (Best Supporting Actor), Donna Reed (Best Supporting Actress). Other Academy Award Nominations: George Duning (Best Musical Score), Burt Lancaster and Montgomery Clift competed for Best Actor, Deborah Kerr (Best Actress). Burt Lancaster was voted Best Actor by the New York Film Critics.

Three Sailors and a Girl. 1953. Warner Bros. Produced by Sammy Cahn. Directed by Roy De Ruth. Screenplay by Roland Kibbee and Deverey Freeman from the play *The Butter and Egg Man* by George S Kaufmann. Photographed by Carl Guthrie in Technicolor. Music by Sammy Fain and Sammy Cahn. Cast: Jane Powell, Gordon Macrae, Gene Nelson, with guest appearance by Burt Lancaster. 95 minutes.

His Majesty O'Keefe. 1954. Warner Bros/Norma. Produced by Harold Hecht. Directed by Byron Haskin. Screenplay by Borden Chase and James Hill. Photographed by Otto Heller in Technicolor. Music by Robert Farnon. Cast: Burt Lancaster, Joan Rice, André Morell, Abraham Sofaer, Benson Fong, Tessa Prendergast. 92 minutes.

Apache. 1954. United Artists/Hecht-Lancaster. Produced by Harold Hecht. Directed by Robert Aldrich. Screenplay by James R Webb from the novel *Bronco Apache* by Paul I Wellman. Photographed by Ernest Laszlo in Technicolor. Music by David Raksin. Cast: Burt Lancaster, Jean Peters, John

McIntire, Charles Buchinski (later Charles Bronson), Monte Blue, John Dehner. 91 minutes.

Vera Cruz. 1954. United Artists/Hecht-Lancaster. Produced by James Hill. Directed by Robert Aldrich. Screenplay by Roland Kibbee, James R Webb and Borden Chase. Photographed by Ernest Laszlo in Superscope and Technicolor. Music by Hugo Friedhofer. Cast: Gary Cooper, Burt Lancaster, Denise Darcel, Cesar Romero, Sarita Montiel, Jack Elam. 94 minutes.

The Kentuckian. 1955. United Artists/Hecht-Lancaster. Produced by Harold Hecht. Directed by Burt Lancaster. Screenplay by A B Guthrie from the novel *The Gabriel Horn* by Felix Holt. Photographed by Ernest Laszlo in Technicolor and Cinemascope. Music by Bernard Hermann. Cast: Burt Lancaster, Diana Lynn, Dianne Foster, John McIntire, Una Merkel, Walter Matthau. 104 minutes.

The Rose Tattoo. 1955. Paramount. Produced by Hal Wallis. Directed by Daniel Mann. Screenplay by Tennessee Williams from his own play. Photographed by James Wong Howe. Music by Alex North. Cast: Anna Magnani, Burt Lancaster, Marisa Pavan, Ben Cooper, Virginia Grey, Jo Van Fleet. 117 minutes.

Academy Awards: James Wong Howe (Best Photogaphy in Black and White), Anna Magnani (Best Actress), Best Art Direction. Other Academy Award Nominations: Best Picture, Alex North (Best Music, Marisa Pavan (Best Supporting Actress).

Trapeze. 1956. United Artists/Hecht-Lancaster. Produced by James Hill. Directed by Carol Reed. Screenplay by James R. Webb from the novel *The Killing Frost* by Max Catto. Photographed by Robert Krasker in Cinemascope and Color by De Luxe. Music by Malcolm Arnold. Cast: Burt Lancaster, Tony Curtis, Gina Lollobrigida, Thomas Gomez, Katy Jurado, John Puleo. 105 minutes.

The Rainmaker. 1956. Paramount. Produced by Paul Nathan and Hal Wallis. Directed by Joseph Anthony. Screenplay by N. Richard Nash from his own play. Photographed by Charles Lang in VistaVision and Technicolor. Music by Alex North. Cast: Katharine Hepburn, Burt Lancaster, Wendell Corey, Lloyd Bridges, Earl Holliman, Cameron Prud'homme, Wallace Ford. 121 minutes.

Academy Award Nominations: Katharine Hepburn (Best Actress), Alex North (Best Music).

Gunfight at the OK Corral. 1957. Paramount. Produced by Hal Wallis. Directed by John Sturges. Screenplay by Leon Uris. Photographed by Charles Lang in VistaVision and Technicolor. Music by Dimitri Tiomkin. Cast: Burt Lancaster, Kirk Douglas, John Ireland, Frank Faylen, Jo Van Fleet, Rhonda Fleming, De Forrest Kelley, Earl Holliman, Lyle Bettger, Dennis Hopper, Lee Van Cleef. 122 minutes.

Sweet Smell of Success. 1957. United Artists/Norma-Curtleigh. Produced by James Hill. Directed by Alexander MacKendrick. Screenplay by Ernest Lehman and Clifford Odets. Photographed by James Wong Howe. Music by Elmer Bernstein. Cast: Burt Lancaster, Tony Curtis, Susan Harrison, Martin Milner, Sam Levene, Emile Meyer, Barbara Nichols, Jeff Donnell, Laurene Tuttle, Edith Atwater, Queenie Smith. 96 minutes.

Run Silent Run Deep. 1958. United Artists/Hecht-Hill-Lancaster. Produced by William Schorr. Directed by Robert Wise. Screenplay by John Gay from the novel by Edward L Beach. Photographed by Russell Harlan. Music by Franz Waxman. Cast: Clark Gable, Burt Lancaster, Jack Warden, Brad Dexter, Nick Cravat, Don Rickles, Eddie Foy III. 93 minutes.

Separate Tables. 1958. United Artists/Hecht-Hill-Lancaster. Produced by Harold Hecht. Directed by Delbert Mann. Screenplay by John Gay and Terence Rattigan from the play by

Rattigan. Photographed by Charles Lang. Music by David Raksin. Cast: Burt Lancaster, Rita Hayworth, David Niven, Wendy Hiller, Deborah Kerr, Gladys Cooper, Cathleen Nesbitt, Rod Taylor. 98 minutes.

Academy Awards: David Niven (Best Actor), Wendy Hiller (Best Supporting Actress). Other Academy Award Nominations: Best Picture, John Gay and Terence Rattigan (Screenplay), Charles Lang (Photography), David Raksin (Music), Deborah Kerr (Actress).

The Devil's Disciple. 1959. United Artists/Bryna/Hecht-Hill-Lancaster. Produced by Harold Hecht. Directed by Guy Hamilton (who replaced Alexander MacKendrick). Screenplay by John Dighton and Roland Kibbee from the play by George Bernard Shaw. Photographed by Jack Hildyard. Music by Richard Rodney Bennett. Cast: Burt Lancaster, Kirk Douglas, Laurence Olivier, Eva Le Gallienne, Harry Andrews, Basil Sydney, George Rose, Janette Scott, Neil McCallum. 82 minutes.

The Unforgiven. 1960. United Artists/Hecht-Hill-Lancaster. Produced by James Hill. Directed by John Huston. Screenplay by Ben Maddow from the novel *The Siege at Dancing Bear* by Alan le May. Photographed by Franz Planer in Panavision and Technicolor. Music by Dimitri Tiomkin. Cast: Burt Lancaster, Audrey Hepburn, Audie Murphy, Charles Bickford, Lillian Gish, Doug McClure, John Saxon, Albert Salmi, Joseph Wiseman. 125 minutes.

Elmer Gantry. 1960. United Artists. Produced by Bernard Smith. Directed by Richard Brooks. Screenplay by Richard Brooks from the book by Sinclair Lewis. Photographed by John Alton in Eastmancolor. Music by André Previn. Cast: Burt Lancaster, Jean Simmons, Arthur Kennedy, Shirley Jones, Dean Jagger, Patti Page, Edward Andrews, Philip Ober, Rex Ingram. 146 minutes.

Academy Awards: Burt Lancaster (Best Actor), Shirley Jones

(Supporting Actress), Richard Brooks (Screenplay). Other Academy Award Nominations: Best Picture, André Previn (Music). Burt Lancaster was voted Best Actor by the New York Film Critics.

The Young Savages. 1961. United Artists/Contemporary. Produced by Pat Duggan. Directed by John Frankenheimer. Screenplay by Edward Anhalt and J P Miller from the novel *A Matter of Conviction* by Evan Hunter. Photographed by Lionel Lindon. Music by David Amram. Cast: Burt Lancaster, Shelley Winters, Dina Merrill, Edward Andrews, Telly Savalas, Milton Selzer. 103 minutes.

Judgment at Nuremberg. 1961. United Artists/Roxlom. Produced and directed by Stanley Kramer. Screenplay by Abby Mann from his television play. Photographed by Ernest Laszlo. Music by Ernest Gold. Cast: Spencer Tracy, Marlene Dietrich, Burt Lancaster, Richard Widmark, Maximilian Schell, Judy Garland, Montgomery Clift, William Shatner, Edward Binns, Werner Klemperer, Torben Meyer, Alan Baxter, Ray Teal. 190 minutes.
  Academy Awards: Abby Mann (Best Screenplay), Maximilian Schell (Best Supporting Actor). Academy Award Nominations: Best Picture, Stanley Kramer (Director), Ernest Laszlo (Photography), Spencer Tracy (Best Actor), Judy Garland (Supporting Actress), Montomgery Clift (Supporting Actor).

Birdman of Alcatraz. 1962. United Artists/Hecht-Hill-Lancaster. Produced by Stuart Miller and Guy Trosper. Directed by John Frankenheimer. Screenplay by Guy Trosper from the book by Thomas E Gaddis. Photographed by Burnett Guffey. Music by Elmer Bernstein. Cast: Burt Lancaster, Karl Malden, Thelma Ritter, Edmond O'Brien, Betty Field, Neville Brand, Hugh Marlowe, Telly Savalas, James Westerfield. 148 minutes.
  Academy Award Nominations: Burnett Guffey (Photo-

graphy), Burt Lancaster (Best Actor), Thelma Ritter (Supporting Actress), Telly Savalas (Supporting Actor). Burt Lancaster was voted Best Actor by the New York Film Critics.

A Child Is Waiting. 1963. United Artists. Produced by Stanley Kramer and Philip Lagner. Directed by John Cassavetes. Screenplay by Abby Mann from his television play. Photographed by Joseph La Shelle. Music by Ernest Gold. Cast: Burt Lancaster, Judy Garland, Bruce Ritchey, Steven Hill, Gena Rowlands, Paul Stewart, Lawrence Tierney. 104 minutes.

The List of Adrian Messenger. 1963. Universal/Joel. Produced by Edward Lewis. Directed by John Huston. Screenplay by Anthony Veiller from the novel by Philip MacDonald. Photographed by Joe MacDonald. Music by Jerry Goldsmith. Cast: George C Scott, Kirk Douglas, Clive Brook, Dana Wynter, Jacques Roux, Walter Tony Huston, Herbert Marshall, Bernard Archard, Gladys Cooper, quest appearances by Robert Mitchum, Frank Sinatra, Burt Lancaster and Tony Curtis. 98 minutes.

The Leopard (Il Gattopardo). 1963. Titanus/20th Century-Fox/ Pathe Cinema/SGC. Produced by Goffredo Lombardo. Directed by Luchino Visconti. Screenplay by Luchino Visconti, Suso Cecchi d'Amico, Pasquale Festa Campanile, Enrico Medioli, Massino Franciosa, from the novel by Giuseppe Tomasi di Lampedusa. Photographed by Giuseppe Rotunno in Technirama and Technicolor. Music by Nino Rota. Cast: Burt Lancaster, Claudia Cardinale, Alain Delon, Paolo Stoppa, Serge Reggiani, Leslie French, Romelo Valli. 205 minutes.

Seven Days in May. 1964. Paramount/Joel. Produced by Edward Lewis. Directed by John Frankenheimer. Screenplay by Rod Serling from the novel by Fletcher Knebel and Charles W Bailey II. Photographed by Ellsworth Fredericks. Music by Jerry Goldsmith. Cast: Kirk Douglas, Burt Lancaster, Fredric March, Ava Gardner, Martin Balsam, Edmond O'Brien,

George Macready, John Houseman, Whit Bissell, Hugh Marlow, Andrew Duggan, Malcolm Atterbury, Colette Jackson. 120 minutes.

The Train. 1965. United Artists/Ariane/Dear Films. Produced by Jules Bricken. Director by John Frankenheimer, who replaced Arthur Penn. Screenplay by Franklin Coen, Frank Davis and Walter Bernstein from the book *Le Front de l'Art* by Ross Valland. Photographed by Jean Tournier. Music by Maurice Jarre. Cast: Burt Lancaster, Paul Scofield, Jeanne Moreau, Michael Simon, Wolfgang Preiss, Suzanne Flon, Albert Remy. 140 minutes.

The Hallelujah Trail. 1965. United Artists/Mirisch/Kappa. Produced and directed by John Sturges. Screenplay by John Gay from the novel by Bill Gulick. Photographed by Robert Surtees in Technicolor and Ultra Panavision 70 (Cinerama). Music by Elmer Bernstein. Cast: Burt Lancaster, Lee Remick, Jim Hutton, Pamela Tiffin, Donald Pleasence, Brian Keith, Martin Landau, Dub Taylor, Whit Bassell, Val Avery. 167 minutes.

The Professionals. 1966. Columbia/Pax. Produced and directed by Richard Brooks. Screenplay by Richard Brooks from the novel *A Mule for the Marquesa* by Frank O'Rourke. Photographed by Conrad Hall in Technicolor and Panavision. Music by Maurice Jarre. Cast: Burt Lancaster, Lee Marvin, Robert Ryan, Claudia Cardinale, Jack Palance, Woody Strode, Ralph Bellamy. 123 minutes.

Academy Award Nominations: Richard Brooks (Screenplay), Conrad Hall (Photography).

The Scalphunters. 1968. United Artists/Bristol/Norlan. Produced by Jules Levy, Arthur Gardner and Arnold Laven. Directed by Sydney Pollack. Screenplay by William Norton. Photographed by Duke Callaghan and Richard Moore in Panavision and Color by De Luxe. Music by Elmer Bernstein.

Cast: Burt Lancaster, Shelley Winters, Telly Savalas, Ossie Davis, Dabney Coleman, Nick Cravat, Paul Picerni. 102 minutes.

The Swimmer. 1968. Columbia. Produced by Frank Perry and Roger Lewis. Directed by Fank Perry. Screenplay by Eleanor Perry from the short story by John Cheever. Photographed by David L Quaid in Technicolor. Music by Marvin Hamlisch. Cast: Burt Lancaster, Janice Rule, Kim Hunter, Diana Muldaur, Cornelia Otis Skinner, Marge Champion, Joan Rivers, John Garfield Jnr, House Jameson, Jan Milner, Dolph Sweet, Louise Troy, Diana Van de Vlis, Rose Gregorio. 94 minutes.

Castle Keep. 1969. Columbia. Produced by Martin Ransohoff and John Calley. Directed by Sydney Pollack. Screenplay by Daniel Taradash and David Rayfiel from the novel by William Eastlake. Photographed by Henri Decaë in Technicolor and Panavision. Music by Michel Legrand. Cast: Burt Lancaster, Peter Falk, Jean Pierre Aumont, Patrick O'Neal, Al Freeman Jnr, Scott Wilson, Tony Bill, Bruce Dern, Astrid Heeren, Michael Conrad. 107 minutes.

The Gypsy Moths. 1969. Metro-Goldwyn-Mayer. Produced by Hal Landers and Bobby Roberts. Directed by John Frankenheimer. Screenplay by William Hanley from the novel by James Drought. Photographed by Philip Lathrop in Metrocolor. Aerial photography by Carl Boenisch. Music by Elmer Bernstein. Cast: Burt Lancaster, Deborah Kerr, Gene Hackman, Scott Wilson, William Windom, Bonnie Bedelia, Sheree North. 110 minutes.

Airport. 1970. Universal/Ross Hunter. Produced by Jacques Mapes. Directed by George Seaton. Screenplay by George Seaton from the novel by Arthur Hailey. Photographed by Ernest Laszlo in Technicolor and Todd-AO. Music by Alfred Newman. Cast: Burt Lancaster, Dean Martin, Jean Seberg,

Helen Hayes, Van Heflin, Jacqueline Bisset, George Kennedy, Maureen Stapleton, Barry Nelson, Dana Wynter, Lloyd Nolan, Barbara Hale, Gary Collins, Jessie Royce Landis. 136 minutes.

Academy Awards: Helen Hayes (Best Supporting Actress). Other Academy Award Nominations: Best Picture, George Seaton (Best Screenplay), Ernest Laszlo (Best Photography), Alfred Newman (Best Music), Maureen Stapleton (Best Supporting Actress).

Valdez Is Coming. 1971. United Artists/Norlan. Produced by Ira Steiner. Directed by Edwin Sherin. Screenplay by Roland Kibbee and David Rayfiel. Photographed by Gabor Pogany in Color by De Luxe. Music by Charles Gross. Cast: Burt Lancaster, Susan Clark, Jon Cypher, Barton Heyman, Frank Silvera, Richard Jordan, Hector Elizondo. 90 minutes.

Lawman. 1971. United Artists/Scimitar. Produced and directed by Michael Winner. Screenplay by Gerald Wilson. Photographed by Robert Paynter in Technicolor. Music by Jerry Fielding. Cast: Burt Lancaster, Robert Ryan, Lee J Cobb, Sheree North, Robert Duvall, Joseph Wiseman, John McGiver, Albert Salmi, J D Cannon, Richard Jordan, John Beck. 99 minutes.

Ulzana's Raid. 1972. Universal. Produced and directed by Robert Aldrich. Screenplay by Alan Sharp. Photographed by Joseph Biroc in Technicolor. Music by Frank de Vol. Cast: Burt Lancaster, Bruce Davison, Jorge Luke, Richard Jaeckel, Lloyd Bochner. 103 minutes.

Scorpio. 1973. United Artists/Scimitar. Produced by Walter Mirisch. Directed by Michael Winner. Screenplay by David W. Rintels and Gerald Wilson. Photographed by Robert Paynter in Technicolor. Music by Jerry Fielding. Cast: Burt Lancaster, Alain Delon, Paul Scofield, J D Cannon, John Colicos, Gayle Hunnicutt. 114 minutes.

Executive Action. 1974. National General/Wakefield Orloff. Produced by Edward Lewis. Directed by David Miller. Screenplay by Dalton Trumbo from a story by Mark Lane and Donald Freed. Photographed by Robert Steadman (in colour). Music by Randy Edelman. Cast: Burt Lancaster, Robert Ryan, Will Geer, Gilbert Green, John Anderson, Ed Lauter. 91 minutes.

The Midnight Man. 1974. Universal/Norlan. Produced and directed by Roland Kibbee and Burt Lancaster. Screenplay by Roland Kibbee and Burt Lancaster from the novel *The Midnight Lady and the Mourning Man* by David Anthony. Photographed by Jack Priestley in Technicolor. Music by Dave Grusin. Cast: Burt Lancaster, Susan Clark, Cameron Mitchell, Morgan Woodward, Ed Lauter. 117 minutes.

Conversation Piece (*Gruppo di Famiglia in un Interno*). 1975. Rusconi/Gaumont/International. Produced by Giovanni Berto-lucci. Directed by Luchino Visconti. Screenplay by Luchino Visconti, Suso Cecchi d'Amico and Enrico Medioli. Photo-graphed by Pasqualino de Santis in Technicolor. Music by Franco Mannino. Cast: Burt Lancaster, Silvano Mangano, Helmut Berger, Claudia Marsani, Dominique Sanda, Claudia Cardinale. 122 minutes.

The Cassandra Crossing. 1976. ITC/ICP. Produced by Carlo Ponti and Lew Grade. Directed by George Pan Cosmatos. Screenplay by Tom Mankiewicz, Robert Katz and George Pan Cosmatos. Photographed by Ennio Guarnieri in Technicolor and Panavision. Music by Jerry Goldsmith. Cast: Sophia Loren, Richard Harris, Ava Gardner, Burt Lancaster, Martin Sheen, Ingrid Thulin, Lee Strasberg, John Philip Law, Lionel Stander, Ann Turkel, O J Simpson, Alida Valli. 129 minutes.

Buffalo Bill and the Indians. 1976. United Artists. Produced and directed by Robert Altman. Screenplay by Alan Rudolph and Robert Altman from the play *Indians* by Arthur Kopit.

Photographed by Paul Lohmann in colour and Panavision. Music by Richard Baskin. Cast: Paul Newman, Burt Lancaster, Joel Grey, Kevin McCarthy, Geraldine Chaplin, Harvey Keitel, John Considine, Denver Pyle, Pat McCormick, Shelley Duvall, Will Sampson. 125 minutes.

1900 (Novecento). 1977. 20th Century-Fox/Paramount/United Artists/PEA/Artemis. Produced by Alberto Grimaldi. Directed by Bernardo Bertolucci. Screenplay by Bernardo Bertolucci, Franco Arcalli and Giuseppe Storaro. Photographed by Vittorio Storaro in Technicolcor. Music by Ennio Morricone. Cast: Burt Lancaster, Robert de Niro, Gérard Depardieu, Dominique Sanda, Donald Sutherland, Sterling Hayden, Alida Valli. Two-part version was 245 minutes. Complete version, 320 minutes.

The Island of Dr Moreau. 1977. Cinema 77/AIP. Produced by John Temple-Smith and Skip Steloff. Directed by Don Taylor. Screenplay by John Herman Shaner and Al Ramrus from the novel by H G Wells. Photograhed by Gerry Fisher in Movielab Color. Music by Laurence Rosenthal. Cast: Burt Lancaster, Michael York, Nigel Davenport, Barbara Carrera, Richard Basehart, Nick Cravat. 98 minutes.

Twilight's Last Gleaming. 1977. Lorimar/Hemdale/Bavaria Studios. Produced by Merv Adelson and Helmut Jedele. Directed by Robert Aldrich. Screenplay by Ronald M Cohen and Edward Huebsch from the novel *Viper Three* by Walter Wager. Photographed by Robert Hauser in Technicolor. Music by Jerry Goldsmith. Cast: Burt Lancaster, Richard Widmark, Charles Durning, Melvyn Douglas, Paul Winfield, Burt Young, Joseph Cotten, Roscoe Lee Brown, Gerald S O'Loughlin, Charles Aidman. 146 minutes.

Go Tell the Spartans. 1978. Mar Vista Productions. Produced by Allan F. Bodoh and Mitchell Cannold. Directed by Ted Post. Screenplay by Wendell Mayes from the novel *Incident at Muc*

Wa by Daniel Ford. Photographed by Harry Stradling Jnr in CFI Color. Music by Dick Halligan. Cast: Burt Lancaster, Craig Wasson, Jonathan Goldsmith, Marc Singer, Joe Unger, Dennis Howard, David Clenner, Evan King, Dolph Sweet. 114 minutes.

Zulu Dawn. 1979. Samarkand/Lamitas. Produced by Nate Kohn and Barrie Saint Clair. Directed by Douglas Hickox. Screenplay by Cy Enfield and Anthony Storey. Photographed by Ousama Rawi in Technicolor and Panavision. Music by Elmer Bernstein. Cast: Burt Lancaster, Denholm Elliott, Peter O'Toole, John Mills, Simon Ward, Nigel Davenport, Michael Jayston, Ronald Lacey, Freddie Jones, Christopher Cazenove, Ronald Pickup, Anna Calder-Marshall. 117 minutes.

Cattle Annie and Little Britches. 1980. Hemdale/Monday. Produced by Rupert Hitzig and Alan King. Directed by Lamont Johnson. Screenplay by Robert Ward and David Eyre. Photographed by Larry Pizer in CFI Color. Music by Richard Greene. Cast: Burt Lancaster, Rod Steiger, Amanda Plummer, Diane Lane, John Savage, Scott Glenn. 96 minutes.

Atlantic City. 1981. Paramount/Cine-Neighbour/Selta Films-EK. Produced by Denis Heroux. Directed by Louis Malle. Screenplay by John Guare. Photographed by Richard Ciupka (in colour). Music by Michel Legrand. Cast: Burt Lancaster, Susan Sarandon, Kate Reid, Michel Piccoli, Hollis McLaren, Robert Joy. 105 minutes.

Academy Award Nominations: Burt Lancaster (Best Actor), John Guare (Best Screenplay), Best Picture, Susan Sarandon (Best Actress), Louis Malle (Best Director). British Film and Television Academy Awards: Louis Malle, Burt Lancaster. Burt Lancaster was voted Best Actor by the New York Film Critics, also by the National Society of Film Critics and the Los Angeles Film Critics Association.

The Skin (*La Pelle*). 1981. Opera/Gaumont. Produced by Renzo Rosselini. Directed by Liliana Cavani. Screenplay by Robert Kotz and Liliana Cavani from the novel by Curzio Malaparte. Photographed by Armando Nannuzzi (in colour). Music by Lalo Schifrin. Cast: Burt Lancaster, Claudia Cardinale, Marcello Mastroianni, Alexander King, Ken Marshall. 131 minutes.

Local Hero. 1983. Enigma-Goldcrest/Twentieth Century-Fox. Produced by David Puttnam. Directed and written by Bill Forsyth. Photographed by Chris Menges (in colour). Music by Mark Knopfler. Cast: Burt Lancaster, Peter Riegert, Denis Lawson, Peter Capaldi, Fulton Mackay, Jenny Seagrove, Jennifer Black. 111 minutes.
    BAFTA Award: Bill Forsyth (Best Direction).

The Osterman Weekend. 1983. Twentieth Century-Fox. Produced by Peter S Davis and William N Panzer. Directed by Sam Peckinpah. Screenplay by Alan Sharp from the novel by Robert Ludlum. Photographed by John Coquillon in Color by De Luxe. Music by Lalo Schifrin. Cast: Burt Lancaster, Rutger Hauer, John Hurt, Craig T Nelson, Dennis Hopper, Chris Sarandon, Meg Foster, Helen Shaver. 105 minutes.

Little Treasure. 1985. Tri-Star/Vista. Produced by Herb Jaffe. Directed and written by Alan Sharp. Photographed by Alex Phillips in Metrocolor. Music by Leo Kottke. Cast: Burt Lancaster, Margot Kidder, Ted Danson. 95 minutes.

Tough Guys. 1986. Silver Screen/Bryna/Touchstone. Produced by Joe Wizan. Directed by Jeff Kanew. Screenplay by James Orr and Jim Cruikshank. Photographed by King Baggot in Colour by De Luxe and Panavision. Music by James Newton Howard. Cast: Burt Lancaster, Kirk Douglas, Charles Durning, Alexis Smith, Eli Wallach. 102 minutes.

The Betrothed (*I Promissi*). 1987. (No information available.)

Rocket Gibraltar. 1988. Columbia/Ulick Mayo Weiss. Produced by Jeff Weiss. Directed by Daniel Petrie. Screenplay by Amos Poe. Photographed by Jost Vacano in Duart Color. Music by Andrew Powell. Cast: Burt Lancaster, Suzy Amis, Patricia Clarkson, Sinead Cusack, John Glover. 100 minutes.

The Jeweller's Shop. 1989. PAC/RAI/Alliance/IMP. Produced by Mario Bregni and Pietro Bregin. Directed by Michael Anderson. Screenplay by Mario di Nardo and Jeff Andrews from the play by Karol Wojtyla. Cast: Burt Lancaster, Daniel Olbrychski, Ben Cross, Olivia Hussey, Andrea Occhipinti. 90 minutes.

Field of Dreams. 1989. Carolco/Universal. Produced by Lawrence Gordon and Charles Gordon. Directed by Phil Alden Robinson. Screenplay by Phil Robinson from the book *Shoeless Joe* by W P Kinsella. Photographed by John Lindley and Ricky Bravo in Colour by De Luxe. Music by James Horner. Cast: Kevin Costner, Amy Madigan, James Earl Jones, Burt Lancaster, Timothy Busfield, Ray Liotta. 106 minutes.

Television Dramas

Moses, the Lawgiver. 1975. A TV series in six two-hour episodes, abridged to 141 minutes for release in cinemas. ITC/RAI. Produced by Vincenzo Labella. Directed by Gianfranco de Bosio. Screenplay by Anthony Burgess and Vittorio Bonicelli. Cast: Burt Lancaster, Anthony Quayle, Ingrid Thulin, Irene Papas, Mariangela Melato, William Lancaster, Aharon Ipale.

Victory at Entebbe. 1976. A taped TV play disastrously transferred onto film for cinema release to compete with two other film versions of the Entebbe hostage incident. Marvin J Chomsky directed and the star cast included Burt Lancaster, Richard Dreyfuss, Elizabeth Taylor, Kirk Douglas, Anthony Hopkins, Helen Hayes and Theodore Bikel.

Marco Polo. 1982. A co-production by NBC Television/RAI.

Scandal Sheet. 1985. A 95-minute film for ABC TV, directed by David Lowell Rich and starring Burt Lancaster, Pamela Reed, Lauren Hutton, Robert Urich and Max Wright.

On Wings Of Eagles. 1986. a 225-minute two-part film produced by NBC Television and directed by Andrew V McLaglen. Cast included Burt Lancaster, Richard Crenna, Paul LeMat and Esai Morales.

Barnum. 1986. A 95-minute film produced by CBS TV, directed by Lee Phillips and starring Burt Lancaster, Hanna Schygulla, Sandor Raski, Patty Maloney and Michael Higgins.

Sins of the Fathers, UK title: *Fathers and Sons*. 1986. A German 240-minute film made for television by Bavaria Atelier/Bernhard Sinkel. Directed by Bernhard Sinkel and starring Burt Lancaster, Julie Christie, Tina Engel, Bruno Ganz and Dieter Laser.

Control. 1987. A 90-minute film produced for Italian cable TV, directed by Guiliano Montaldo, starring Burt Lancaster, Ben Gazzara, Kate Nelligan, Kate Reid and Ingrid Thulin.

Phantom of the Opera. 1990, A two-part 180-minute TV production directed by Tony Richardson, starring Burt Lancaster, Charles Dance, Teri Polo, Ian Richardson, Andrea Ferreol and Adam Stroke.

Films produced by Hecht-Lancaster (later Hecht-Hill-Lancaster) in which Lancaster did not appear.

The First Time. 1952. Columbia. Directed by Frank Tashlin. Cast: Barbara Hale, Robert Cummings, Jeff Donnell, Mona Barrie.

Marty. 1955. United Artists. Directed by Delbert Mann. Cast: Ernest Borgnine, Betsy Blair, Esther Minciotti, Joe Mantell, Karen Steele, Jerry Paris.

Academy Awards: Best Picture, Paddy Chayevsky (Best Screenplay), Delbert Mann (Best Director), Ernest Borgnine (Best Actor). Other Academy Award Nominations: Joseph La Shelle (Best Cinematography), Betsy Blair (Best Supporting Actress), Joe Mantell (Best Supporting Actor).

The Bachelor Party. 1957. United Artists. Directed by Delbert Mann. Cast: Don Murray, Carolyn Jones, E G Marshall, Jack Warden, Phillip Abbott, Nancy Marchand.

Academy Award Nomination: Carolyn Jones (Best Supporting Actress).

Take a Giant Step. 1959. United Artists. Directed by Philip Leacock. Cast: Johnny Nash, Estelle Hemsely, Ruby Dee, Frederick O'Neal, Beah Richards.

Index

AD, 232, 233
Adler, Buddy, 74
Airport, 186, 187
Alamo, The, 131, 132, 164
Aldrich, Robert, 84–7, 194, 195, 216
Alexander, Fay, 96
All My Sons, 37
Allen, Lewis, 29
Alpert, Hollis, 66
Altman, Robert, 210
Anastasia, 102
Andersen, Maxwell, 190
Anderson, Norma, 17–20, 30, 33, 36, 39, 40, 43, 48–50, 56, 59, 79, 81, 82, 92, 97, 120, 146, 160, 163, 175, 176, 180
Andrews, Harry, 121
Anhalt, Edward, 133
Apache, 83–5, 88
Asphalt Jungle, The, 124
Astor, Mary, 29
Atlantic City, 220–22, 224, 226, 228, 245

Babenco, Hector, 232
Bacall, Lauren, 54
Bachelor Party, The, 102, 132
Bacon, James, 143
Bad for Each Other, 74
Bad News Bears, The, 213
Barnum, 240
Basehart, Richard, 215

Bellamy, Ralph, 168
Ben Hur, 118, 164, 203, 239
Bent, Charles 'Curly', 8
Berger, Helmut, 206, 207
Bergman, Ingmar, 209, 210
Bergman, Ingrid, 101, 147
Bertolucci, Bernardo, 208, 209, 211, 212, 221
Betrothed, The, 240
Bettger, Lyle, 107
Bickford, Charles, 31, 60, 124
Birdman of Alcatraz, The, 138–46, 152, 157, 161
Blair, Betsy, 98
Blyth, Ann, 31
Bodoh, Allen F, 217
Boenisch, Carl, 181
Bogart, Humphrey, 54
Bone, Jackie, 175–7, 180, 184, 185, 192, 198, 220, 227, 228, 232, 238
Booth, Shirley, 67–9
Borgnine, Ernest, 74, 77, 88, 91, 98, 231
Bowman, Lee, 38
Boyd, Stephen, 118
Boys of Autumn, The, 223, 224, 236
Brand, Neville, 144
Brando, Marlon, 38, 57, 58, 117
Breezy, 247
Brick Foxhole, The, 31
Bricken, Jules, 159
Bronson, Charles, 84, 85

Brooks, Richard, 31, 32, 102, 103, 127–31, 168–73
Brute Force, 31–3, 48, 102, 138
Buffalo Bill and the Indians, 210, 211
Burgess, Anthony, 203
Burns, George, 233
Bush, George, 241

Cabot, Bruce, 86
Caesar, Sid, 122
Cannold, Mitchell, 217
Capoanno, Maria Teresa, 223
Cardinale, Claudia, 152, 156, 168, 170, 206, 222, 223
Carerra, Barbara, 215
Carney, Art, 229
Carpenter, John, 232, 233
Casablanca, 42
Cassandra Crossing, The, 213–15
Cassavetes, John, 147, 148
Castle Keep, 178–80, 183
Cat Ballou, 169
Cattle Annie and Little Britches, 219
Cavini, Liliana, 222
Chambers, John, 216
Chandler, Jeff, 239
Chariots of Fire, 225
Chase, Borden, 71
Chayevsky, Paddy, 88, 102
Child is Waiting, A, 147, 148
Christie, Julie, 237
Cinerama, 163–5, 167
Cirque d'Hiver, 96
Clark, General Mark, 16, 222
Clark, Susan, 188, 201
Clayton, Jack, 147
Clift, Montgomery, 73, 75, 77, 78, 80, 119
Cobb, Lee J, 189, 190
Coca, Imogene, 122
Cohn, Harry, 48, 53, 60, 61, 72–4, 76, 79
Cole Brothers Circus, 10, 44
Collinge, Pat, 77
Come Back Little Sheba, 67–9, 94

Control, 240
Conversation Piece, 206, 207
Convoy, 230
Cooper, Gary, 86–8, 114, 180
Cooper, Gladys, 116
Cosmatos, George Pan, 214
Costner, Kevin, 241
Cravat, Nick, 4, 8–13, 31, 44, 48, 49, 56, 57, 64, 81, 193, 201, 215
Crenna, Richard, 237
Crichton, Charles, 139
Crimson Pirate, The, 63–5, 69, 70, 78
Criss Cross, 41, 42, 95
Cronyn, Hume, 31
Cruikshank, Jim, 236
Cummings, Robert, 70
Curtis, Tony, 42, 95–8, 110, 112, 113, 148, 236
Curtiz, Michael, 60, 67

Dance, Charles, 242
Darcel, Denise, 86, 87
Dark City, 53
Dassin, Jules, 31–3
Davenport, Nigel, 215, 218
Davies, Ossie, 176, 177
Davison, Bruce, 194
de Bosio, Gianfranco, 204, 205
de Carlo, Yvonne, 31, 42
de Laurentiis, Dino, 233
De Mille, Cecil B, 66, 67, 204
De Niro, Robert, 208, 209, 211
de Scaffa, Francesca, 87, 91, 92
Defiant Ones, The, 123
Dehner, John, 61
Delon, Alain, 150, 196, 237
Depardieu, Gérard, 208, 209, 211
Dern, Bruce, 179
Desert Fury, 25–9, 31, 33, 36
Devil's Disciple, The, 118–23
Dietrich, Marlene, 15, 79, 80, 141, 142, 235
Dighton, John, 119
Douglas, Kirk, 3, 35, 36, 40, 99, 100, 104–8, 118–23, 142, 148, 156–60,

162, 166, 167, 184, 193, 223, 224,
231, 232
Dru, Joanne, 57
Dunne, Philip, 54
Durning, Charles, 216

Eastwood, Clint, 40, 86, 185
Elektra, 198
Elliott, Denholm, 218
Elmer Gantry, 31, 102, 103, 127–31,
141, 168, 191, 245
Enfield, Cy, 218
Entertainer, The, 119, 120
Ernst, June, 11
Erskine, Chester, 37
Executive Action, 199, 200

Fairbanks, Douglas Sr, 2
Farrell, Bernard, 159
Faylen, Frank, 107
Field, Betty, 144
Field of Dreams, 241
55 Days at Peking, 157
Firestarter, 232, 233
First Time, 60, 61, 69
Flame and the Arrow, The, 48, 52, 53,
61, 63
Fleming, Rhonda, 107
Fonda, Henry, 224, 235
Fonda, Jane, 241
Fontaine, Margot, 198
Ford, John, 106, 124
Forsyth, Bill, 225–8, 242
Frankenheimer, John, 133–6,
139–42, 157–62, 181–3
Franzone, Vincent, 5
From Here to Eternity, 72–80, 88,
183, 191, 245
Fry, Christopher, 118
Full Metal Jacket, 217

Gable, Clark, 75, 114, 115, 180
Gaddis, Thomas E, 138
Garbo, Greta, 235
Gardner, Ava, 27, 62, 75, 156–8, 214

Garfield, John Jr, 175
Garner, James, 183
Garrison, Jim, 199
Gay, John, 164
Gazzara, Ben, 240
Geer, Will, 199
Gielgud, John, 12
Gish, Lillian, 124, 127
Go Tell the Spartans, 217
Godfather II, 212
Goetz, Augustus, 96
Goetz, Ruth, 96
Goetz, William, 56, 57
Goldbeck, Wallis, 61
Goldwyn, Sam, 66
Good, the Bad and the Ugly, The, 209
Gorman Brothers, 10, 96
Grade, Lew, 203, 204, 213, 214
Graham, Sheilah, 27, 28, 36, 42, 56,
66, 92, 104, 105
Granger, Farley, 49–52
Grant, Cary, 86, 235
Grant, Lee, 134, 135
Great Escape, The, 164, 165
Great White Hope, The, 194
Greatest Story Ever Told, The, 164
Green Berets, The, 217
Gregory's Girl, 225
Griffin, Tess, 232
Griffith, Hugh, 56
Guare, John, 224
Guffey, Burnett, 80
Gulick, Bill, 164, 167
Gunfight at the OK Corral, The, 99,
100, 104–8, 173
Gwenn, Edmund, 53
Gypsy Moths, The, 181–3

Hackman, Gene, 181, 183
Hailey, Arthur, 186
Hale, Barbara, 70, 186
Hall, Conrad, 173
Hall, William, 179, 189
Hallelujah Trail, The, 108, 163–8,
173

Hamilton, Guy, 120
Hardy, Phil, 173
Harris, Richard, 214
Harrison, Robert, 91
Haskin, Byron, 25, 36, 79
Hauer, Rutger, 230
Hayden, Stirling, 211
Hayes, Helen, 186
Hayworth, Rita, 115–17
Hecht, Harold, 21, 22, 24, 25, 30, 38,
    40, 41, 64–6, 70, 83, 87, 88, 91,
    108, 112, 114, 120, 121, 124,
    132–4, 140, 247 (*see also* Hecht-
    Norma Productions, Hecht-
    Lancaster Company and Hecht-
    Hill-Lancaster)
Hecht-Hill-Lancaster, 95, 96, 102,
    108, 119, 120, 123–5, 127, 137,
    146, 219
Hecht-Lancaster Company, 83, 85,
    92, 95
Hecht-Norma Productions, 48, 53,
    60, 70, 71, 83
Heeren, Astrid, 178
Heflin, Van, 186
Hellinger, Mark, 26, 28, 31, 33–5, 41
Henried, Paul, 42
Hepburn, Audrey, 124–7
Hepburn, Katharine, 101
Heston, Charlton, 40, 53, 66, 74, 118,
    203
Higgins, Alex, 228
Hiller, Wendy, 116, 117
Hills, James, 30, 71, 87, 93, 112, 114,
    115, 124, 132, 133, 247 (*see also*
    Hecht-Hill-Lancaster)
His Majesty O'Keefe, 71, 72, 78, 80,
    87, 108
Holden, William, 80, 247
Holliman, Earl, 107
Hopper, Dennis, 107
Hopper, Hedda, 42, 43
Horse Feathers, 21
Houdini, 95
House Un-American Activities Com-
mittee, 53, 54, 64
How the West Was Won, 164
Howe, James Wong, 98
Humphrey, Hubert, 184
Hunter, Kim, 175
Hunter, Ross, 186, 187
Hurt, John, 230
Huston, John, 54, 123–6, 129, 148,
    176

I Walk Alone, 35, 100
Indian Fighter, The, 166
Inge, William, 67
Ipale, Aharon, 204
Ireland, John, 107
Island of Dr Moreau, The, 215, 216

Janssen, David, 185
Jeweller's Shop, The, 240
JFK, 199
Jim Thorpe, All-American, 59, 60, 83
Jones, Carolyn, 102
Jones, James, 72, 96
Jones, James Earl, 241
Jones, Shirley, 131
Joy, Robert, 222
Judgement at Nuremberg, 140–42,
    145, 149
Julia, Raul, 232
Jurado, Katy, 96

Kay Brothers Circus, 9, 10
Kazan, Elia, 38, 74
Kelly, Gene, 54, 243
Kelly, Grace, 86
Kennedy, George, 186
Kennedy, John F, 157, 159, 199
Kentuckian, The, 89–91, 93, 201, 217
Kerr, Deborah, 73, 75, 76, 78, 80,
    115, 117, 181–3
Kibbee, Roland, 63, 65, 119, 201, 202
Kidder, Margot, 235
Killers, The, 26–9, 31, 74
King, Stephen, 232

Kinski, Nastassia, 232
Kiss of the Spider Woman, The, 232
Kiss the Blood Off My Hands, 40, 41
Knickerbocker Glory, 190–92
Kopit, Arthur, 242
Korchalovsky, Andrei, 232
Kovacs, Ernie, 184
Kovacs, Kippe, 184
Kramer, Stanley, 140, 147, 148, 164

Lancaster, Burt, birth of, 1, 2; temper
    and violent streak, 3, 7, 8, 30, 50,
    87, 91–3, 135, 136, 145, 146, 205,
    247; love of music, 3, 6, 7, 177,
    197, 198, 242; acrobatics and
    fitness training, 4, 8, 9, 31, 44, 52,
    56, 57, 82, 96, 175, 179, 197, 246;
    hydrophobia, 5, 168, 174, 175,
    185; religion, 5, 6, 118, 203;
    marriage and divorce, 11, 30, 184,
    242, 243; circus and fairground
    career, 9–13, 44; injuries and
    health problems, 9, 13, 161, 216,
    219, 220, 232, 233, 239, 243, 244;
    military service, 14–19; difficult
    reputation, 30, 32, 35, 64, 65, 78,
    84, 86, 101, 104, 105, 115, 130,
    134, 139, 141, 142, 150, 157, 158,
    178, 182, 189, 190; infidelity, 27,
    39, 40, 44–52, 55–9, 62, 156,
    175–7, 180; awards, 80, 98, 117,
    131, 132, 141, 146, 152, 224, 228;
    art collection, 83, 143, 185, 217,
    223; death of, 244
Lancaster, James H (father), 1, 3, 4, 5,
    30
Lancaster, James Jr (brother), 2, 3, 30,
    35, 38, 140
Lancaster, James Stephen (son), 30,
    143, 163, 243
Lancaster, Jane (sister), 2, 7
Lancaster, Mrs James H (mother), 1,
    2, 4, 5, 6, 7
Lancaster, Joanna (daughter), 59,
    143, 163, 184, 213, 226, 238, 243

Lancaster, June (*see* Ernst, June)
Lancaster, Norma (*see* Anderson,
    Norma)
Lancaster, Sighle-Ann (daughter), 82,
    143, 163, 184, 243
Lancaster, Susan (*see* Schere, Susan)
Lancaster, Susan Elizabeth (daughter),
    43, 163, 184, 243
Lancaster, William (brother), 2, 31
Lancaster, William Henry (son), 33,
    47, 82, 143, 163, 184, 201, 204,
    205, 213, 232, 243
Labella, Vincenzo, 204, 205
Laine, Frankie, 107
Lampedusa, Guiseppe, 149
Landford, Janet, 175
Lane, Diane, 219
Lane, Mark, 199
Lang, Charles, 106
Last Tango in Paris, 208, 209, 211
Laszlo, Ernest, 90
Laughton, Charles, 215, 216
Lauter, Ed, 193, 194, 200, 201
Lawman, 189, 190
Lawrence, Jodie, 61, 62
Lawson, Denis, 227, 229, 230
Lear, Norman, 230
Lehman, Ernest, 96, 109, 110
Leigh, Janet, 96, 97, 110
Leigh, Vivien, 109, 115, 120, 121
Leighton, Margaret, 109, 115
Leone, Sergio, 86, 209
Leopard, The, 62, 149–56, 209, 223,
    234–5, 245
Leroux, Gaston, 242
Lester, Mark L, 233
Levene, Sam, 20, 21, 70, 71
Lewis, Sinclair, 31, 102, 128, 130
Life of Verdi, The, 231
List of Adrian Messenger, The, 148
Littin, Miguel, 235
Little Treasure, 235
Local Hero, 225–30
Loden, Barbara, 176
Lollobrigida, Gina, 95–7

Lombardo, Goffredo, 148, 149
Loren, Sophia, 95, 109, 214
Lorre, Peter, 42
Lubin, Arthur, 70
Lynn, Diana, 89

McCarthy, Joseph, 53, 54
McGovern, George, 196
McGuire, Dorothy, 53
MacKay, Fulton, 229
MacKendrick, Alexander, 111, 112, 120, 121
McLaren, Hollis, 222
Macrae, Gordon, 70
Maddow, Ben, 124
Magnani, Anna, 89, 94, 96, 98
Magnificent Seven, The, 164, 186
Mahlor, Jack, 19
Mailer, Norman, 45–7
Malden, Karl, 144
Mangano, Silvano, 206
Malle, Louis, 220–22
Mann, Daniel, 67, 94
Mann, Delbert, 91, 102, 116
Mann, Roderick, 198
Mantell, Joe, 98
Marchand des Quatre Saisons, Le, 235
Marco Polo, 222, 223
Maria's Lovers, 232, 233
Mark of Zorro, The, 2
Marlowe, 183
Martin, Dean, 186, 187
Marty, 88, 91, 94, 98, 102
Marvin, Lee, 160–73
Mason, James, 233
Mastroianni, Marcello, 222
Matthau, Walter, 89, 213
Mayo, Virginia, 48, 70
Merrill, Dina, 133
Midnight Man, The, 201, 202
Miller, David, 199
Miller, JP, 133
Mills, John, 218
Mister 880, 53

Mitchum, Robert, 74, 148, 220, 231, 233
Moore, Keiron, 61
Morath, Inge, 125
Moreau, Jeanne, 161, 162
Morris, Wayne, 26
Moses – The Lawgiver, 203–6
Muldaur, Diana, 175
Murphy, Audie, 124–6
Murray, Don, 102
My Darling Clementine, 106

Naked and the Dead, The, 45, 61
Nash, Johnny, 123
Nelligan, Kate, 240
Nelson, Barry, 186
Newman, Paul, 184, 210
Newton, Robert, 41
1900, 208, 209, 211, 212
Niven, David, 115–17
Nixon, Richard, 53, 184
Nolan, Lloyd, 186
Norlan Productions, 219
North, Alex, 98
Nureyev, Rudolph, 198

O'Brien, Edmond, 159
Odets, Clifford, 54, 110, 112
Office, The, 132
Old Gringo, 241
Olivier, Laurence, 109, 115, 119–23, 149
On Golden Pond, 224, 235, 240
On Wings of Eagles, 237
Once Upon a Time in America, 209
Once Upon a Time in the West, 209
Orr, James, 236
Osterman Weekend, The, 230
Otello, 198
Othello, 119
O'Toole, Peter, 218

Palance, Jack, 168
Paleface, The, 165
Papas, Irene, 204

Patton, 186
Pavan, Marisa, 98
Peck, Gregory, 146, 231, 241
Peckinpah, Sam, 230
Pelle, La, 222
Penn, Arthur, 159, 160
Perkins, Gil, 57
Perry, Eleanor, 175, 176
Perry, Frank, 175, 176
Peters, Jean, 85
Petrie, Daniel, 240
Phantom of the Opera, The, 242
Pickup, Ronald, 231
Place in the Sun, A, 51, 55
Planer, Franz, 125
Planet of the Apes, The, 216
Platoon, 217
Plowright, Joan, 120
Plummer, Amanda, 219
Poe, Amos, 240
Poitier, Sidney, 242
Pollack, Sydney, 135, 136, 176–80
Ponti, Carlo, 214
Post, Ted, 217
Postman, Eric, 109
Powell, Jane, 70
Preston, Billy, 126
Previn, André, 131
Professionals, The, 168–73, 186
Putnam, David, 225, 226, 228, 240

Quayle, Anthony, 204

Rachevasky, Zina, 92
Raft, George, 185
Raines, Ella, 31
Rainmaker, The, 100–102, 108, 128
Rains, Claude, 42
Rattigan, Terence, 108, 109, 116
Ray, Nicholas, 157
Reed, Carol, 95–7, 211
Reed, Donna, 74, 78, 80
Reed, Pamela, 236
Remick, Lee, 166
Rice, Joan, 79

Richardson, Tony, 242
Riegert, Peter, 227–9
Ringling Brothers Circus, 11, 12, 96
Ritchey, Bruce, 148
Ritter, Thelma, 144
Rivers, Joan, 175
Robinson, Edward G, 37, 38, 54, 184
Robinson, Robert, 122
Rocket Gibraltar, 240
Roland, Gilbert, 61
Rope of Sand, 42
Rose Tattoo, The, 89, 93, 94, 98
Rossen, Robert, 29, 54
Rozsa, Miklos, 29
Rule, Janice, 175
Run Silent, Run Deep, 114, 115
Ruthless People, 238
Ryan, Robert, 170–73, 189, 190, 199, 200

Sabatini, Enrico, 223
Sanda, Dominique, 209
Salt, Waldo, 48
Sarandon, Susan, 221, 222, 224
Savage, John, 232
Savalas, Telly, 144, 176, 177
Scalphunters, The, 173, 176–8
Scandal Sheet, 236
Schaffner, Franklin, 186
Schell, Maximilian, 141, 142
Schere, Susan, 237, 238, 242–4
Schiffer, Bob, 93, 94
Schnabel, Artur, 98
Schneider, Maria, 209
Scofield, Paul, 159
Scorpio, 196–8
Scott, Lizabeth, 29, 33, 35, 36, 53, 74
Seagrove, Jenny, 227
Searchers, The, 124
Seaton, George, 187
Seberg, Jean, 186
Separate But Equal, 242, 243
Separate Tables, 108, 109, 115–17, 119, 121
Sesame Street, 196

Seven Days in May, 156–60, 224
Sharp, Alan, 194, 195
She Done Him Wrong, 21
Sheen, Martin, 214, 233
Sherin, Edwin, 188
Simmons, Jean, 128, 130
Sinatra, Frank, 74, 75, 77, 78, 80,
    148, 191
Sins of the Fathers, 237
Siodmak, Robert, 27, 28, 42, 63–5
Smith, Ian, 226, 230
Sorry, Wrong Number, 38, 39
Sound of Hunting, A, 20, 22, 24, 25,
    71
South Sea Woman, 70, 71
Spartacus, 158
Spiegal, Sam, 176
Stalag 17, 80
Stanwyck, Barbara, 39
Stapleton, Maureen, 89, 186
Steiger, Rod, 219
Steloff, Skip, 215
Stevens, George, 164
Stone, Oliver, 199
Streetcar Named Desire, A, 39
Striepke, Dan, 219
Strode, Woody, 170, 172, 173–6
Stroud, Robert, 138–40
Sturges, John, 100, 104–8, 164–7
Susan Productions, 95
Sutherland, Donald, 208
Sweet Smell of Success, The, 30, 42,
    109–14, 236, 245

Take a Giant Step, 123
Taradash, Frank, 70
Taylor, Don, 215
Taylor, Sam, 96
Temple-Smith, John, 215
Ten Tall Men, 60–62
Thaxter, Phyllis, 60
Thing, The, 233
Thomas, Cal, 230
Thomas, J Parnell, 53
Thomas, Lowell, 163

Thorpe, Jim, 59, 60
Thorpe, Richard, 57
Three Pills in a Bottle, 4
Three Sailors and a Girl, 70
Thulin, Ingrid, 204, 214, 240
Tiomkin, Dimitri, 107
To Kill a Mockingbird, 146
Tobias, George, 61
Tough Guys, 99, 236–9
Tracy, Spencer, 108, 109, 141, 142
Train, The, 159–62
Trapeze, 42, 95–8, 109, 110, 122
Treasure of the Sierra Madre, The,
    235
Trosper, Guy, 194
Trumbo, Dalton, 54, 158, 199
Turner, Don, 52
Twilight's Last Gleaming, 216
Two for the Seesaw, 134, 135

Ulzana's Raid, 194–6
Unforgiven, The, 123–7, 176
Urich, Robert, 236
Uris, Leon, 99, 100

Valdez is Coming, 188, 192
Van Cleef, Lee, 185
Van Druten, John, 108
Van Fleet, Jo, 106, 107
Vance, Jim, 223
Variety Girl, 33
Veiller, Anthony, 26, 29
Vengeance Valley, 57
Vera Cruz, 85–9, 173
Visconti, Luchino, 149–54, 157, 206,
    207, 209, 221

Wallace, Mike, 145
Wallach, Eli, 74
Wallis, Hal B, 22, 23, 28, 29, 33,
    35–9, 42, 48, 53, 63, 66, 67, 73,
    89, 94, 99–101, 104–7, 203, 204
Walker, Robert, 57
Ward, Eddie, 96, 97
Ward, Simon, 218

Warner, Jack, 48, 49
Wayne, John, 40, 131, 132, 176, 189, 217, 224
Webb, James, R, 84, 96
Weill, Kurt, 190
West Side Story, 137
Widmark, Richard, 141, 142, 216
Wild Geese, The, 218
Wilde, Cornel, 66
Wilder, Billy, 54
Williams, Bill, 166, 167
Williams, Tennessee, 38, 89, 94, 95
Wilson, Scott, 181–3
Winner, Michael, 189, 190, 196, 197
Winters, Shelley, 39, 40, 44–52, 55–9,

62, 79, 95, 132–6, 177
Wise, Robert, 114, 115
Wojtyla, Karol, 240
Woodward, Joanne, 184
Wyler, William, 54, 118
Wynter, Dana, 186

York, Michael, 215, 220
Young, Gig, 185
Young Savages, The, 132–7, 176, 177
Young Stranger, The, 133

Zinnemann, Fred, 73–6, 78–80
Zulu, 218
Zulu Dawn, 218